BECOMING A WORD LEARNER

COUNTERPOINTS: *Cognition, Memory, and Language*

STRETCHING THE IMAGINATION
Representation and Transformation in Mental Imagery
C. Cornoldi, R. Logie, M. Brandimonte, G. Kaufmann, D. Reisberg

MODELS OF VISUOSPATIAL COGNITION
M. de Vega, M. J. Intons-Peterson, P. N. Johnson-Laird,
M. Denis, M. Marschark

WORKING MEMORY AND HUMAN COGNITION
J. T. E. Richardson, R. W. Engle, L. Hasher,
R. H. Logie, E. R. Stoltzfus, R. T. Zacks

RELATIONS OF LANGUAGE AND THOUGHT
The View from Sign Language and Deaf Children
M. Marschark, P. Siple, D. Lillo-Martin,
R. Campbell, V. Everhart

GENDER DIFFERENCES IN HUMAN COGNITION
P. J. Caplan, M. Crawford, J. S. Hyde,
J. T. E. Richardson

FIGURATIVE LANGUAGE AND THOUGHT
A. Katz, C. Cacciari, R. W. Gibbs, M. Turner

BECOMING A WORD LEARNER
A Debate on Lexical Acquisition
R. Michnick Golinkoff, K. Hirsh-Pasek, L. Bloom, L. B. Smith,
A. L. Woodward, N. Akhtar, M. Tomasello, G. Hollich

BECOMING A WORD LEARNER

A Debate on Lexical Acquisition

ROBERTA MICHNICK GOLINKOFF

KATHY HIRSH-PASEK

LOIS BLOOM

LINDA B. SMITH

AMANDA L. WOODWARD

NAMEERA AKHTAR

MICHAEL TOMASELLO

GEORGE HOLLICH

OXFORD

UNIVERSITY PRESS

2000

OXFORD

UNIVERSITY PRESS

Oxford   New York

Athens   Auckland   Bangkok   Bogotá   Buenos Aires   Calcutta
Cape Town   Chennai   Dar es Salaam   Delhi   Florence   Hong Kong   Istanbul
Karachi   Kuala Lumpur   Madrid   Melbourne   Mexico City   Mumbai
Nairobi   Paris   São Paulo   Shanghai   Singapore   Taipei   Tokyo   Toronto   Warsaw

and associated companies in
Berlin   Ibadan

Published by Oxford University Press, Inc.
198 Madison Avenue, New York, New York 10016

Oxford is a registered trademark of Oxford University Press.

Library of Congress Cataloging-in-Publication Data
Becoming a word learner : a debate on lexical acquisition /
Roberta Michnick Golinkoff . . . [et al.].
p.   cm.—(Counterpoints)
Includes bibliographical references and index.
ISBN 0-19-513031-6; ISBN 0-19-513032-4 (pbk.)
1. Language acquisition.   2. Vocabulary.   I. Golinkoff, Roberta M.
P118.B424 2000
401'.93 21—dc21   99-045882

1 3 5 7 9 8 6 4 2

Printed in the United States of America
on acid-free paper

Contents

Contributors

Nameera Akhtar, University of California, Santa Cruz

Lois Bloom, Teachers College, Columbia University

Roberta Michnick Golinkoff, University of Delaware

Kathy Hirsh-Pasek, Temple University

George Hollich, Temple University

Linda B. Smith, Indiana University

Michael Tomasello, Max-Planck Institute and Emory University

Amanda L. Woodward, University of Chicago

BECOMING A WORD LEARNER

CHAPTER 1

Word Learning

Icon, Index, or Symbol?

Roberta Michnick Golinkoff
Kathy Hirsh-Pasek

A word is a microcosm of human consciousness. (L. S. Vygotsky, *Thought and Language*)

He first evidenced comprehension by responding to sentences uttered in context. For example, as he began to associate the light switch with the word "light," he rushed over and flipped the switch anytime someone mentioned the word. Later, he simply looked over at the switch, as though visually forming the pairing. (E. S. Savage-Rumbaugh, "Language Acquisition in a Nonhuman Species")

Because the word "light" is uttered so often upon entering a room and the effects of flipping a light switch are so dramatic, babies often recognize "light" as one of their first words. Shortly after recognizing the causal connection between the manipulation of the switch and the appearance and disappearance of the light, babies become fascinated with producing the effect themselves. Although the light switch experience described in the epigraph above involved a pygmy chimpanzee called Kanzi, it bears a great resemblance to the experiences of a human child at the beginning of word learning (Savage-Rumbaugh et al., 1993). The reports of Kanzi's learning (Savage-Rumbaugh, 1990), as well as the work by Pepperberg (1990) and by Pepperberg and McLaughlin (1996) on a parrot; by Herman, Kuczaj, and Holder (1993) and by Herman, Morrel-Samuels, and Pack (1990) on dolphins; by Marler (1982) on vervet monkeys; and by researchers studying such chimpanzees as Nim (Terrace, 1985), Sherman and Austin (Savage-Rumbaugh, 1986), and Sarah (Premack, 1988, 1990) force us to ask whether words are the exclusive province of human beings. To date, experiments on infrahuman species have suggested that their ability to use a syntactic system in no way approaches that of humans. The jury is still out, however, on whether infrahuman species have *words*. In this introduction to a text that examines how *humans* break the word-learning barrier, it is important to ask, "What is a word?" Consideration of this question, especially in light of whether other species in language-learning laboratories or in the wild have words may offer us a new perspective on how humans cross the word-learning barrier. Beginning with a look at the complex skills that children must master helps us appreciate the task of word learning.

WHAT IS A WORD?

Words are minimal free forms in the languages of the world and therefore, unlike phonemes or syllables, they are units par excellence. As individuated elements capable of recombination, words are the building blocks of language. Consider their power. They can seal a contract, destroy a marriage, and move nations to war. Words are powerful tools in human social interactions. They are used to express emotion as well as to describe states of affairs and give directions. A word uttered by a baby can delight a roomful of adoring adults. The meaning of a single word may or may not connect with an object in the world: The word can stand for a tangible entity, such as a table; for a complex process such as pasteurization; or for an idea, such as truth or beauty, whose extensions in the real world we can pinpoint much more easily than its intentions. Yet all words have several characteristics in common.

Natural language words have a phonological form.[1] Even the words of an extinct language such as Latin can be pronounced. The acoustic properties of a word are the first aspect that a child must notice; the word emanates from the mouth, stands in contrast with the silence around it, and is spatially separated from its referent. In fact, from the time that babies are born, linguistic stimuli appear to be processed in different parts of the brain than are nonlinguistic stimuli (Molfese & Molfese, 1979), which suggests that, at least for humans, our brain has evolved to expect to respond to linguistic stimuli.

At first, babies are intrigued solely by the acoustic properties of words (for reviews see Hirsh-Pasek & Golinkoff, 1996; Aslin, Jusczyk, & Pisoni, 1998; and Jusczyk, 1997). But development occurs quickly. By about 4½ months, they begin to recognize the sound patterns of their own names (Mandel, Jusczyk, & Pisoni, 1995). By the time a baby has reached about 6 months of age, some of the phonological forms are already infused with meaning. Tincoff and Jusczyk (1999) have shown that, when infants are tested in the Intermodal Preferential Looking Paradigm (Golinkoff, Hirsh-Pasek, Cauley, & Gordon, 1987; Hirsh-Pasek & Golinkoff, 1996), a baby who hears, "mommy" will look to his or her own mother and a baby who hears "daddy" will look to his or her own father. How children derive the meanings of the rest of their words is an issue addressed by a number of the essays in this volume.

In addition, at least for skilled speakers of a language, words do not usually refer to a single object, property, or event.[2] Rather, words refer mostly to categories—from a range of reds to a variety of tables. As Brown (1958) pointed out, even such proper nouns as "Fido" can be said to refer to a category. Although the lexical category "Fido" is narrower than, say, the category "dog," "Fido" does not look exactly the same each time the name is used. Yet word learning is complicated even further by the fact that the same word can have *multiple* meanings. "Table" refers not only to the four-legged surfaces in our houses but to something that we do with motions at meetings. As Miller (1999) has pointed out, it is often the linguistic context that resolves potential ambiguities in word meaning.

This fact brings us to the realization that words have connections to many other words. Although linguists debate about whether true synonyms exist (e.g., Bollinger, 1980), it is certain that words have close cousins. "Happy" and "delighted" are very close in meaning, whereas "unhappy" and "delighted" are antonyms. Yet focusing on antonyms and synonyms treats the connections between words too narrowly. Although there are single-word sentences—as when we yell, "Fire" or tell our dog, "Sit!"—words do not usually stand in isolation in sentences.

Words do more than refer; they participate in a web of relations within the grammar of a language (Frawley, 1992). Thus, words also have a part of speech—and sometimes more than one; the word "kiss," for example, can be a noun or a verb. Moreover, a word's part of speech can be readily changed by adding a derivational morpheme. Thus, "happy" (the adjective) can become "happi*ness*" (the noun) or "happi*ly*" (the adverb). By virtue of its syntactic part of speech and its meaning, a word plays a particular role in a sentence. Words can, for example, modify each other, as in the "*happy* camper," and they can take different types of arguments. Thus, the adverb "happily" takes a verb argument (as in "She sang happily"). The transitive verb "tickle" requires a tickler and a ticklee (two noun arguments), whereas the transfer verb "give" requires a giver, something to give, and a receiver (three noun arguments). In order to use words correctly in their sentences, children must identify all of these requirements.

Given the myriad properties a word may have, it is impressive that children around two years of age already seem to know so many of them. We presuppose that the words used by adult humans are symbolic in nature. Yet we often finesse the fact that there is little agreement among psychologists, philosophers, and linguists about what constitutes a symbol. Equipped with some sense of how words work for skilled users of a language, we need to step back and explore where human and animal learners begin. Is it possible that the range of infrahuman species used in various language-learning experiments have words in this complex sense? Do even human infants' words have these properties when the children first break the word-learning barrier? And how are words learned to begin with? Are they learned purely by association, with the requirement of temporal contiguity between a word and a referent, or do other variables such as the intention of the speaker influence the mapping between word and world for humans and animals? As the size of this text indicates, none of these questions is simple to answer.

We continue our inquiry by examining whether species other than human beings can be credited with using symbols—and this leads us to the question: Does our own species operate with words as symbols from the outset?

ICON, INDEX, AND SYMBOL

Bates (1979) and Deacon (1997) began to sketch the theoretical landscape of icon, index, and symbol by expanding on insights from the philosopher Charles Sanders Peirce (1932). Peirce's main contribution lies in the recognition that "different modes of reference can be understood in terms of *levels* of interpretation" (Deacon, p. 73). It is this hierarchical aspect of reference that distinguishes human words from animal calls; however, they differ in more than just complexity. Briefly, icon, index, and symbol fall along a continuum. On the continuum, icons bear a *physical* resemblance to what they represent, and indices relate to what they represent by association forged from experience (as when smoke is an index for a fire or a shriek is an index for fear). By the time the continuum reaches the term "symbol," the relationship between the referent and the sign is purely arbitrary, based neither on physical similarity nor on functional or causal relations.

In Peirce's system, the first level of reference, an *icon,* is mediated by a similarity between a sign and an object. To put it more simply, a sign is something like a sculpture or a picture or an image in one's mind. The icon *resembles* what it stands for. It is not the resemblance per se, however, that makes it an icon. Instead, it is the inferential process that goes on in the mind that causes one to recognize the similarity. Icons are not "out there," in the world; icons are created by our interpretation of external stimuli that remind us of other stimuli. A good icon can tell us something new about something familiar because it highlights interesting relations we may not have noticed. A caricature, an icon, of the actor Liza Minelli might lead the viewer to realize that the performer has very large eyes. Interestingly, the comprehension of icons—even those that closely resemble what they stand for—does not happen automatically. DeLoache, Pierroutsakos, Uttal, Rosengren, and Gottlieb (1998) have shown that at 9 months—but not at 19 months—of age babies try to handle pictures of objects the way they handle the objects themselves.

The second level of reference, an *index,* is mediated by a physical or a temporal connection between a sign and an object, as when a thermometer goes up and down to indicate the temperature. Indexes are learned through condition-ing, either classical or operant. For example, dolphins can be trained to respond to signs that their trainers produce (Herman, Kuczaj, & Holder, 1993). The dol-phins are shaped to know that an upraised fist means "Go to the left of the tank." The fist becomes an index because it is associated with receiving reinforcement (fish) for movements to the left. Then the fist alone can elicit leftward move-ments. The fist becomes a signal for the reinforcement that will come with the correct response. This is standard conditioning. Recall that classical condition-ing has also been called "signal learning," because the unconditioned stimulus comes to serve as a sign of the unconditioned reinforcer that follows. On Deacon's view, the fist has the status of index, but not of symbol, because when the unconditioned reinforcer following the sign stops, the organism's response to the sign will cease. Thus, indices are not examples of what Deacon would call genuine reference.

Nim (Terrace, 1985) and other animals have used sign-context combinations in ways that look like symbols. For example, when Nim wanted something, he would sign, "Want x." But is there any evidence that Nim understood what he was doing? Or was he merely using the phrase "Want x" to get something? Deacon gave the example of a person learning to use a social phrase in differ-ent social contexts—for example, "How are you today?" Here we might be fooled into thinking that the person knew what he or she was saying when the individual really did not. By itself, decontextualization is just another example of stimulus generalization. In the same way, being able to use a sign for a range of objects, that is, categorically, is insufficient. Using a word in a range of con-texts could be accomplished merely by iconic overlap. Upon seeing an apple and hearing the word "apple," the person or animal may be reminded of another of the same type with which it shares features. This then becomes a matter of recognizing an item in memory and is not by itself symbolic. Thus, it is diffi-cult to be sure that reference is symbolic rather than indexical, since the two of-ten look the same.

Many scientists have questioned whether Marler's (1982) vervet monkeys' three different calls for three different kinds of prey (leopards, eagles, and snakes) constitute an instance of symbol use. Although each call has a unique acoustic character and is used in a unique situation, they function indexically by invit-ing the listener to recall a previous experience in memory when a particular call was followed by a particular type of predator. Thus, the eagle alarm may make the vervet think of prior eagle incidents and react by fleeing for cover. Moreover, these three distinct calls cannot be combined or modified. Other than by call-ing very vigorously out of great fear (even at its most frantic, an imprecise mode of signaling compared to language), vervets cannot indicate that an eagle is very big and very close and that the listener should run for its life. There is no sys-tem that houses these three calls and allows their modulation. Further, it is not clear that these calls are used with the intention to communicate. And there is some evidence that the ability to make these calls has an innate component and that the variable the vervet responds to is prey orientation: If it comes from above, give the eagle alarm; if it comes from below, give the snake alarm (Deacon, 1997). Although vervet juveniles have to learn to constrain their calls to avoid, for example, producing the eagle alarm in the instance of falling leaves, the fact that they appear to make the calls as juveniles suggests that the calls may have been shaped through evolution. Vervets with the abilities to give and readily comprehend the calls would certainly be in a better position to survive than those without them.

As Deacon wrote, "learned association, arbitrariness, reference, and transmission of information from one individual to another—are not sufficient to define symbolic reference" (1997, p. 66). Although each of these behaviors is true of symbols, even taken together they provide insufficient evidence for symbols as opposed to indices. All can be accounted for by means of lower level, indexical explanations.

WHAT IS A SYMBOL?

As DeLoache, Miller, and Pierroutsakos (1998, p. 816) pointed out:

> Symbolic relations are distinguished from other kinds of relations . . . in two main ways. One is intentionality; for something to be a symbol, someone must intend that it be interpreted primarily in terms of something other than itself (DeLoache, 1995). . . . There is always a qualitative difference between symbol and referent; they are different kinds of things.

Symbols are useful to us because they allow us to "represent, draw inferences from, and make predictions about objects and events we have never directly experienced" (DeLoache, Miller, & Pierroutsakos, p. 816). We are fairly well stuck in reality with indices; with symbols, thought takes wings.

Deacon (1997) has said that, although symbols may start out as indexical (that is, based in associations), they go beyond mere associative relationships. In indexical relations, a sign triggers the memory of a referent. In symbolic relations, a symbol may trigger the memory of a referent or—and here is the crucial distinction—the memory of other symbols. Symbols are organized into *systems* that are rule governed. Symbols are not just "accumulations of symbols in unstructured collections that can be arbitrarily shuffled in different combinations" (Deacon, p. 100). And symbols do not lose their meaning even when their referents disappear or the reinforcement that follows their use no longer occurs (Deacon, 1997). For example, despite the fact that dodos are extinct, the word "dodo" still has a clear meaning. This phenomenon is connected to the fact that words are organized into systems of relations. The fact that we can tell someone that a dodo was a kind of bird gives the word "dodo" its meaning. Because words can be organized into sentential relations, they allow us to discuss such impossible states of affairs as "This sentence will run four miles tomorrow."

Individual symbols are also organized into higher-order relations. This is different from using a symbol to label items in the same category (e.g., "shoe" for different kinds of shoes), because that can come about in an indexical way. According to Deacon (1997), the ability to inhibit this indexical link and to recognize the higher-order connection between the word "shoe" and the word "clothes" indicates that a symbolic level has been reached. "Clothes" does not refer to a single type of clothing (e.g., a skirt or pants) and therefore cannot be narrowly indexical. Deacon described how Savage-Rumbaugh's (1986) chimpanzees Sherman and Austin were successful in inhibiting first-learned indexical signs in order to learn symbols for the superordinate categories "food" and "tool." Lana, a chimpanzee who knew an equally large number of indexical signs, could not seem to master this higher-order relationship. Lana apparently fell into "learning potholes" (Savage-Rumbaugh, p. 136) by focusing on individual sign-object associations (indexes) and was unable to rise above these local relationships to grasp nonlocal, symbol-symbol regularities (as in the relationship between items called "hammer" and "pliers," which came under the category of "tools"). Like Sherman and Austin, Premack's (1988, 1990) Sarah was also able to treat symbols as labeling categories. In fact, Sarah operated as preschoolers do, selecting a taxonomically related item over a thematically related item in a forced-choice task (Premack, 1990; Markman & Hutchinson, 1984).

Other chimpanzees, such as Washoe (Gardner & Gardner, 1974) and Nim (Terrace, 1985; Seidenberg & Petitto, 1979), like Lana, show less skill with their signs than do Sherman, Austin, and Sarah. The seemingly less-skilled chimpanzees appear to have sizeable vocabularies (although Washoe's sign use has been criticized as imitating that of her trainers), but there is little evidence that they recognize the relationships between their signs or the way the signs form a system. As Karmiloff-Smith (1992, p. 62) put it, describing some of the work on chimpanzees, "A list of lexical items, however long, does not constitute naming and bears little or no relationship to the linguistic competence of even a 2- or 3-year-old."

Is there any evidence that any of the infrahuman species that have been studied function with symbols rather than with indices? Premack's (1988, 1990) Sarah is probably in possession of symbols. Although Sarah required thousands of conditioning trials to select the correct object in response to the presentation of a plastic symbol, eventually she treated her plastic symbols as transparent and relational. That is, when asked to describe "apple," Sarah did not select properties that described the symbol for apple; rather, she selected properties that characterized real apples. Thus, Sarah was treating the plastic symbol as though it arbitrarily stood for the real apple. Even this behavior, impressive as it is, is an insufficient criterion for the claim that the chimpanzee has true symbols. Sarah is however, capable of computing *relations between symbols.* When asked "same as" and "different from" questions, she is capable of comparing the symbols that appear on either side of the question and answering correctly. Her impressive ability to evaluate relations between symbols suggests that Sarah is operating on more than just an indexical level where the appearance of a particular plastic symbol predicts the appearance of a specific object. Did Sarah, like human children, experience a vocabulary spurt? Did she show any evidence of "learning to learn" with symbols?

The chimpanzee Kanzi seems to have symbols as well (Savage-Rumbaugh et al., 1993). Kanzi has been shown to understand novel combinations of symbols, such as "Put the sparklers in the potty" or "Give the sweet potato a shot." With these objects—and many more—arrayed before him, Kanzi was able to, first, select the correct objects and, second, place them into relations as specified by the sentences he hears. This is tantamount to understanding that the sentence is more than the sum of its parts—that it specifies a particular event in the world. Kanzi could have simply selected each of the items and carried out the requested action on something else. But he did not. By recreating in action the relations he heard in language, he showed an understanding of language on at least a parallel with 13- to 15-month-old humans. At that age, when babies are shown a pair of events on videotape, they will look for a significantly longer time at the event that matches the sentence they are hearing than at a very similar event that does not match the sentence (Hirsh-Pasek & Golinkoff, 1996).

In sum, most infrahuman species, according to Deacon (1997), fail to use their "words" as symbols. Nonhuman species lack three characteristics of immature humans. First, they lack large prefrontal cortexes that allow them to suppress thoughts about indexical relationships in order to look for relationships at a higher level. Deacon has claimed that the enlarged prefrontal cortex in the human brain is capable of entertaining some form of "not." That is, humans (at least) can rise above local indexical relations and recognize that a sign is being used in another, more global, way. He has used the example of psychological experiments where both infrahuman and human subjects are able to stop using a response strategy that worked previously and grasp that the strategy required for reward has changed. Being able to form a "not" relation is important because "nots" can represent the world in a way that goes counter to our sense impressions. Therefore, "not" must come from meaning—meaning outside the world of the senses.

Second, nonhumans do not seem to have the learning constraints and biases that encourage them to look for nonlocal relations. Here Deacon (1997) endorsed Newport's (1990) "less is more" hypothesis, claiming that languages have the properties that they do because they need to be learned by immature minds. Citing the putative critical period is the same as saying that the immature organism must start small, since it is unable to deal with the whole language problem at once. The learning constraints posed by starting small favor the discovery of nonlocal relations. Deacon explained the symbolic success of Kanzi (Savage-Rumbaugh et al., 1993) in the same way: Kanzi started learning lexical items as an infant, in an incidental way, without being explicitly trained; he learned over 200 lexical items and even recognized that strings of words map to particular relations in the world.

Third, symbols are only symbols because they can be embedded in an organized system that permits symbol-to-symbol relations. In this sense, infrahuman communication (whether in the wild or in our laboratories) is not language *minus* grammar and syntax. On Deacon's (1997) view, without an organized system that permits symbol-to-symbol links, there are no true symbols—only indices. This is because symbols are embedded in a nexus of relationships, some indexical (hence the hierarchical nature of reference) and some not, because they capture higher-order relations. With the exception of Kanzi and Sarah—and to a much more limited degree, Sherman and Austin—nonhuman words (or their signed equivalents), therefore, are indexical.

WHAT DO HUMANS START OUT WITH?

Let us examine for a moment whether symbols are in fact acquired in the same way as indices, as Bates (1979) and Deacon (1997) both have suggested. Bates claimed that "from the perspective of the novice knower, objective indices and objective symbols are equally arbitrary . . . and the process by which the two are acquired is identical." This does not seem accurate. Symbol acquisition seems to require more than does the acquisition of indices. The listener's knowledge of the *intention* of the speaker is required for the acquisition of a symbol; otherwise the listener will not realize that the sounds emanating from the speaker's mouth are about something in the world removed from the speaker. Bates has given the example of a child recognizing that a mother putting on her coat is an index of the fact that she is likely to leave. Since these events (putting the coat on and leaving) are linked by contiguity, and the first predicts the second, there is nothing symbolic there. The child may begin to cry upon seeing the mother put on her coat because he or she remembers that this action precedes the action of leaving.

This seems very different from understanding the word "coat." "Coat" may be used in a range of contexts, not all of which mean that Mother will leave imminently. "Coat" refers not only to Mother's coat but to a range of coats.[3] The word "coat" has the same meaning even in the summertime when Mother does not wear one, and it would continue to mean a garment worn on the upper body and the arms even if, for some reason, coats went out of fashion and capes replaced them. The question comes down to whether the child appreciates these aspects of "coat" from the start or whether "coat" functions initially as the index of seeing Mother put her coat on. Although there is surely an associative element in learning the index and the symbol "coat," further research may reveal that *from the start* the learning of symbols differs from the learning of indices. At 12 months of age (chapter 6 in this volume) and certainly by 18 months (Baldwin, 1991, 1993; Tomasello & Barton, 1994), temporal contiguity is not sufficient to create associations between words and referents. Even at 12 months of age, babies will apparently not create mismappings between a word and a powerfully attractive potential referent if the speaker does not indicate that he or she means to label that referent. Similar results in the domain of imitation have been found by Meltzoff (1995): Eighteen-month-olds will imitate only those actions that seem to be performed "on purpose." They will then complete the actor's intended goal even if they did not see it carried out. These studies tell us that word learning is tied in with intention very early, if not from the start. That is, the child seems to be sensitive to the social cues that indicate that the speaker *means* to label something or *means* to carry out some action. If the speaker's intention to label a referent is missing, the word is not learned, even if it is repeated many times (Hollich, Hirsh-Pasek, & Golinkoff, in press).

Another difference between how an index and a symbol are learned is that a symbol, because of its arbitrariness, can be mismapped, whereas an index, linked to real events, cannot. Using the previous example, a mother putting on her coat is an index (a predictor) of Mother leaving. The link between an index and what it represents is not as arbitrary as the link between a symbol and a referent. Putting on a coat, like the Pavlovian ringing of a bell, is a reliable predictor of an impending event. It is also—in the case of the coat—functionally linked to the impending event of leaving. Coats keep you warm outside, just as the index of smoke is produced by fire. On the other hand, the word "coat" could be mismapped to a part of the coat (the collar) or perhaps to the hat that usually accompanies the coat. And there is no functional or causal link between the object coat and the word "coat." As Bates (1979, p. 58) has written, "Icons are mastered through a perception of similarity; indices and symbols are mastered through perception of contiguity (i.e., by association)." We have argued that symbols are mastered through the perception of contiguity as well as through an additional perception—the perception of the social cues that herald a speaker's intention (Grice, 1975).

Eventually human children will reach an even more impressive level of symbolic use, a level not observed in any of the nonhumans that have received language training. Humans, according to Karmiloff-Smith (1992), can reflect on what they know about the symbols they possess. Karmiloff-Smith has referred to this process as "representational redescription" or the ability of humans to analyze their own representations as objects. As the following example shows (Karmiloff-Smith, p. 31), humans are capable of thinking about the symbols they know:

YARA (4 YEARS OLD): What's that?

MOTHER: A typewriter.

YARA: No, you're the typewriter; that's a typewrite.

This discussion has left us with a host of questions about how young children approach the language-learning task. Although we may have come closer to analyzing the difference between true symbols on one hand and indices and icons on the other, the question of which components of symbols babies begin word learning with is still unclear. For example, is there a time, say, prior to the vocabulary spurt, when words are used indexically, or are humans symbol users from the start? We know, for example, that 13- to 15-month-old infants, many of whom have no words in their productive vocabularies, can nonetheless compute the relations in a sentence well enough to watch one of two television screens that depicts a matching event (Hirsh-Pasek & Golinkoff, 1996). If children were not sensitive to the relations that underlie language use, how could they know which was the correct screen? Could it be that human infants are ready to interpret words symbolically from the start? If infants *are* predisposed to interpret words symbolically, perhaps it would not be surprising to learn that they are prepared to accept a wider range of signs as symbols than are older children. Namy and Waxman (1998) reported that 18-month-old infants learned novel symbolic gestures as names for objects in addition to learning new words. However, by 26 months, babies preferred names over gestures. Woodward and Hoyne's (1999) data suggested that at 13 months, but not at 18 months, babies are willing to treat object noises (such as a whistle) as a name for an object. On the other hand, Hollich, Hirsh-Pasek, & Golinkoff (in press) found that although 12-month-olds do not prefer to learn object noises as names, they can do so under certain conditions. Furthermore, it seems that any speechlike sound that emanates from the mouth (such as "psst") can be used by 12-month-olds to name an object as readily as can a word.

Although some of the essays in this volume touch upon these issues, most seem to presuppose that human infants begin by learning words as symbols. But there are many questions still to be answered. Why is it, for example, that 1-year-olds learn words so laboriously, whereas just 8 months later 20-month-olds can acquire, on average, 10 new words a day? Do children go through a naming insight akin to that experienced by Helen Keller? Clearly, future research needs to address whether words start out indexical and become symbolic only later.

OVERVIEW OF THE VOLUME

Word learning is a very active area of research in developmental psycholinguistics. This volume offers a panoramic view of the research that is defining the field. To explain the problem of word learning, leading researchers in the area of first-language acquisition include chapters from their own unique theoretical perspectives. The contributors to this volume met in Atlanta, Georgia, in spring 1998 at the meetings of the International Society for Infant Studies to decide on a format for this book. Because the Counterpoints series prides itself on creating dialogue among researchers from various theoretical perspectives, we agreed not only to present each chapter but also to have the authors provide commentaries on all the other chapters. In addition, in spring 1999, we all participated in a symposium on word learning at the meetings of the Society for Research in Child Development. At this lively session, each chapter's author presented his or her theoretical views—especially as they contrasted with the views of other panelists—and each was queried by other members of the panel and by the audience. In this volume, we invite the reader to enter into the debate on early word learning. We hope that some of the excitement of our exchanges comes through on these printed pages.

The first six chapters of the volume introduce the reader to the wealth of research in this area. Chapter 7 contains the authors' reactions to the previous chapters and highlights the similarities and differences between these theoretical views.

Chapter 2 discusses word learning in the context of the whole child. Lois Bloom emphasizes how word learning forms a part of language development and how language emerges out of a nexus of other developments in emotion, cognition, and social connectedness. Bloom presents her views as an antidote to the MIT perspective, which emphasizes a language acquisition device instead of a real child. She consistently argues (e.g., Bloom, 1970) that language development must not be studied in isolation as the acquisition of a formal system.

Chapter 3 takes a different tack. Linda B. Smith is concerned with how associative mechanisms drive word learning and, more importantly, how they allow the child to build up biases that engender additional word learning. In particular, Smith and her colleagues (e.g., Landau, Smith, & Jones, 1988) argue that children develop a "shape bias" when they encounter new count nouns and learn that object-based lexical categories are organized by shape. Thus, Smith's position differs from that of Amanda Woodward in the next chapter: Smith emphasizes the role that learning plays in developing biases, whereas Woodward emphasizes the role of a priori constraints on word learning.

In chapter 4, Amanda L. Woodward summarizes the bounty of research that claims that constraints play a role in word learning from the earliest stages. Woodward argues, for example, that there exists a bias to interpret words as labeling whole objects (Markman & Wachtel, 1988; Golinkoff, Mervis, & Hirsh-Pasek, 1994; Woodward, 1993). On Woodward's view, word learning would be very difficult indeed if it were not biased in some way.

Chapter 5 is devoted to describing research findings from the social-pragmatic approach. Nameera Akhtar and Michael Tomasello's dramatic findings show how word learning occurs in some fairly complex, nonostensive situations amid the flow of social interaction. Current models of word learning, they suggest, undervalue the role of social interaction. Because language has social goals as its ultimate purpose, social interactions are the sine qua non of word learning.

Chapter 6, by Kathy Hirsh-Pasek, Roberta Michnick Golinkoff, and George Hollich, takes the perspective that multiple cues are necessary for word learning. In their emergentist coalition model, the authors argue that the intricacies of word learning demand a complex theory that presupposes an active child who integrates cues from the social, cognitive, perceptual, and social domain. Using a new method—the Interactive Intermodal Preferential Looking Paradigm—they present a case for the transformation of the word-learning process over the 2nd year of life as the child comes to weigh the available cues differently with development.

The commentaries that follow in chapter 7 highlight the differences between these perspectives even further. Part of the debate concerns whether the first words are more like the indexical signs of most nonhumans or like the symbols of the human 4-year-old. Although there are marked contrasts between the views, the work of all of the authors focuses on a central issue: an understanding of how infants break the language barrier by learning words.

ACKNOWLEDGMENTS

Preparation of this chapter was supported in part by a grant from NSF (SBR9601306) to the authors and by a grant from NICHHD (HD25455-07) to Kathy Hirsh-Pasek. We thank Bill Frawley, Lou Mosberg, and Fred Adams for their helpful comments on this essay.

NOTES

1. Although this chapter focuses on how hearing children learn words, we recognize that words "spoken" with the hands in the sign language of people who are deaf have semantic and syntactic properties similar to those of pronounced words.

2. We specify "usually" since, on occasion, words can refer to unique events. For example, December 7, 1941 (the invasion of Pearl Harbor), is a date with great significance. We thank F. Adams for calling our attention to this point.

3. Research in our laboratory suggests, however, that the notion that a word applies to a category does not come for free. Twelve-month-olds do not automatically extend newly learned object labels and can do so only if they are given more experience with the members of the lexical category (Hollich, 1999; Hennon, Rocroi, & Chung, 1999). Just 2 months later, at 14 months of age, babies can automatically extend a newly learned word.

REFERENCES

Aslin, R. N., Jusczyk, P. W., & Pisoni, D. B. (1988). Speech and auditory processing during infancy: Constraints on and precursors to language. In W. Damon (Ed.), *Handbook of child psychology: Cognition, perception, and language* (pp. 147–198). New York: John Wiley & Sons.

Baldwin, D. A. (1991). Infants' contribution to the achievement of joint reference. *Child Development, 62,* 875–890.

Baldwin, D. A. (1993). Infants' ability to consult the speaker for clues to word reference. *Journal of Child Language, 20,* 394–419.

Bates, E. (1979). *The emergence of symbols: Cognition and communication in infancy.* New York: Academic Press.

Bloom, L. M. (1970). *Language development: Form and function in emerging grammars.* Cambridge, MA: MIT Press, 1970.

Bolinger, D. (1980). *Language—The loaded weapon.* London: Longman Press.

Brown, R. (1958). *Words and things.* Glencoe, IL: Free Press.

Deacon, T. W. (1997). *The symbolic species: The co-evolution of language and the brain.* New York: W. W. Norton.

DeLoache, J. S. (1995). Early symbol understanding and use. In D. Medin (Ed.) *The psychology of learning and motivation* (pp. 65–114). New York: Academic Press.

DeLoache, J. S., Miller, K. F., & Pierroutsakos, S. L. (1998). Reasoning and problem solving. In W. Damon (Ed.), *Handbook of child psychology: Cognition, perception, and language* (pp. 801–850). New York: John Wiley & Sons.

DeLoache, J. S., Pierroutsakos, S. L., Uttal, D. H., Rosengren, K. S., & Gottlieb, A. (1998). Grasping the nature of pictures. *Psychological Science, 9,* 205–210.

Frawley, W. (1992). *Linguistic semantics.* Hillsdale, NJ: Erlbaum.

Gardner, B. T., & Gardner, R. A. (1974). Comparing the early utterances of child and chimpanzee. In A. Pick (Ed.), *Minnesota Symposia on Child Psychology.* Minneapolis: University of Minnesota Press.

Golinkoff, R. M., Hirsh-Pasek, K., Cauley, K. M., & Gordon, L. (1987). The eyes have it: Lexical and syntactic comprehension in a new paradigm. *Journal of Child Language, 14,* 23–45.

Grice, H. P. (1975). Logic and conversation. In P. Cole & J. Morgan (Eds.), *Speech acts: Syntax and semantics. Vol. 3.* (pp. 41–58). New York: Academic Press.

Hennon, E., Rocroi, C., & Chung, H. (1999, April). Testing the principle of extendibility: Are new words learned as proper nouns or category labels? Paper presented at the meeting of the Society for Research in Child Development, Albuquerque, NM.

Herman, L. M., Kuczaj, S. A. I., & Holder, M. D. (1993). Responses to anomalous gestural sequences by a language-trained dolphin: Evidence for processing of semantic relations and syntactic information. *Journal of Experimental Psychology: General, 122.* 184–194.

Herman, L. M., Morrel-Samuels, P., & Pack, A. A. (1990). Bottlenosed dolphin and human recognition of veridical and degraded video displays of an artificial gestural language. *Journal of Experimental Psychology: General, 119,* 215–230.

Hirsh-Pasek, K., & Golinkoff, R. M. (1996). *The origins of grammar: Evidence from early language comprehension.* Cambridge, MA: MIT Press.

Hollich, G. (1999). Mechanisms of "word learning": A computational model. Unpublished doctoral dissertation, Temple University.

Hollich, G. J., Hirsh-Pasek, K., & Golinkoff, R. M. (with Hennon, E., Chung, H. L., Rocroi, C., Brand, R. J., & Brown, E.) (in press). Breaking the language barrier: An emergentist coalition model for the origins of word learning. *Society for Research in Child Development Monographs.*

Jusczyk, P. W. (1997). *The discovery of spoken language.* Cambridge, MA: MIT Press.

Karmiloff-Smith, A. (1992). *Beyond modularity: A developmental perspective on cognitive science.* Cambridge, MA: MIT Press.

Landau, B., Smith, L. B., & Jones, S. S. (1988). The importance of shape in early lexical learning. *Cognitive Development, 3,* 299–321.

Mandel, D. R., Jusczyk, P. W., & Pisoni, D. B. (1995). Infants' recognition of the sound patterns of their own names. *Psychological Science, 6,* 314–317.

Markman, E. M., & Hutchinson, J. E. (1984). Children's sensitivity to constraints on word meaning: Taxonomic versus thematic relations. *Cognitive Psychology, 16,* 1–27.

Marler, P. R. (1982). Avian and primate communication: The problem of natural categories. *Neuroscience and Biobehavioral Reviews, 6,* 87–94.

Meltzoff, A. N. (1995). Understanding the intentions of others: Re-enactment of intended acts by 18-month-old children. *Developmental Psychology, 31,* 838–850.

Miller, G. A. (1999). On knowing a word. *Annual Review of Psychology, 50,* 1–19.

Molfese, D. L., & Molfese, V. J. (1979). Hemisphere and stimulus differences as reflected in the cortical responses of newborn infants to speech stimuli. *Developmental Psychology, 15,* 505–511.

Namy, L. L., & Waxman, S. R. (1998). Words and gestures: Infants' interpretations of different forms of symbolic reference. *Child Development, 69,* 295–308.

Newport, E. L. (1990). Maturational constraints on language learning. *Cognitive Science, 14,* 11–28.

Peirce, C. S. (1932). Collected papers. In C. Jartshorne & P. Weiss (Eds.), *Collected papers.* Cambridge, MA: Harvard University Press.

Pepperberg, I. M. (1990). Some cognitive capacities of an African grey parrot. *Advances in the Study of Behavior, 19,* 357–410.

Pepperberg, I. M., & McLaughlin, M. A. (1996). Effect of avian-human joint attention on allospecific vocal learning by grey parrots (Psittacus erithacus). *Journal of Comparative Psychology, 110,* 286–297.

Premack, D. (1988). Minds with and without language. In L. Weiskrantz (Ed.), *Thought Without Language* (pp. 46–65). New York: Oxford University Press.

Premack, D. (1990). Words: What are they, and do animals have them? *Cognition, 37,* 197–212.

Savage-Rumbaugh, E. S. (1986). *Ape language: From conditioned response to symbol.* New York: Columbia University Press.

Savage-Rumbaugh, E. S. (1990). Language acquisition in a nonhuman species: Implications for the innateness debate. *Developmental Psychobiology, 23,* 599–620.

Savage-Rumbaugh, E. S., Murphy, J., Sevcik, R. A., Brakke, K. E., Williams, S. L., & Rumbaugh, D. M. (1993). Language comprehension in ape and child. *Monographs of the Society for Research in Child Development, 58* (3–4, Serial No. 233).

Seidenberg, M. S., & Petitto, L. A. (1979). Signing behavior in apes: A critical review. *Cognition, 7,* 177–215.

Terrace, H. S. (1985).In the beginning was the "name." *American Psychologist, 40,* 1011–1028.

Tincoff, R., & Jusczyk, P. W. (1999). Some beginnings of word comprehension in 6-month-olds. *Psychological Science, 10,* 172–175.

Tomasello, M., & Barton, M. (1994). Learning words in non-ostensive context. *Developmental Psychology, 30,* 639–650.

Woodward, A. L., & Hoyne, K. L. (1999). Infant's learning about words and sounds in relation to objects. *Child Development, 70,* 65–77.

CHAPTER 2

The Intentionality Model of Word Learning

How to Learn a Word, Any Word

Lois Bloom

The central force in word learning is the mind of the child and its development rather than external mechanisms such as the social context, neural networks, or lexically specific constraints, principles, and biases. Early language is a succession of transformations of the adult target language by the child, under the child's control. The child's agency and directionality toward the target language apply to both its lexicon and grammar in the course of acquisition, and one is not learned apart from the other. Moreover, the acquisition of language is, itself, embedded in other cognitive, social, and emotional developments that occur at the same time. Efforts to explain word learning, therefore, must involve broad principles that account for both developmental process and changes in behavior over time. I have proposed three such principles as explanatory concepts *that focus on the agency and action of the child as mechanism* (L. Bloom, 1993, 1998). These principles describe the moment-to-moment adjustments between a child's intentional states in consciousness and the child's perceptions of changing circumstances in the context—adjustments that are required for all development. Here the principles are applied to language development in general and to word learning in particular.

According to the principle of *relevance,* language learning is enhanced when the words a child hears bear upon and are pertinent to the objects of engagement, interest, and feelings that are the child's contents of mind. Relevance is determined by the things children care about in the real world and provides the *direction* for word learning, determining the words children say and understand and, thereby, the words they learn. Relevance, according to Sperber and Wilson (1986, p. 46) "is the single property that makes information worth processing."[1]

According to the principle of *discrepancy,* a language has to be acquired when the child's contents of mind differ from what is already evident to other persons and clues from the context are not available for shared understanding. As children become able to anticipate new events and recall past events not part of the here and now, they need to learn a language for expression and interpretation in order to resolve discrepancies between what they and others have in mind. Discrepancy provides the *motivation* for word learning: why children learn words and procedures for sentences in the first place.

According to the principle of *elaboration,* children will have to learn increasingly more of the language—its words and its syntax—in order to express and articulate the increasingly elaborated contents of mind made possible by developments in the symbolic capacity and conceptual structure. Language must keep up with the increasing number of elements, roles, and relationships that are represented in intentional states for expression and interpretation. Elaboration of intentional states provides the *impetus* for propelling the progress of language acquisition forward.

Together, the principles of relevance, discrepancy, and elaboration have two essential consequences in the intentionality theory of language learning. First, other aspects of the child's development contribute to the process of language learning. Language emerges out of a nexus of developments in cognition, emotion, and social connectedness in the first 3 years of life (L. Bloom, 1993, 1998), and its acquisition is not reducible to neural networks, lexical constraints and biases, or the actions of other persons. Second, word learning depends on the essential agency of the child. Although such general learning strategies as discrimination and association are required, these are driven by the child's cognitive and affective processes. Language is learned by a child who is poised to act, to influence, to gain control—a child who is reaching out to a world of persons and objects to embrace the learning of language for the power of expression it provides.

In contrast, most of the constraints theories that have been proposed depend on mechanisms for learning words that are isolated from the rest of language— particularly its grammar—and from the rest of a child's development. Explanatory principles are constraints, theories, biases, default assumptions, and the like that are presumed to guide the child through the word-learning process, outside of a child's control and apart from the child's actions and interactions in the world (e.g., Markman, 1989). Moreover, the constraints that have been offered focus on how children learn the nouns of the language. To the extent that verbs are addressed, for example, different explanatory principles specific to verbs (or other parts of speech) need to be invoked. But a child's lexicon is not simply lists of nouns, verbs, and adjectives. Rather, the lexicon has an inherent organization with respect to both itself and emerging knowledge of the syntactic constructions in which words are experienced. Lexical organization and word learning cannot be independent of the knowledge that the child is also gaining about syntax and morphological processes, and nouns are not privileged.

In social pragmatic theories, a language tutor/caregiver in the child's social context is the mechanism for word learning. In the ordinary give-and-take of activities of daily living, such ostensive signals as a caregiver's gaze, gesture, and smile point the child to things in the context that can offer clues to what an unknown word might mean. Pragmatic theories are descended, at least tacitly, from socially driven theories more generally (notably Vygotsky, 1962, 1978; Bruner, 1983). In social theories of language development, the major emphasis is on the part adults play in constructing and guiding the interpersonal context and how children learn to interpret what adults do for clues to what the adult might have in mind. To be sure, the child is the novice—the child is the apprentice to the adult in language learning. But that fact cannot obscure the child's agency in acts of expression and interpretation directed toward other persons—acts that embody, make manifest, express what *the child has in mind.*

The goal of this chapter is to present a model of language acquisition that shifts the balance of influence from the adult to the child for the social dynamics of their interaction (e.g., see L. Bloom, 1993, 1998; Bloom, Margulis, Tinker, & Fujita, 1996). It is the *child's* agenda that creates the language-learning scenario more often than not, and that sets the pace for language learning in everyday interactions. It is *the child's contents of mind* that determine which words are learned and whether what an adult does is useful for word learning.

Chapters 1 and 4 in this book marry pragmatic theories to constraints theories in an effort to contextualize the operation of lexically specific principles or biases as mechanisms of word learning. In Hirsh-Pasek and Golinkoff's coalition model (1991, and chapter 1 in this volume), word-learning principles operate in conjunction with pragmatic cues from the context to determine not only how words are learned but how the principles themselves develop over time. This view was echoed, more recently, by Woodward and Markman (1997). Still missing, however, in models of lexical principles-plus-pragmatics is the *internal* component: the child's contents of mind that prompt and exploit the pragmatic cues from a caregiver for word learning and that kindle and fuel the interactions in which such cues occur and words are learned.

Connectionist learning models invoke mechanisms that can, potentially at least, explain acquisition of morpho-syntactic processes and structures as well as word learning. The mechanism in connectionist models depends on the neurological architecture and functioning of the brain and is not far removed conceptually from the hard wiring in the "language acquisition device" that Chomsky proposed in 1965—however much the two kinds of theories might differ in the specifics of what it is that is being acquired. In the world according to MIT, language is acquired by a device, not a child, and research begins with a theory of adult grammar and asks what aspects of that theory of grammar are learnable. In connectionist models, language acquisition is reduced to the neural connections in the brain that are the effects of linguistic experience. Both kinds of theory are specific to language learning, and both kinds of theory bypass the child, who is simply the vehicle in which such a device or connections work.

All of these efforts to understand the mechanisms of word learning focus on one or another version of the "mapping problem": how children attach the forms of language to concepts of objects, events, and relations in the world. This emphasis on the mapping problem has, by and large, been product oriented rather than process oriented. The products emphasized in research and theory are concepts, the forms of language, connections between concepts and language forms, and how those connections are represented in the brain/mind. In fact, I think it is fair to say that most language study, with adults as well as children, is not ordinarily concerned with process—with the on-line, moment-to-moment thinking that goes into actually saying and understanding words and sentences.

A focus on the mentally constructed, unobservable representations that individuals express when they talk and that result from interpreting the speech of others connects a theory of language development to theories of intentionality in philosophy (in the sense of Brentano, 1966;Danto, 1973; Searle, 1983; Taylor 1985, among others). Intentional states are the representations we construct in consciousness as we talk and listen, and they are the critical aspect of thinking for language and for the process of language acquisition. These representations are cognitive not linguistic constructions, but "language does not come without them" (Fauconnier, 1985, p. 1). Still, most theories of word learning bypass the intentionality of the child.

Theories of word learning have ignored the essential fact about what language is and what it does. Language exists in a society to embody and make public our intentional states—the goals and plans, the beliefs and desires, and the feelings we have that are, themselves, unobservable but that determine how we connect to one another in everyday events. "What comes about through the development of language in the broadest sense is the coming to be of expressive power" (Taylor, 1985, p. 238). The power of expression comes from using the conventional, linguistic meanings in words and grammar to express the private, personal meanings in a mind. These personal meanings—the contents of our beliefs, desires, and feelings—are unobservable unless we can somehow embody them and make them manifest. In this perspective the focus is squarely on the mind of the child, to be sure, but that is not to deny the critical part played by the social world. Children learn language for acts of expression, in the effort to make known to others what their own thoughts and feelings are about, and for acts of interpretation, in the effort to share the thoughts and feelings of other persons.

Intentionality is central to the model of language acquisition that I describe in this chapter (L. Bloom, 1993, 1998; Bloom and Tinker, 1999). The principles of relevance, discrepancy, and elaboration explain the dialectic transactions between a child's intentional states in conscious states of mind and the external social and physical contexts in which language is discovered by the child for learning. Invoking a child's intentionality in a model of language acquisition places the essential agency of the child at the center of the developmental process and locates language within a nexus of developments in cognition, emotion, and social connectedness.

INTENTIONALITY AND LEARNING

Virtually all developmental accounts of children's word learning have noted the strong association between word and object, word and action, or word and event. More than a century ago, Thorndike (1898) pointed out that the importance of words comes from "their connections with real things, qualities, acts, events, and relations. . . . The[se] connections operate in a mental 'set' and under the influence of more or less of the hearer-reader's entire mental equipment." He was the original "connectionist." The title of an anthology of his papers published in 1949, the year that he died, is *Selected Writings from a Connectionist's Psychology*. He pointed to the strength or weight of connections in terms of their "potency" and the resulting probabilities with which they influence what animals, including children and other persons, actually do. The relative ease with which connections are formed depends upon three basic facts: the frequency with which an act is performed, the attention the individual gives to the action, and, perhaps even more important, the intention in the act or what Thorndike called "the impulse to act." Invoking attention and intention in a theory of learning anticipated the principle of relevance.

Good old-fashioned associative learning has to play a fundamental role in almost anybody's theory of how words are learned (L. Bloom, 1993), and associationism is the centerpiece of chapter 3 in this volume. Although association clearly contributes to the process of learning, it is just one component of the word-learning process. Still missing are the affective and motivational components of word learning captured by the principle of relevance, which determines the particular words a child learns, and the principle of discrepancy, which determines why words are learned. Also missing is the cognitive impetus captured by the principle of elaboration, which propels a child's progress in language development forward and determines why more words and eventually a grammar must be acquired.

I have described the part played by associations in word learning in *One Word at a Time* (1973) and *The Transition from Infancy to Language* (1993), and pointed out, in particular, that children experience words (or signs) as one part of a complex event. When a child hears a word (and perhaps a larger speech unit such as a phrase or sentence), the linguistic units are entered in memory along with other perceptual and personal data about their circumstances of use. The data for these associations come from the perceptual and functional contingencies experienced with the word, which can include many elements in addition to an object in the context—such as something that someone does or other transformations of persons, objects, and relationships between them. Hearing a word is one element in an episode along with such other elements as persons, objects, actions, and the relations between them.

At the start, the word is not separate from the episode in which it was first encountered, and it enters the memory system as a virtual fusion of form and content—a "word-image representation" that provides the basis for proceeding to consolidate the word's meaning in subsequent encounters (L. Bloom, 1973). Because word and episode are at first linked in memory, recalling the word is interdependent with recalling other aspects of the episode. In *One Word at a Time*, I described how the earliest words can be highly restricted in their use—for example the word "car" said only when cars went by under the bedroom window and not extended to cars seen in any other circumstances. And I cited similar examples of such underextensions from the early diary studies (see, more recently, examples reported by Dromi, 1987). Thus, when some aspect of the same or similar episode reappears, these reencounters are cues for reactivating and recalling the word/episode compound from memory. In sum, early words are strongly "context bound," because the word is represented in memory along with something of the circumstances of its first encounter, before aspects of still other, succeeding, encounters are added to it. Abstractions of word and episode are stored together in word-learning encounters. Repeated encounters with a word both sharpen the boundaries of its meaning and broaden its extension to like circumstances. Thus, words are not mapped to isolated representations as the typical word-learning experiment would have it.

The importance of ostensive naming and association has always figured in descriptions of early language learning, beginning at least with St. Augustine in the 4th century, who professed to recall and recount his own personal history of language acquisition (see L. Bloom, 1993). Ostensive-inferential pragmatic signals—a glance, a shrug, a frown—are pervasive, and language does not occur without them (Sperber & Wilson, 1986). Infants and their caregivers both depend on these signals before language, and their exchanges provide contexts in which words are acquired. The pragmatic signals available to the language-learning child figure prominently in several theories of word learning (e.g., Baldwin, 1993; Tomasello, 1992a) and have been incorporated into theories of lexical principles and constraints (Hirsh-Pasek & Golinkoff, 1991; Woodward & Markman, 1997). But these signals go in both directions, and the adult in an interaction depends on the cues to relevance that the child provides as much as the child depends on cues from the adults. Ostensive learning depends on a speaker and listener having the same contents of mind, and both child and caregiver provide relevant cues for creating shared contents of mind. Children do not "wait around for someone to name what they have in mind" (as someone pronounced in criticism of the intentionality model), but neither do they wait around for other persons to point items out to them and name them. Indeed, much of language acquisition occurs outside of ostensive episodes, at least as these have been typically described, and extends far beyond the paradigm case in child language research of "pointing out" (see Gopnik & Meltzoff, 1987, for discussion).

Children begin to acquire words slowly at first, in the second year, and their early words are fragile, tentative, and imprecise as they grope to find the associations that connect the different circumstances in which words are experienced (L. Bloom, 1973). But sometime toward the end of the 2nd year, with a spurt in vocabulary, they begin to use many different words and to use them more frequently and more easily. The words learned in the 2nd year do not replace the pragmatic signals and emotional displays that served the infant so well in the 1st year. Children continue to express their feelings through displays of emotion as they learn the words to articulate what their feelings are about—the words that name the objects and circumstances of their emotional experiences, such words as "more," "gone," "Mama," "cookie," "fall down" (L. Bloom, 1993). Because these words give public expression to a child's private meanings, other persons can know them, share them, and perhaps do something about them. The basic assumption in my intentionality model of language development is that children learn language to express contents of mind and to interpret what others have in mind.

THE CHILD'S INTENTIONALITY AND LANGUAGE DEVELOPMENT

The intentionality model shown in Figure 2.1 (from Bloom & Tinker, 1999) has at its core the tripartite model of language content, form, and use that Margaret Lahey and I introduced in the late 1970s. Linguistic forms—sounds, words, syntax—are only part of what language is. *Form* requires *content,* because language is always *about something.* And form and content require the pragmatics of language *use,* because language is used differently in different situations according to pragmatic circumstances and communication goals. One or the other of these components, notably form alone, cannot by itself be a language—rather, language is, necessarily, the *convergence* of content, form, and use (Bloom & Lahey, 1978). The child's theory of language is always directed at the target language, but what the child knows and is learning about language at

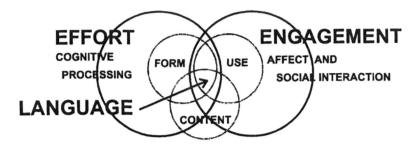

FIGURE 2.1. Intentionality Model of Language Acquisition (Bloom & Tinker, 1999).

any point in time is contextualized in everything else the child knows and is learning about the world of persons, objects, and events.

A model of language that encompasses language content and use as well as linguistic form means that language will never be acquired in the first place without *engagement* in a world of persons, objects, and events—the world that language is about and in which language is used. A model of language development, therefore, needs to embrace the part played by the social and emotional factors in language learning, which are conceptualized in Figure 2.1 as engagement. Children are engaged, from the beginning of life, with other persons, and the intersubjectivity that develops between infant and caregivers in the 1st year is the foundation for a child's social connectedness throughout life. Virtually from birth, emotional expressions are available for sharing and for creating and maintaining intersubjectivity. By the time language begins, toward the end of the 1st year, infants' emotional expressions are well established for sharing what they and others feel and think.

However, the result of cognitive developments in the 1st year is that children have contents of mind that are increasingly elaborated and discrepant from what other persons can see and hear in the context. As infants remember past events and anticipate new events, they have intentional states with beliefs, desires, and feelings about things that other persons cannot yet know and that cannot be expressed by emotional expressions. A child will have to acquire a language when emotional expressions cannot be explicit enough and caregivers cannot exploit clues from the context in order to understand—when the objects of the child's belief, desire, and feeling are not already evident. Language not only expresses contents of mind but also articulates the objects, roles, and relationships represented in intentional states in ways that emotional displays cannot. Children learn language, therefore, because they strive to maintain intersubjectivity with other persons—language has to be learned when what the child has in mind differs from what someone else has in mind and must be expressed in order to be shared.

While engagement encompasses the child's emotional and social directedness for learning a language, the component of *effort* captures the work it takes to learn a language and the cognitive processes that are required. Learning and using words for interpretation and expression put demands on a young child's essentially limited cognitive resources. For example, at a minimum, *learning a word* requires that the child construct an intentional-state representation out of data from perception and data recalled from memory, associate the word with an element or elements in that representation, and encode the word and its associated contingencies in memory. At a minimum, *using a word* requires that the child both construct and hold in mind an intentional-state representation, retrieve the word from memory for expressing an element or elements in the intentional state, and articulate the word in an expression.

These processes for word learning and expression often occur together, which compounds the effort that each requires. In addition, because words are not expressed apart from a child's emotional responses and other actions or interactions in the world, the cognitive resources available for words must be shared with—among other things—emotional expression, learning about objects and relationships between objects in play, responding to what someone else says in conversation, and so forth. The effort required by learning and using the units of language tends to be overlooked, especially when the processes involved are attributed to mechanisms external to the child, such as the social context, or a language-acquisition device, or neural networks, or lexical principles, constraints, and biases.

In sum, language is learned in a dialectical tension between engagement and effort. *Engagement,* which provides the motivation for learning language, together with the cognitive *effort* required for language draw on the young child's affective and cognitive resources. The principles of relevance, discrepancy, and elaboration mediate between engagement and effort. Relevance determines what captures a child's engagement for linguistic learning and linguistic interaction. Discrepancy between what the child and others have in mind determines the need to exert the effort required to learn and use language. And increasing elaboration of the contents of mind causes effort to be extended toward learning and using increasingly more complex and abstract language forms and functions.

Engagement and Word Learning

A word that the child hears is relevant when its target is part of what the child has in mind, part of the representations in consciousness that are the child's intentional states—what the child is feeling and thinking at the time. Children surely hear many words that are not relevant to what they have in mind, but the words they will learn are those that are relevant to the persons, objects, events, actions, states, relationships, and the like that they do care and know about and that are, therefore, the objects of their engagement. Relevance is not the same as salience. For example, the Empire State Building at 34th Street in New York City is salient to people riding the Fifth Avenue bus downtown, but it is not necessarily *relevant* unless they are reminded to meet someone on the corner of 34th Street. What is salient in the context becomes useful to the child only when it is pertinent and bears upon the elements, roles, and relationships in the configuration in the child's mind—that is, when it is "information worth processing." To be sure, what the child has in mind changes on hearing words, and the child's attention can be drawn to something new, which then becomes relevant, but that is the consequence of all acts of interpretation.

A recurrent claim in the literature, following Quine (1960), is that a new word could theoretically have many different meanings in the situations in which a child hears it: How is the child to know that the meaning of "rabbit" is not "hop," "ears," "tail," "furry" or any one of the meanings it could have? When the child sees a second rabbit hop by and hears, "more," why should the word "more" mean something other than "rabbit"? The answer is that the principle of relevance narrows the range of possible meanings the word could have on the occasion of the child's hearing it. Relevance in word-learning scenarios has three determinants: The first is the child's *engagement* in whatever is the focus of attention. The extent to which a child finds a task interesting will determine the level of engagement that the child brings to the task (Renninger, 1990; Renninger & Wozniak, 1985). The second determinant is *conceptual structure* in the knowledge base and the concepts of objects (such as rabbits) and relationships (such as recurrence) that the child is also learning. Children more readily learn words that name things they are learning about and they are more likely to become engaged when learning something new than when presented with what is already familiar and well-known. The third determinant of relevance is the child's *focus of attention* and the extent to which an adult shares that focus of attention when saying words. If the child's focus is on the whole object, then he or she will provide signals to an adult to assure a connection between the word and the whole object, and that is what the child will take the word "rabbit" to mean. But if the focus is the rabbit's ears, then the child will assume that the word "rabbit" means "ears" until persuaded otherwise.

Invoking the Quinean dilemma simply does not fit the typical situations for either word learning by infants (Nelson, 1988) or language use by adults.

> The speaker-listener does not consider all the interpretations of a sentence and then discard the inappropriate ones. . . . Starting from the [mental] configuration already available . . . the potential of a sentence is always far less than its general potential for all possible configurations. (A brick could theoretically occupy any position in a wall, but at any stage of the actual building process, there is only one place for it to go.) (Fauconnier, 1985, pp. 168–169)

Fortunately, like Fauconnier's brick, the word a child hears will already have its target in the child's mind, more often than not, because caregiver speech to children is overwhelmingly *responsive* (Bloom et al., 1996). In actual word-learning scenarios, a child hears words that name elements, roles, and relations already in mind or called to mind in the situation. Children are not—as in the typical word-learning experiment—depending on adults to direct their attention to an object and then name it.

Evidence for the principle of relevance for word learning is abundant in the literature. Studies have revealed again and again that communication between infants and mothers occurs in contexts of "joint attention," which assure that the adult's contribution to the exchange will be relevant. The importance of joint attention (Bruner, 1977; Tomasello, 1992a), is one aspect of language development virtually everyone agrees on by now. The extent to which caregivers name the object that a child is attending to determines the words a child learns and influences subsequent vocabulary size. Children evidently learn more words when caregivers tune into and say something about the objects of attention (Masur, 1982; Tomasello & Akhtar, 1995). Similarly, an optimum occasion for learning language forms occurs when caregivers fail to understand an infant's expression and "negotiate" the form of the message in subsequent exchanges (Golinkoff, 1986). In these instances, infants are presented with the forms that can more successfully articulate what they have in mind.

In studies of joint attention between child and caregiver, however, the focus is rarely on the importance of attentional processes for language development *from the child's point of view.* The emphasis is typically on the part played by the adult, who does or does not take the child's attentional focus into account in the interaction, rather than on the child, who provides the signals that direct the adult's attention. However, the child's intentional state determines joint attention more often than not, as children invariably take the lead in their everyday conversations with adults (L. Bloom et al., 1996; Harris, 1992; Howe, 1981) as well as in their play activities (L. Bloom & Tinker, 1999). Even mothers' efforts at setting up routines, games, and formatting in their exchanges with their infants (the prototypical kinds of scaffolding events) are prompted most often by something a child looks at, touches, or says (Maher, Lucariello, & Bloom, 1999). Evidence is now accumulating to show that it is a caregiver's *responsiveness* to a child, rather than the adult's direction or external scaffolding of the interaction that determines the interaction between them (L. Bloom, 1993, 1998; Bloom, Margulis, Tinker, & Fujita, 1996). Moreover, the extent to which caregiver speech is responsive is a much stronger predictor of word learning than is the mere quantity or amount of speech a child hears (Bornstein, Tamis-LeMonda, & Haynes, 1999).

Since feelings and emotions are central to engagement with the personal and physical world, we might expect children to talk about those things their feelings are about, and this expectation was borne out in a study of the timing relationship between saying words and expressing emotion. Children were most likely to express emotion during and immediately after the moments when they were also talking—when compared with their baseline rates of emotional expression, which was how often they might be expected to express emotion at any particular time. (Bloom & Beckwith, 1989; see Fig. 2.4). However, instead of naming the individual emotions and learning emotion labels, they talked about topics that were relevant to the objects, causes, and circumstances of their feelings, using words *to express what their feelings were about* while they continued to express how they were feeling through displays of positive and negative affect. In other words, they talked about what they cared about, providing evidence of their engagement and affirming the principle of relevance. But the results of this study also showed the effects of effort: The engagement evident when children expressed more emotion around speech than was predicted by their baseline rates was qualified by the effects of the effort that both saying words and expressing emotion can require, as will be described below.

Effort and Word Learning

The mental processes for saying a word or sentence begin with a plan. That mental plan entails several things (at least), including constructing an intentional state for the child's mental meaning, and then accessing the words, syntax, and other linguistic forms and procedures for articulating and expressing the mental meaning. In an earlier study, we showed the effects of the effort required for this on-line processing in the variable length and completeness of 2-year-olds' early sentences (Bloom, Miller, & Hood, 1975). When a child's sentence included words that were newly learned or certain kinds of complexity such as negation or prepositions in a verb complement, or when the sentence did not have support in the accompanying discourse, the effect was an increase in cognitive load. The result was that children said such sentences as "Mommy read book" and "No read book," rather than the more complete sentence "Mommy no read book." Negative sentences, or sentences with newly learned words, or sentences without discourse support were shorter, because using negation and using new words in a sentence cost the child extra cognitive effort. The converse was also true: Using frequent, earlier-learned words with accompanying discourse support and without added complexity increased the probability that sentences would be longer and more complete (Bloom, Miller, & Hood; see also, P. Bloom, 1989; Valian, 1991).

Thus, learning something of the language does not mean that access for expression is automatic—far from it. Rather, the probabilities of saying words and sentences in one or another situation are determined by at least the ability to construct a mental meaning, how familiar and frequent the linguistic forms and their meanings are, and either support or competing demands from accompanying discourse. There is considerably more to language development, therefore, than just acquiring the words and procedures for sentences.

To begin with, engagement is required. Children will be guided in their language learning by that portion of the input that is relevant to what they have in mind, and they will be motivated to learn the language in order to express contents of mind that cannot otherwise be known by other persons—the principles of relevance and discrepancy that build on corresponding developments in emotionality and social connectedness. But effort is required as contents of mind become increasingly elaborated. Children need to learn increasingly more complex and abstract aspects of the language for expressing as well as articulating more elements, roles, and relationships that are represented in intentional states.

The original study by Bloom, Miller, and Hood (1975) and subsequent studies of such "competition" effects, however, looked only at aspects of linguistic behavior: lexicon, syntactic complexity, and discourse. More recently, we have studied children's early word learning in relation to nonlinguistic behaviors and actions, including emotional expression, play with objects, and conversations with mothers (Bloom & Beckwith, 1989; Bloom & Tinker, 1999; Bloom, Margulis, Tinker, & Fujita, 1996). The relationships of these several kinds of behavior to a child's language, on-line in the moment-to-moment temporal contingencies of everyday events, showed the effects of both effort and engagement and provided evidence to support the centrality of the child's intentionality for word learning.

EVIDENCE FOR THE INTENTIONALITY MODEL OF LANGUAGE DEVELOPMENT

The evidence for the intentionality model supports, in particular, the generality of the principles that guide word learning, the child's agency in word learning, and the engagement and effort entailed in the process of word learning.

Generality of Word-Learning Principles

Children learn many different kinds of words in addition to object names; in fact, for many 1-year-olds, more than half the words they know are not object names. However, with rare exceptions, the principles, biases, or predispositions that have been offered to explain word learning are not only language-specific and, more particularly, *lexically* specific (having to do only with learning words) but lexical principles and constraints are also typically *object* specific (having to do only with how children learn names for objects). Important examples are the whole-object assumption (Markman, 1989, 1992) and the principle of object scope (Golinkoff, Mervis, & Hirsh-Pasek, 1994; Golinkoff, Shuff-Bailey, Olguin, & Ruan, 1995). On hearing a new word, a child will assume that it names a whole object rather than a part of the object, one of its properties, or something related to it. Object specific lexical principles (constraints, biases, or assumptions) are consistent, however, with much of the history of research in word learning in their emphasis on object names, since nouns are the largest syntactic class of words in the adult language and they are relatively easy to study experimentally.

The importance of words in children's early vocabularies that are not names of objects was first described in L. Bloom, 1973, with respect to relational words and person names, and in Nelson, 1973, with respect to individual differences. These early results have since been confirmed by many others (e.g., Bates, Dale, & Thal, 1995; Gopnik, 1982; Hampson, 1989; Lieven, Pine, & Barnes, 1992; McCune-Nicolich, 1981). In our study of children's early vocabulary (Bloom, Tinker, & Margulis, 1993), we sampled the words of 14 children every month, starting with mothers' diaries begun before the children said their first words in our playroom observations (on average, at about 13 months of age) and continuing through the succeeding months until 1 month after they showed a vocabulary spurt (at about 20 months of age, on average). If object-specific lexical principles help get word learning off the ground, as has been claimed, then we might expect more object words to be learned early in this period, followed by a decline in object names, as children learn to "override" a constraint such as the whole-object assumption (as Markman [1992] suggested). However, plotting the average percentage of object names among the new words the children learned from month to month revealed that object names made up, on average, less than 40% of new words learned each month. Object names also made up less than half of all the words, new and old, in the children's total vocabularies each month. Even after eliminating the child whose percentage of object words was consistently the lowest each month, the result was the same. On average, 30% to 39% of the different words (word types) said each month by the remaining 13 children were object words. Thus, object words did not predominate in the single-word period for these children (Bloom, Tinker, & Margulis, 1994).

A similar result was obtained for the more than 11,000 word tokens the children said in this period: only 33.3% of the tokens were object names. The continuum of word learning was divided into two periods, one period encompassing the months up to and including the month before the vocabulary spurt, and the other period encompassing the month of the vocabulary spurt and the following month. In the periods before and after the vocabulary spurt, 34.8% and 32.5% of word tokens (respectively) were, on average, object names, consistent with the rates of object names among word types reported overall. Thus, object words were not more likely to be learned earlier or later in the period of word learning and were not more likely to be learned either before or after the vocabulary spurt.

When person names (including "Mama" or its equivalent) were included along with object words, both object words and person names together accounted for 40.6% of word types and 43% of word tokens in all the children's words up to and including the month after the vocabulary spurt. When the size of the children's vocabularies reached 50 words—often used as a milestone in word learning—the mean percentage of object words was 36.3%, with a range from 10% to 50% for the individual children, and object names represented 50% of the first 50 words for only one child. These findings from L. Bloom, Tinker, & Margulis (1993) are consistent with many other studies of early vocabulary, whether from observation of spontaneous speech or from mothers' reports (e.g., Bates, Bretherton, & Snyder, 1988; L. Bloom, 1973; Fenson et al., 1994; Gopnik, 1982, 1988; Gopnik, Choi, & Baumberger, 1996; Hampson, 1989; Hampson & Nelson, 1993; McCarthy, 1930; Nelson, 1973; Pine, 1992; Tardif, 1996).

Moreover, object words do not necessarily become more important as children learn procedures for sentences. We have now extended the analysis to the children's vocabularies at the time of their transition to multiword speech (MW), the month in which mean length of utterance reached or passed 1.5 words; the findings are presented in Figure 2.2 along with the original results reported by L. Bloom, Tinker, & Margulis (1993). Most of the words in the children's spontaneous speech were still not the names for objects—in fact, an even smaller percentage of the vocabularies that they were using consisted of object nouns. In the 3-month window around vocabulary spurt (VS), object names represented, on average, about 37% of the new words that appeared each month. But at the time the children were making their transition to sentences, object words represented only about 26% of the new words they were using. Evidently, the children had a lot to learn about the language, and learning object names was not necessarily the top priority.

The mean number of words in the children's vocabularies through MW + 1 was 204. In the normative data based on the Communication Development Inventory (Bates et al., 1994), a decline in the proportion of object names also occurred when total vocabulary was about 200 words, which may well have coincided with the transition to syntax by the children in that study. Many studies have reported the increase in verbs relative to nouns at about this time. Learning object names, therefore, seems to become less, not more, important as acquisition progresses. If we had used the Communication Development Inventory and asked the mothers which words they thought their children knew, we expect they would have reported many more object names in their children's vocabularies (as well as more of other kinds of words). In some studies, particularly those using mother-report measures, the proportion of nouns reported has been as high as 60%. However, even when mothers relate that 60% or even 70% of the words their children know are object names, a theory of word learning must account for how those children learned 30%–40% of their words. In

Mean Number of New Words

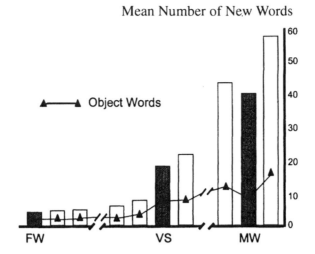

Months between Language Achievements

FIGURE 2.2. Frequency of Object Words among New Words Each Month. From first words (FW) through vocabulary spurt (VS), to month following transition to multiword speech (MV), the breaks in the continua indicate differences among the children in the number of months between the language achievements. Data from FW through VS + 1 correspond to 14 children (L. Bloom, Tinker, & Margulis, 1993); data in the 3-month window around MW correspond to 11 of the same children (L. Bloom, unpublished data).

sum, because children are not just learning object names, theories of word learning must be considerably more general; they must explain *how a child can learn any kind of word.*

The representation of object names in the vocabularies of the 1-year-olds we studied was also consistent with the relative frequency of object names in the speech these children heard from their mothers in the same observation sessions (L. Bloom, unpublished data). Moreover, the distribution of nouns we found in both child and mother speech is consistent with analyses of a variety of both adult and child written and spoken texts, which showed that common nouns make up about 37% of all word tokens (Hudson, 1994). It does not seem to matter whether the sample consists of words used in adult or child texts or in written or spoken texts; the relative frequency of common nouns remains under 40%.

The message is clear: Object names represent less than half of the words in the everyday texts of either spoken or written discourse from both adults and children. How, then, can object-specific lexical principles explain word learning? If many or most of the words that children acquire, and most of the words that they use in their running speech, are not names of objects, then more general principles are required to explain how a child will learn any kind of word, not just object words (L. Bloom, 1993, 1997).   ·

Invoking object-specific principles to explain word learning also separates the acquisition of the lexicon from the rest of the language a child is learning, particularly the procedures for sentences. Grammar is inherently *relational* in that the function of sentences is to specify the relationships within and between objects, states, and events. Before children begin to use syntax, words such as "more," "up," and "on," which name relationships, figure prominently in their single-word vocabularies. Toward the end of the single-word period, in anticipation of the transition to syntax, verbs, which are quintessentially relational, increase in frequency and number (e.g., Bates, Bretherton, & Snyder, 1988; L. Bloom, 1973, 1993; L. Bloom, Tinker, & Margulis, 1993; Gentner, 1982; Goldin-Meadow, Seligman, & Gelman, 1976; Tomasello, 1992a). We have proposed repeatedly that acquiring the structures of grammar goes hand in hand with learning the words of the language, particularly verbs (e.g., L. Bloom, 1981, 1991; Bloom, Lifter, & Hafitz, 1980; Bloom, Lightbown, & Hood, 1975; Bloom, Merkin, & Wootten, 1982; Bloom, Rispoli, Gartner, & Hafitz, 1989; see also, Pinker, 1984, 1989; Tomasello, 1992b). Clearly, children need to learn different kinds of words for their early vocabularies, not just object names, and general principles, such as the three principles of the intentionality model of language development described here, are required to explain language learning.

The principles of relevance, discrepancy, and elaboration explain more than just the variation in the kinds of words that children learn. For the children in our studies, developments also occurred from first words to vocabulary spurt in the mental meanings that their words expressed (L. Bloom, 1993, 1994; Bloom, Beckwith, Capatides, & Hafitz, 1988). If the principle of elaboration is correct, then development ought to occur in the expression of intentional states with multiple elements, roles, and relations between elements, such as in mental meanings that include an action. Dynamic meanings directed at actions have several elements with different roles and relations between them, according to the details of the action. These can include an actor or agent of the action, an object affected by the action, an instrument for the action, the place to which an object is moved, and so forth. Static, stative meanings without an action, other than one of "picking out," usually focus on the single element that the child has in mind while showing, giving, pointing, or otherwise presenting. Expression of both sorts of meaning increased in the period from first words to vocabulary spurt. But the development that occurred at vocabulary spurt was the relatively greater increase in expression of dynamic, action meaning compared to presentational, stative meanings. This increase in expression of action meanings anticipated the subsequent transition to simple sentences.

Thus, one development in the single-word period was an increase in the number of elements, roles, and relations attributable to mental meanings directed at actions, consistent with the principle of elaboration. We looked also at whether the elements attributed to mental meanings expressed by the children's words were already evident in the circumstances in which the words were said. According to the principle of discrepancy, children will acquire words and the grammar of a language as their mental meanings become increasingly discrepant from the data of perception and must be expressed in order to be shared. *Development in mental meanings ought to proceed in the direction of expressing what is anticipated rather than what is already evident in the context.* Most of the children's words expressed meanings that were evident, directed as they were to what was already present or in progress. The greater frequency of evident expression overall, at both first words and vocabulary spurt, was what one might expect from the often cited "here and now" characterization of children's early speech. However, development occurred from first words to vocabulary spurt in the relative frequency of *anticipated* expression, with a greater increase in words expressing something about *imminent* actions and events.

In sum, development in the single-word period was in words that expressed mental meanings that were both increasingly elaborated (having multiple objects, roles, and action relations) and increasingly discrepant (having meanings that could not otherwise be known to a listener because they were anticipated by the child—imminent but not yet evident). The general principles of relevance, discrepancy, and elaboration, therefore, account for the meanings that children's words express in addition to differences in the kinds of words they are learning. Lexical- and object-specific principles of word learning can account for neither.

Child Agency in Word Learning: Who's in Charge?

By themselves, lexical principles (or biases or constraints) as well as theories based on neurological architecture and brain function imply an essentially passive child, one who depends on external mechanism rather than active mental and affective process in the course of development. A cornerstone of the intentionality theory of language development is that word learning is the product of the active mind of a child. Children strive to learn the words that can express what they have in mind. They work hard at interpreting the social and pragmatic cues in contexts of everyday living, first, to be able to attribute intentional states to other persons in order to share what others have in mind and, second, so they can "read" the cues to particulars associated with a word that can yield its linguistic meaning. However, young children provide a rich array of cues to their own intentionality, so that other persons can make attributions of what they have in mind, and, indeed, caregivers depend on these cues for their caregiving and other interactions with infants and toddlers.

Recognizing inherent limitations on lexically specific learning principles or constraints, theorists have now acknowledged that these principles alone can-not account for word learning. Young children's impressive ability to make use of pragmatic cues in their social interactions has now been acknowledged and incorporated into lexical-principles theories (Hirsh-Pasek & Golinkoff, 1991; Woodward & Markman, 1997; chapters 1 and 4 in this volume). The impor-tance of pragmatic cues for word learning cannot be underestimated; in fact, pragmatics was a dominant influence on theories of language acquisition a gen-eration ago (e.g., Bates, 1976; Bruner, 1975, 1983; Dore, 1975; Ervin-Tripp, 1973; McShane, 1980; Ryan, 1974) as well as more recently (e.g., Clark, 1991; Tomasello, 1992b; Zukow, 1990). The fact is that children depend on hearing words as one part of a complex interpersonal event. The circumstances of word use in everyday occurrences are rich in visual and auditory cues—gazes, ges-tures, emotional displays, intonation, and the like—that point children to un-derstanding the significance of the words they hear (L. Bloom, 1973). Most re-cently, such pragmatic cues have been validated in experimental studies, and children's interpretive abilities have been richly demonstrated (Baldwin, 1993; Tomasello & Akhtar, 1995).

Most research on the importance of pragmatic cues for word learning has as-sumed that it is the adult in an interaction who is responsible for constructing the word-learning scenario and supplying the necessary cues to the child. To be sure, interested others are sensitive to the child's cues and tune in to the child's focus of attention, *but it is the child who provides the lead more often than not.*

The child's agency in the typical word-learning scenario has been evident in two recent studies of 1-year-olds and their mothers: one a study of the tem-poral and functional relationship between child and mother messages in their spontaneous conversations (Bloom, Margulis, Tinker, & Fujita, 1996) and the other a study of those particular interactions that included mothers' formatting routines (Maher, Lucariello, & Bloom, 1999). The structure of the discourse context has long been invoked as the basis for word learning, but the typical as-sumption has been that word learning depends on the caregiver for both con-structing the discourse and scaffolding the child's participation in it. We have shown, however, that conversations between children and their mothers are generated by the children, from the beginning of word learning, and neither the interactions themselves nor learning words in an interaction depends on adults' creating the dialog between them.

Child-Mother Conversations. In the study of the on-line temporal con-tingencies between child and mother speech, the tendencies for each to be talk-ing before, during, and after the other were compared to the respective baseline rates of child and mother speaking. The results at the time of the vocabulary spurt (mean age about 19 months), for the 12 children and mothers we studied, are presented in Figure 2.3. The horizontal line in the figure represents the base-

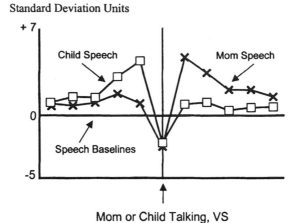

FIGURE 2.3. Temporal Patterns of Child-Mother Conversations. The figure shows the tendency for child or mother to be speaking during the other's speech (S) and in the five 1-second intervals before and after, relative to their respective baseline rates of speech overall (differences from baseline rates are in standard deviation units) (Bloom, Margulis, Tinker, & Fujita, 1996).

line rates of either child or mother speaking. The baseline rate was the incidence of either child or mother speech overall, as it was distributed throughout the entire observation, and was, therefore, the chance probability of either one speaking in any given 1-second interval. The vertical line in the figure represents the target events—speech (S)—the times when either mother or child was speaking. The data points represent deviations from baseline rates (in standard deviation units) *during* the target event and in each of the five 1-second intervals *before* and *after* the target (averaged here for the 12 child-mother pairs). Data points above the baseline meant that the observed speech was greater than was expected; data points below baseline meant that observed speech was less than predicted by the baseline rate.

All 12 of the child-mother pairs in this study showed the same profile as the group. Compared with their baseline rates of talking overall, children were most likely to be talking before mothers' speech, less likely to be talking after, and least likely to be talking at the same time. Relative to their baselines, mothers, in contrast, were more likely to be talking immediately after a child said something and less likely to be talking before the child's speech. The result is shown in Figure 2.3 for the vocabulary spurt; however, the same pattern of interaction occurred at first words but with greater excursions from baseline rates at vocabulary spurt than at first words. The temporal contingency of turn taking, a highly relevant dimension of conversational interaction, was already evident at first words but was consolidated in the period of word learning between first words and vocabulary spurt. Other research has also shown that mothers are more likely to respond than to initiate conversations (Harris, 1992, with infants 16 months old and younger; Howe, 1981, with 20- to 25-month-olds). One-year-old French-speaking Swiss children initiated the majority of talk about immediate past events in a study by Veneziano and Sinclair (1995), whereas talk about distant past events was more often initiated by adults, who might be expected to have more prior knowledge (see Lucariello & Nelson, 1987; Sachs, 1977).

When mothers shared the child's topic in responding, they typically simply repeated or otherwise acknowledged what the child had just said, and they were more likely to make a statement than to ask a question. Only about one-third of all child speech occurred in response to something mothers said. Thus, although the mothers of these 1-year-olds were taking a turn to keep the conversation going, they were not likely to make "extended replies," such as has been described with older children (e.g., Howe, 1981). Children, in turn, shared the topic most often when mothers' prior speech functioned as discourse commentary and less often when mothers encouraged or discouraged their actions.

This study of early conversations provided evidence of the kinds of experiences with language that young children have in their spontaneous, everyday interactions for learning words. Participation in these earliest conversations was motivated largely by a child's own cognitive agenda to express something in mind, and conversations functioned to allow the children to direct the flow of the interaction in order to express and thereby share what was relevant to them. Mothers, in turn, were primarily responsive. Thus, the results support a model of language development that takes a young child's intentional states as the starting point for conversations in particular and for word learning more generally, and that depends on responsivity as an important contribution that mothers make to their interactions with young children. Most recently, Bornstein, Tamis-LeMonda, and Haynes (1999) have shown that the extent to which mothers responded to their young children in this same developmental period was the most important influence on word learning, even more important than the number of words the mothers said.

Formats and Routines. From our study of conversations in children's 2nd year, we concluded that the children were the ones who set the pace and controlled the agenda of their interactions; they did not depend on their mothers to set up linguistic formats and scaffold their exchanges. However, the scaffolding model has been an important one in language-acquisition theory, and mothers' linguistic formatting has been considered vital to word learning in particular (e.g., Ninio & Bruner, 1978; Snow & Goldfield, 1983). For this reason we've recently looked specifically at those interactions that could be considered as "scaffolding" in the by-now classic sense in which the term is used: episodes that consisted of games, routines, songs, and play themes in which mothers might be deliberately or otherwise "teaching" their children words (Maher, Lucariello, & Bloom, 1999).

The analysis used the data at first words and the vocabulary spurt for eight of the same children in the conversations study. In spite of the liberal definition of scaffolding that we used, formatting episodes represented only 18% of the interactions at first words and 15% at vocabulary spurt. The frequency of mothers' formatting was simply related to how often mothers talked—mothers who talked more also produced more formatting episodes. However, formatting did not encourage children to talk more: The frequency of child speech was unrelated to frequency of formatting episodes. Formatting also did not play a leading role in word learning, because the children of mothers who least often formatted said proportionally more of the target words in format episodes than did children of mothers who formatted more often. Most important, however, formats were effective for word learning to the extent that they were child driven. Approximately two-thirds of the successful format episodes, in which a child eventually said a target word in an episode, were initiated by a child either looking at, touching, acting on, or saying something. Finally, one-third of the words the mothers targeted in format episodes at the vocabulary spurt had already appeared in the children's speech in the earlier months—they were not new words. Thus, if formats contribute to word learning, they might function to consolidate the vocabulary of words that children have already learned, instead of teaching new words.

The formatting results confirmed our earlier conclusion that children are "in charge" more often than not, taking the lead and setting the agenda for language learning in their interactions. They do this by providing cues to their intentionality—to that which they find relevant. Mothers differ in how well or how often they pick up on a child's cues and the extent to which they act on and respond to a child's cues. But it is mothers' *responsiveness* rather than prior scaffolding that influences word learning. Whatever social, interpersonal, or affective function that routines, games, and other formatting interactions might have, scaffolding is not the engine of word learning. Rather, word learning is driven by the agency and action of the child in the expression of intentionality.

Our studies of conversations and formatting were based on naturally occurring, spontaneous interactions between children and their mothers, who were provided with groups of toys and a snack and given the opportunity to do what they do in everyday situations. Mothers were asked neither to engage in picture book reading or such scripted activities as tea parties nor to "teach" a child how to perform a task (as in the typical study of formats and scaffolding). These are the sorts of scripted activities in which mothers have the upper hand, and they might well be expected to initiate and direct the activity. However, these practices can be expected to make up only a small part of the interactions between caregivers and young children in the course of a typical day. In contrast, by studying activities in which mothers did not necessarily have an advantage in the exchange, we were able to demonstrate the importance of their children's contribution to the interactions. The picture that emerged differed from traditional accounts of scaffolding and conversational asymmetry. Both child and mother contributed to the architecture of the early conversations between them, but it was, in fact, the children who were "in charge" (L. Bloom, Margulis, Tinker, & Fujita, 1996).

Engagement and Effort: Getting It Together

By now virtually everyone recognizes the importance of the larger linguistic contexts and social exchanges in which words occur and the critical contribution from conceptual development to word learning. However, little attention has been given to the dynamic processes of a child's thinking or to how other developments in cognition, affect, and social connectedness contribute to that thinking with respect to learning and using language. This is what the intentionality model is about. In our most recent research, Erin Tinker and I have looked, therefore, to the on-line convergence of several behaviors in the stream of a child's activities to see how linguistic expression converges with other behaviors at the same time. We looked at both the on-line, microgenetic relationships between different kinds of behavior in real time and changes in the patterns of these relationships across developmental time in the 2nd year. Three achievements in language provided the window on development that we used: first words, vocabulary spurt, and early sentences (Bloom & Tinker, 1999).

If a target behavior, such as saying a word, was unrelated to a second behavior, such as expressing emotion, then the emotional expression should not differ around a child's words from the baseline rate of occurrence of emotional expression overall; we should see an essentially random interaction between expressing emotion and saying words. As I have already reported, that was not the case; the result (from Bloom & Beckwith, 1989) is reproduced in Figure 2.4. The children were most likely to be expressing emotion, relative to their baseline rates of expression, immediately after and during the interval of time in which they said words, with the same pattern at both of the language achievements.

The results of this study provided evidence of both engagement and effort. The increased likelihood of emotional expression relative to baseline around words, particularly at vocabulary spurt, was described earlier as evidence of *engagement*. The children were learning to talk, in general, about those things that were *relevant* to them. However, the two systems of expression came together

Standard Deviation Units

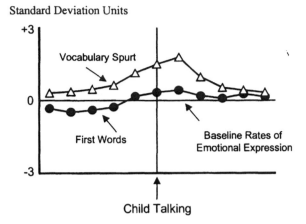

FIGURE 2.4. Tendency to Express Emotion. The figure shows the expression of emotion during speech (S) and in the five 1-second intervals before and after, relative to baseline rates of emotional expression overall, at first words and vocabulary spurt (differences from baseline rates are in standard deviation units) (Bloom & Beckwith, 1989).

with certain constraints that indicated the effort involved. First, the emotion expressed when saying words was primarily positive emotion rather than negative emotion and was most likely to be at low levels of intensity, therefore requiring less *effort*. Expressions of positive emotion pertain to the attainment of a desired end state and require less cognitive effort than do the negative emotions, which require the construction of a plan either to remove an obstacle to a goal (in the case of anger) or to construct a new goal (when a desired end state is lost, as with sadness) (see the discussion in Stein & Levine, 1989). Second, the words said with emotional expression were the words that children knew best: the earliest learned or most frequent words in their vocabularies that were presumably more "automatic." The excursions above baseline increased significantly at vocabulary spurt, which is a time of consolidation in word learning, compared to first words, which is a time of emergence. The smaller deviations above baseline at first words, along with the suppression of emotional expression below baseline rates in the 2–5 seconds before saying words, indicated the greater effort required to coordinate the two forms of expression when words first began.

We have now extended this analysis to the later transition to saying sentences, in the studies reported in Bloom and Tinker (1999). In contrast to the vocabulary spurt, when the children had been much more likely to express emotion relative to the baseline around speech, emotional expression was suppressed and was below baseline levels when the children were beginning to say sentences, indicating the effort that the transition to sentences required.

Moreover, when the group of 12 children was divided according to their ages at the time of the transition to sentences, with 6 children older than the mean age (the later learners) and 6 children younger than the mean (the earlier learners), the two groups differed significantly. The emotional expression of the younger learners did not differ from their baseline rates, but the emotional expression of the children who were older when they started to say sentences was substantially below their baselines. Greater effort was evidently required to coordinate the two kinds of expression, emotion and speech, for children who made the transition to saying sentences somewhat later and perhaps with more difficulty (Bloom & Tinker).

All of these analyses looked at the children's words and emotional expressions throughout a half-hour of play and interaction with their mothers, regardless of what else they were doing. We have also looked at the convergence of children's speech and emotional expression along with the occurrence of their mothers' speech in the moments around episodes in play—in particular, in those episodes in which the children were constructing thematic relationships between objects (such as putting one block on another, connecting train cars, or feeding a doll with a spoon). (The results of this study can be described only briefly here, but they are reported in full in Bloom & Tinker, 1999.) The findings provided evidence of the effort required for children to coordinate saying words, expressing emotion, and attending to what their mothers were saying at the same time that they were also learning to construct thematic relationships between objects in their spontaneous play.

As with the previous studies, data consisted of the likelihood of mother speech, child speech, and child emotion relative to the respective baselines of each, during and around target episodes of object play: a child putting objects together to construct a thematic relationship between them. Evidence of effort was apparent in two ways. First, the children were speaking and expressing emotion less often than expected in these play episodes. Speech and emotional expression were both below baseline, indicating a need to conserve affective and cognitive resources for the attention and thinking required to construct thematic relationships between objects in the same window of time. And second, effort was also evident in a trade-off between the two forms of expression, with the children more likely to be talking than expressing emotion during the act of constructing (between its times of onset and offset). Thus, even though the children were much more likely to express emotion during and immediately after saying words in general at the time of a vocabulary spurt, regardless of whatever else was going on (as we saw in Figure 2.4), the two forms of expression were dissociated during constructing activity.

Mothers, whom we have already seen as primarily responsive to their children in their conversations, were more likely to be responsive in play as well:

Relative to their baseline levels of speech, mothers were least likely to say something during the child's constructing activity and most likely to talk 1 and 2 seconds immediately after. In sum, the results of these studies of on-line temporal contingencies revealed the intricate adjustments required between engagement and effort for at least some of the different kinds of behaviors and activities that provide the contexts for word learning. Word learning is integrated in the stream of expression and other behavior. It is not an isolated activity, and no one would argue that it is. Nevertheless, most explanations offered to explain word learning ignore how the many elements involved simultaneously in the affective and cognitive life of the child contribute to the process.

CONCLUSION

Language is created by a child in the dynamic contexts and circumstances that make up the child's world, and the *heart of language acquisition* is in the dialectical tension between the two psychological components of effort and engagement. A language will never be acquired without *engagement* in a world of persons, objects, and events. The concept of engagement embraces the social, affective, and emotional factors that figure in language learning. Other persons and the *social* context are required in language development, not only as the source of the linguistic objects to be acquired but also because the motivation for learning a language is to express and interpret intentional states so that the child and others can share what each is thinking and feeling (the principle of discrepancy). *Affect* and emotional expression are required not only for establishing intersubjectivity and sharing between child and caregiver before language but also for motivating a child's attention and involvement with people, objects, and events for learning language. Language is learned when the words a child hears relate to the objects of engagement, interest, and feelings that the child has in mind (the principle of relevance).

And language will never be acquired without effort. Our studies have only begun to tap the complex ways in which word learning is an effortful activity. The young language-learning child is essentially a limited information processor, and available cognitive and affective resources have to be distributed among competing demands on those resources. All words are not equally accessible for learning, and all of a child's cognitive and affective resources are not readily available for learning. The principles of relevance, discrepancy, and elaboration mediate between the engagement and effort that are required. While the principle of relevance provides the direction for word learning, and the principle of discrepancy provides the motivation, the principle of elaboration propels the process of language learning forward. In order to keep pace with their increasingly elaborated, complex, and abstract representations in intentional states as a consequence of development, children must learn more words and the procedures for forming sentences. It is the child's intentionality, therefore, that is the driving force for acquiring language and for word learning.

NOTE

1. In the 1995 edition of their book, Sperber and Wilson make clear that their original intent was to highlight a *communicative* principle rather than a *cognitive* principle, and they distinguish between the two kinds of principles. Neither reading of their principle of relevance, however, has to do with learning, with children, with acquisition, or with development. Their principle of relevance is, instead, a theory of how "every act of ostensive communication communicates a presumption of its own optimal relevance" (Sperber and Wilson, 1986 [1995], p. 158); it is explicitly a *pragmatic* principle having to do with the special connections between ostensive communicative signals and language. The principle of relevance that I have proposed for word learning (and language learning more generally) (e. g., L. Bloom, 1993) is a cognitive principle that has pragmatic (and other) consequences for how children acquire language. Although the principle of relevance proposed here incorporates Sperber and Wilson's notion of relevance as the "single property that makes information worth processing," it is not the same principle of relevance that they proposed; theirs is a principle of communication.

REFERENCES

Baldwin, D. (1993). Infants' ability to consult the speaker for clues to word reference. *Journal of Child Language, 20,* 395–418.

Bates, E. (1976). *Language in context.* New York: Academic Press.

Bates, E., Bretherton, I., & Snyder, L. (1988). *From first words to grammar: Individual differences and dissociable mechanisms.* Cambridge, England: Cambridge University Press.

Bates, E., Dale, P., & Thal, D. (1995). Individual differences and their implications for theories of language development. In P. Fletcher & B. MacWhinney (Eds.), *The handbook of child language* (pp. 96–151). Oxford, England: Blackwell.

Bates, E., Marchman, V., Thal, D., Fenson, L., Dale, P., Reznick, S., Reilly, J., & Hartung, J. (1994). Developmental and stylistic variation in the composition of early vocabulary. *Journal of Child Language, 21,* 85–123.

Bloom, L. (1973). *One word at a time: The use of single-word utterances before syntax.* The Hague, Netherlands: Mouton.

Bloom, L. (1981). The importance of language for language development: Linguistic determinism in the 1980s. In H. Winitz (Ed.), *Native language and foreign language acquisition.* Annals of the New York Academy of Sciences (Vol. 379, pp. 160–171). New York: New York Academy of Sciences.

Bloom, L. (1991). *Language development from two to three.* New York: Cambridge University Press.

Bloom, L. (1993). *The transition from infancy to language: Acquiring the power of expression.* Cambridge, England: Cambridge University Press.

Bloom, L. (1994). Meaning and expression. In W. Overton & D. Palermo (Eds.), *The ontogenesis of meaning* (pp. 215–235). Hillsdale, NJ: Erlbaum.

Bloom, L. (1998). Language acquisition in its developmental context. In D. Kuhn & R. S. Siegler (Eds.), *Handbook of child psychology: Vol. 2. Cognition, perception, and language* (pp. 309–370). New York: John Wiley & Sons.

Bloom, L., & Beckwith, R. (1989). Talking with feeling: Integrating affective and linguistic expression in early language development. *Cognition and Emotion, 3.* Reprinted In C. Izard (Ed.) *Development of emotion-cognition relations* (pp. 313–342). Hillsdale, NJ: Erlbaum.

Bloom, L., Beckwith, R., Capatides, J., & Hafitz, J. (1988). Expression through affect and words in the transition from infancy to language. In P. Baltes, D. Featherman, & R. Lerner (Eds.), *Life-Span Development and Behavior* (Vol. 8, pp. 99–127). Hillsdale, NJ: Erlbaum.

Bloom, L., & Lahey, M. (1978). *Language development and language disorders.* New York: John Wiley & Sons.

Bloom, L., Lifter, K., & Hafitz, J. (1980). The semantics of verbs and the development of verb inflections in child language. *Language, 56,* 386–412.

Bloom, L., Lightbown, P., & Hood, L. (1975). Structure and variation in child language. *Monographs of the Society for Research in Child Development, 40* no. 2 (Serial No. 160).

Bloom, L., Margulis, C., Tinker, E., & Fujita, N. (1996). Early conversations and word learning: Contributions from child and adult. *Child Development, 67,* 3154–3175.

Bloom, L., Merkin, S., & Wootten, J. (1982). Wh-questions: Linguistic factors that contribute to the sequence of acquisition. *Child Development, 53,* 1084–1092.

Bloom, L., Miller, P., & Hood, L. (1975). Variation and Reduction as Aspects of Competence in Language Development. In A. Pick (Ed.), *Minnesota Symposia on Child Psychology* (Vol. 9, pp. 3–55). Minneapolis: University of Minnesota Press.

Bloom, L., Rispoli, M., Gartner, B., & Hafitz, J. (1989). Acquisition of complementation. *Journal of Child Language, 16,* 101–120.

Bloom, L., & Tinker, E. (1999). *The coordination of engagement and effort for acquiring a language.* Unpublished manuscript.

Bloom, L., Tinker, E., & Margulis, C. (1993). The words children learn: Evidence against a noun bias in early vocabularies. *Cognitive Development, 8,* 431–450.

Bloom, P. (1989). Subjectless sentences in child language. *Linguistic Inquiry, 21,* 491–504.

Bornstein, M., Tamis-LeMonda, C., & Haynes, O. (1999). First words in the second year: Continuity, stability, and models of concurrent and lagged correspondence in vocabulary and verbal responsiveness across age and context. *Infant Behavior and Development, 22(1),* 67–87.

Brentano, F. (1966). *The true and the evident.* (English ed.: R. Chrisholm, Ed., & R. Chrisholm, I. Politzer, & K. Fischer, Trans.). New York: Humanities Press. (Original work published 1930).

Bruner, J. (1975). The ontogenesis of speech acts. *Journal of Child Language, 2,* 1–19.

Bruner, J. (1977). Early social interaction and language acquisition. In H. Schaffer (Ed.), *Studies in mother-infant interaction* (pp. 271–289). London: Academic Press.

Bruner, J. (1983). *Child's talk: Learning to use language.* New York: W. W. Norton.

Chomsky, N. (1965). *Aspects of the theory of syntax.* Cambridge, MA: MIT Press.

Clark, E. (1991). Acquisitional principles in lexical development. In S. Gelman & J. Byrnes (Eds.), *Perspectives on language and thought* (pp. 31–71). Cambridge, England: Cambridge University Press.

Danto, A. (1973). *Analytical philosophy of action.* Cambridge, England: Cambridge University Press.

Dore, J. (1975). Holophrases, speech acts, and language universals. *Journal of Child Language, 2,* 21–40.

Dromi, E. (1987). *Early lexical development.* Cambridge, England: Cambridge University Press.

Ervin-Tripp, S. (1973). *Language acquisition and communicative choice: Essays by Susan M. Ervin-Tripp.* Stanford, CA: Stanford University Press.

Fauconnier, G. (1985). *Mental spaces: Aspects of meaning construction in natural language.* Cambridge, MA: MIT Press.

Fenson, L., Dale, P. S., Reznick, J. S., Bates, E., Thal, D. J., & Pethick, S. J. (1994). Variability in early communicative development. *Monographs of the Society for Research in Child Development, 59* (5, Serial No. 242).

Gentner, D. (1982). Why nouns are learned before verbs: Linguistic relativity versus natural partitioning. In S. Kuczaj (Ed.), *Language development: Vol. 2. Language, thought, and culture* (pp. 301–333). Hillsdale, NJ: Erlbaum.

Goldin-Meadow, S., Seligman, M., & Gelman, R. (1976). Language in the two-year-old. *Cognition, 4,* 189–202.

Golinkoff, R. (1986). "I beg your pardon?": The preverbal negotiation of failed messages. *Journal of Child Language, 13,* 455–476.

Golinkoff, R. M., Mervis, C. B., & Hirsh-Pasek, K. (1994). Early object labels: The case for a developmental lexical principles framework. *Journal of Child Language, 21,* 125–155.

Golinkoff, R. M., Shuff-Bailey, M., Olguin, R., & Ruan, W. (1995). Young children extend novel words at the basic level: Evidence for the principle of categorical scope. *Developmental Psychology, 31,* 494–507.

Gopnik, A. (1982). Words and plans: Early language and the development of intelligent action. *Journal of Child Language, 9,* 303–318.

Gopnik, A. (1988). Three types of early word: The emergence of social words, names and cognitive-relational words in the one-word stage and their relation to cognitive development. *First Language, 8,* 49–69.

Gopnik, A., Choi, S., & Baumberger, T. (1996). Cross-linguistic differences in early semantic and cognitive development. *Cognitive Development, 11,* 197–227.

Gopnik, A., & Meltzoff, A. (1987). The development of categorization in the 2nd year and its relation to other cognitive and linguistic developments. *Child Development, 58,* 1523–1531.

Hampson, J. (1989). *Elements of style: Maternal and child contributions to the referen-*

tial and expressive styles of language acquisition. Unpublished doctoral dissertation, City University of New York, New York.

Hampson, J., & Nelson, K. (1993). The relation of maternal language to variation in rate and style of language acquisition. *Journal of Child Language, 20,* 313–342.

Harris, M. (1992). *Language experience and early language development: From input to uptake.* Hillsdale, NJ: Erlbaum.

Hirsh-Pasek, K., & Golinkoff, R. (1991). Language comprehension: A new look at some old themes. In N. Krasnegor, D. Rumbaugh, R. Schieffelbusch, & M. Studdert-Kennedy (Eds.), *Biological and behavioral determinants of language development* (pp. 301–320). Hillsdale, NJ: Erlbaum.

Howe, C. (1981). *Acquiring language in a conversational context.* London: Academic Press.

Hudson, R. (1994). 37% of word tokens are nouns. *Language, 70,* 331–339.

Lieven, E., Pine, J., & Barnes, H. (1992). Individual differences in early vocabulary development: Redefining the referential-expressive distinction. *Journal of Child Language, 19,* 287–310.

Lucariello, J., & Nelson, K. (1987). Remembering and planning talk between mothers and young children. *Discourse Processes, 10,* 219–235.

Maher, S., Lucariello, J., & Bloom, L. (1999). The function of formatting for word learning. Poster presented at Biennial Meetings of Society for Research in Child Development, Albuquerque, N.M.

Markman, E. M. (1989). *Categorization and naming in children: Problems of induction.* Cambridge, MA: MIT Press.

Markman, E. M. (1992). Constraints on word learning: Speculations about their nature, origins, and domain specificity. In M. R. Gunnar & M. P. Maratsos (Eds.), *Modularity and constraints in language and cognition: The Minnesota Symposia on Child Psychology* (Vol. 25, pp. 59–101). Hillsdale, NJ: Erlbaum.

Masur, E. (1982). Mothers' responses to infants' object-related gestures: Influences on lexical development. *Journal of Child Language, 9,* 23–30.

McCarthy, D. (1930). *The language development of the preschool child.* Institute of Child Welfare Monograph Series, No. 4. Minneapolis: University of Minnesota Press.

McCune-Micolich, L. (1981). The cognitive basis of relational words in the single word period. *Journal of Child Language, 8,* 15–34.

McSahne, J. (1980). *Learning to talk.* Cambridge, England: Cambridge University Press.

Nelson, K. (1973). Structure and strategy in learning to talk. *Monographs of the Society for Research in Child Development, 38* (Serial No. 149).

Nelson, K. (1988). Constraints on word learning. *Cognitive Development, 3,* 221–246.

Ninio, A., & Bruner, J. (1978). The achievement and antecedents of labeling. *Journal of Child Language, 5,* 1–15.

Pine, J. (1992). How referential are "referential" children? Relationship between maternal report and observational measures of vocal composition and usage. *Journal of Child Language, 19,* 75–86.

Pinker, S. (1984). *Language learnability and language development.* Cambridge, MA: Harvard University Press.

Pinker, S. (1989). *Learnability and cognition: The acquisition of argument structure.* Cambridge, MA: MIT Press.

Quine, W. V. O. (1960). *Word and Object.* Cambridge, MA: MIT Press.

Renninger, A. (1990). Children's play interests, representation, and activity. In R. Fivush & J. Hudson (Eds.), *Knowing and remembering in young children: Emory Symposia in Cognition* (pp. 127–165). New York: Cambridge University Press.

Renninger, A., & Wozniak, R. (1985). Effect of interest on attentional shift, recognition, and recall in young children. *Developmental Psychology, 21,* 624–632.

Ryan, J. (1974). Early language development: Towards a communicational analysis. In M. Richards (Ed.), *The integration of the child into the social world* (pp. 185–213). London: Cambridge University Press.

Sachs, J. (1977). Talking about the there and then. *Papers and Reports in Child Language Development, 13,* 56–63.

Searle, J. (1983). *Intentionality: An essay in the philosophy of mind.* Cambridge, England: Cambridge University Press.

Snow, C. E., & Goldfield, B. A. (1983). Turn the page please: Situation-specific language acquisition. *Journal of Child Language, 10,* 551–569.

Sperber, D., & Wilson, D. (1986). *Relevance: Communication and cognition.* Cambridge, MA: Harvard University Press. 2nd ed. (1995). Malden, MA: Blackwell.

Stein, N., & Levine, L. (1989). The causal organization of emotional knowledge: A developmental study. *Cognition and Emotion, 3,* 343–378.

Tardif, T. (1996). Nouns are not always learned before verbs: Evidence from Mandarin speakers' early vocabularies. *Developmental Psychology, 32,* 492–504.

Taylor, C. (1985). *Human agency and language: philosophical papers* (Vol. 1). Cambridge, England: Cambridge University Press.

Thorndike, E. L. (1898). Animal intelligence. *Psychological Review, Monograph Supplement, 2* (3), 65–109.

Thorndike, E. L. (1949). *Selected writings from a connectionist's psychology.* New York: Appleton-Century-Crofts.

Tomasello, M. (1992a). The social bases of language acquisition. *Social Development, 1* (1), 67–87.

Tomasello, M. (1992b). *First verbs: A case study of early grammatical development.* Cambridge, England: Cambridge University Press.

Tomasello, M., & Akhtar, N. (1995). Two-year-olds use pragmatic cues to differentiate reference to objects and actions. *Cognitive Psychology, 10,* 201–224.

Valian, V. (1991). Syntactic subjects in the early speech of American and Italian children. *Cognition, 40,* 21–81.

Veneziano, E., & Sinclair, H. (1995). Functional changes in early child language: The appearance of references to the past and of explanations. *Journal of Child Language, 22,* 557–581.

Vygotsky, L. S. (1962). *Thought and language.* Cambridge, MA: MI Press.

Vygotsky, L. S. (1978). *Mind in society: The development of higher psychological processes* (M. Cole, V. John-Steiner, S. Scribner, & E. Souberman, Eds.). Cambridge, MA: Harvard University Press. (Originally published 1930)

Woodward, A. L., & Markman, E. M. (1998). Early word learning. In D. Kuhn & R. S. Siegler (Eds.), *Handbook of child psychology: Vol. 2. Cognition, perception, and language* (pp. 371–420). New York: John Wiley & Sons.

Zukow, P. (1990). Socio-perceptual bases for the emergence of language: An alternative to innatist approaches. *Developmental Psychobiology, 23,* 705–726.

CHAPTER 3

Learning How to Learn Words

An Associative Crane

Linda B. Smith

Children produce their first word when they are about a year old. Over the next several months, they add new words to their productive vocabulary slowly, one word at a time. In contrast, children a year older learn words, particularly object names, rapidly. They are so good at this task that upon hearing a single object named, they will correctly generalize that name to other members of the category (e.g., Golinkoff, Mervis, & Hirsh-Pasek, 1994; Markman, 1989; Smith, 1995; Waxman, 1994).

Consider this example drawn from observing the word learning of a child. When the child was 22 months old, she saw her first tractor. It was a big, green John Deere tractor that was working in a field. The adult accompanying the child told her that it was a "tractor." Several days later, the child spontaneously generalized the name "tractor" to another tractor. This new tractor was not green, not a John Deere, and not in a field. Still, the child knew it was a tractor. It was as if the child already knew the kinds of things that are tractors before hearing the first one named. But how could the child know what tractors are before ever seeing one? Moreover, how could the child know from the first naming instance that the adult was talking about tractors rather than farm equipment more generally, or John Deeres more specifically, or big things, or green things, or things in fields? How, from *a single instance of naming,* could this young child so rightly know the category of things to which the name referred? This chapter attempts to answer that question.

First, however, we need to decide what kind of an answer we want. Dennett (1995) offers a guiding metaphor in his discussion of Charles Darwin's theory of evolution. Recall that Darwin's big claim is that the intelligent adaptations of species are created out of the algorithmic workings of natural selection. Dennett characterizes natural selection as the "crudest, most rudimentary, stupidest imaginable process" (1995, p. 75). Nonetheless, by accumulating tiny changes over very long periods of time, natural selection is said to create specialized smart adaptations. The main challenges to Darwin's theory, therefore, are evolutionary changes that seem too fast and too smart for the gradual progress of natural selection.

Here is the metaphor: According to Dennett, explanations of these too-fast, too-smart evolutionary leaps can take the form of either a skyhook or a crane. "Skyhooks" explain evolutionary leaps with mechanisms outside of evolutionary theory. For example, Kurt Gödel denied the plausibility that brains were the product of evolution as follows:

> I don't think the brain came in the Darwinian manner. In fact, it is disprovable. Simple mechanisms can't yield the brain. I think the basic elements of the universe are simple. Life force is a primitive element of the universe and it obeys certain laws of action. These laws are not simple and not mechanical. (quoted in Wang, 1993, p. 133)

The problem with skyhooks such as Gödel's "life force" is that the origin of the skyhook itself is unexplained. "Cranes," in contrast to skyhooks, explain evolutionary leaps with mechanisms consistent with evolutionary theory. Cranes are mechanisms that speed up evolution *but are also mechanisms that are made through the slow progress of natural selection.* Clearly, explanations in terms of cranes are both better and harder than explanations in terms of skyhooks, because the processes that make the crane are also explained.

Here is the relevance to the present chapter: Children's smart learning of object names is like the evolutionary leaps that challenge Darwinian theory. Smart one-trial learning of whole categories defies ordinary psychological mechanisms of trial-and-error learning. Thus, it is not surprising that some have attempted to explain word learning in terms specialized language mechanisms and even preknowledge about the possible meanings of words and possible kinds of categories (see, e.g., Markman, 1989; Soja, Carey, & Spelke, 1991). If word-learning mechanisms are to be cranes and not skyhooks, however, their developmental origins must be explained. This chapter explains how children's too-fast, too-smart learning of object names is the product of a crane, a mechanism that lifts children over the gradual progress of ordinary learning but that is itself made only gradually out of those same ordinary learning processes.

THE SHAPE BIAS

The word-learning crane that forms the centerpiece of this chapter is what is known in the literature as the shape bias. Young word learners often seem to assume that objects that have the same shape have the same name. Landau, Smith, and Jones (1988) reported the original result. They showed 2- and 3-year-old

Exemplar

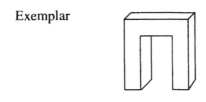

Test Objects

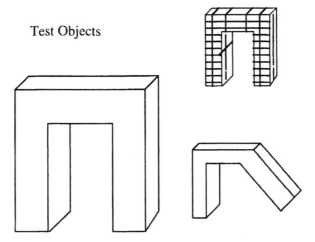

FIGURE 3.1. Examples of the Stimuli Used by Landau, Smith, and Jones (1988). These stimulus objects and all others represented in the figures in this chapter were three-dimensional objects made of wood, clay, metal, cloth, and plastic.

children the novel wooden object illustrated in Figure 3.1. The object was named with a new count noun, "This is a 'dax'." They then presented the children with the test objects, also depicted in Figure 3.1, and asked them about each, "Is this a dax?" Children generalized "dax" to test objects that were the same shape as the exemplar, not to test objects that were different in shape. The degree of children's selective attention to shape was remarkable. Children extended the name "dax" to same-shaped test objects that were 100 times the exemplar in size, as well as to those made of sponge or chicken wire.

Think about what this attention to shape does for young word learners. They do not need to figure out by trial and error what "dax" or "tractor" refers to; they know immediately that the word refers to the shape of the thing—not its color, texture, size, or location. If most of the object names that early word learners need to acquire also refer to categories of same-shaped things, then children can learn object names in one trial with few mistakes. Critically, studies of the structure of basic-level object categories suggest that these categories are well organized by shape (Rosch & Mervis, 1975; Biederman, 1987).

This shape bias in children's object-name learning has been demonstrated in many different studies and by many different experimenters using both specially constructed and real objects (e.g. Imai, Gentner, & Uchida, 1994; Keil, 1994; Gathercole & Min, 1997; Soja, 1992). Moreover, control studies have shown that biased attention to shape is specific to the task of learning an object name and is not evident in other kinds of categorization or similarity-judgment tasks (e.g., Landau, Smith, & Jones, 1988; Imai, Gentner, & Uchida, 1994; Soja, Carey, & Spelke, 1991). This fact tells us that young children do not go around in their everyday lives always attending only to the shapes of objects. Rather, the shape bias appears to reflect specifically a child's knowledge about how words map onto object categories.

The shape bias helps explain how children can, from hearing one object named, learn the category of objects to which the name applies. But how can we explain the shape bias?

AN ASSOCIATIVE-LEARNING ACCOUNT

Associative learning is the most fundamental and universal mechanism of psychological change (e.g., Clark, 1993; Kelly & Martin, 1994; Shanks, 1995). Like natural selection, however, associative learning has its skeptics: It seems too slow, too errorful, too probabilistic, too stupid to be the creative force behind developmental achievements—such as the learning of object names—that are fast and nearly right from the start (e.g., Keil, 1994; Pinker, 1989). This incredulity notwithstanding, this chapter shows that dumb associative learning *is* enough to build the crane that then makes object-name learning smart.

One hundred years of research in psychology tells us that whenever one perceptual cue is regularly associated with another, the presence of the first will come to automatically increase attention to the second (e.g., Allport, 1989; James, 1950; Rescorla & Wagner, 1972). The automatic control of selective attention by associative learning is one of the most widespread and well documented phenomena in all of psychology. The control of attention by associated cues is demonstrated in experimental studies by presenting the organism with some cue (or cluster of cues) that probabilistically predicts the relevance of some other property in the task. For example, bushy eyebrows might predict the relevance of chin shape in classifying faces (e.g., Medin & Wattenmaker, 1987; Medin, Altem, Edelson, & Freko, 1982). The laboratory evidence indicates that if such a predictive relation—even if imperfect and only probabilistically true—is in the input, then whenever the predictive cue is present, attention to the associated property is increased. This is a truly basic process, one that goes forward continuously in infants, children, adults, and nonhuman animals (e.g., Kelly & Martin, 1994; Kruschke, 1992; Lewicki, Hill, & Sasak, 1989; MacIntosh, 1965; Medin & Wattenmaker; Younger, 1990). It is also a process that could create the shape bias. This is an interesting idea: The shape bias—a mechanism that enables children to bypass the gradual progress of ordinary learning—may itself be made by ordinary learning.

Where might children be exposed to cues that reliably predict the category relevance of shape? One possibility is in early word learning itself. Children may begin learning object names with no special mechanisms to speed that learning. Instead they may, at first, have to learn object names through the grinding away of ordinary trial-and-error learning. This idea fits the fact that in its earliest stages, word learning *is* slow and errorful. At first, children *do* make such mistakes as calling all vehicles from bikes to planes "car"; or calling oranges, fingernails, and plates "moon"; or calling swans and robins "duck" (for further examples see Clark, 1973; Macnamara, 1982; Mervis, 1987; Mervis, Mervis, Johnson, & Bertrand, 1992). In the beginning, children apparently need multiple repeated examples to figure out just what is the class of objects that gets called "car" or "moon" or "duck." Critically, however, these early experiences in learning object names may present children with linguistic cues reliably associated with categorization by shape. As these associations are learned, the linguistic cues may shift attention to shape whenever an object is named, such that subsequent learning of object names is neither slow nor errorful. Accordingly, my colleagues and I examined the early vocabularies of young children to determine whether they exemplified the kinds of statistical regularities that could, through ordinary learning, create a shape bias.

STATISTICAL REGULARITIES AMONG
EARLY LEARNED NOUNS

Any claim that some developmental achievement emerges from statistical regularities in the input requires an examination of that input to determine whether it contains the hypothesized regularities. As a first step, the studies summarized below assessed the statistical regularities in the input by measuring the words children *know* rather than the words they *hear.* The reasoning is this: The statistical regularities in the input that are hypothesized to create the shape bias do so neither by their mere existence nor all at once as an atemporal fact about the world. Rather, the statistical regularities in the input can have their effect on individual children only if they are learned. Thus, the early words *known* by children serve as a good starting point for examining the hypothesis that the shape bias is learned.

The First Hundred Nouns

In one study, my colleagues and I (Smith, Gershkoff-Stowe, and Samuelson, 2000) asked the parents of eight children to keep diaries of every word spoken by the children. Children began the study when they had about 20 nouns in productive vocabulary and remained in the study until they had 100 nouns. (One child moved and therefore left the study prior to this point). Table 3.1 presents the mean and range of the ages, number of total words, and number of all nouns (count, mass, and proper) in productive vocabulary at the start of laboratory visits and at the end of the experiment. Table 3.2 lists the frequencies of lexical items of several conceptual kinds at three levels of vocabulary development: 0–25 nouns, 26–50 nouns, and 51 or more nouns. When children produced fewer than 25 nouns, most of those nouns were names of artifacts or animals or were proper nouns. As the number of nouns in productive vocabulary grew, the biggest increase was in names of artifacts—such words as "car," "ball," "pen," "cup," and "book." It is interesting that artifact terms dominate early nouns, because several theorists have suggested that artifact categories are the most robustly organized by shape (Keil, 1994; Jones & Smith, 1998; Soja, Carey, & Spelke, 1991).

To determine the statistical properties manifest in these early noun vocabularies, we classified each noun in the diary records by its syntactic properties in the adult language and by the similarities among the objects to which the noun referred. Syntactic category is relevant because count-noun syntax could be the explicit cue linked to attention to shape (see Landau, Smith, & Jones, 1988; Soja, Carey, & Spelke, 1991). Table 3.3 provides the criteria we used to make the syntactic judgments (see also Gathercole & Min, 1997). Table 3.4 shows the proportion of nouns of different syntactic types as a function of the three levels of noun vocabulary development. As is apparent, count nouns dominate early noun vocabularies from the beginning.

We determined the category structure of each noun by asking adults about the similarities among objects in each category. Specifically, we presented 20 undergraduates with the entire list of nouns from the eight children. We asked them to indicate for each lexical item whether members of that category were

TABLE 3.1. Changes in Children's Productive Vocabulary across the Experiment

	First Laboratory Visit	Last Laboratory Visit
Mean age (months)	17.4	21.4
(Range)	(16–19.75)	(18.5–23.75)
Mean total words	42.1	134.4
(Range)	(27–74)	(82–194)
Mean nouns	17.5	78.8
(Range)	(10–24)	(51–123)

TABLE 3.2. Mean Cumulative Types of Nouns at Three Levels of Children's Productive Vocabulary Development

Types of Nouns	0–25 Nouns	26–50 Nouns	51-Plus Nouns
Proper nouns (includes "mama," "dada")	4.25	6.50	9.88
Character names (e.g., "Ernie," "Big Bird")	0	2.00	5.00
Other people (e.g., "fireman," "boy," "kids")	1.00	1.38	1.75
Artifacts	7.50	17.6	32.75
Animals	4.90	8.62	12.25
Food	3.00	6.25	10.88
Body part	1.62	2.50	4.87
Other (e.g., "dirt," "wind," "snow")	.62	3.00	7.00

similar in shape, color, or material. From these adult judgments, each lexical item was designated as shape based, size based, color based, or material based if 75% of the adults judged the members to be similar on that property. Note that individual lexical items could be deemed by these criteria to be organized by more than one property. For example, by the adult judgments, "bubble" is a shape-based category and a material-based category, whereas "cup" is a shape-based category.

The central result from these analyses is shown in Table 3.5, which gives the proportion of count nouns at three levels of vocabulary development that, by adult judgment, refer to objects similar in shape. As is apparent, almost all of these count nouns refer to shape-based categories. Moreover, fewer than 20% of the count nouns at each level of vocabulary development were deemed to be organized by material or color. These facts mean that children must repeatedly hear count noun frames such as "This is a _____" and "Here is another _____" used to refer to categories of similarly shaped things. The degree of association between count-noun syntax and shape-based categories among first-learned nouns seems certain to teach that count nouns name objects by

TABLE 3.3. Criteria Used to Classify Nouns According to Syntactic Categories (by Adult Usage)

Noun Classification	Criteria
Proper noun	Cannot be preceded by an "a" or by numerals, has no plural form, cannot be preceded by "much"
Count noun	Can be preceded by "a" and by numerals, has a plural form, cannot be preceded by "much"
Mass noun	Cannot be preceded by "a" or by numerals, has no plural form, can be preceded by "much"
Other	Occurs in mass and count forms, such as "cake"; includes also character names, such as "Ernie" that may be used as proper nouns or with count syntax

TABLE 3.4. Proportion of Nouns of Each Syntactic Type at Three Levels
of Vocabulary Development

Cumulative Nouns	Count Nouns	Proper Nouns	Mass Nouns	Other
0–25	.73	.18	.06	.02
26–50	.70	.14	.06	.08
51 plus	.68	.08	.10	.14

shape. Indeed, given all that is known about attentional learning, this correspondence should cause count-noun syntactic frames to become context cues
that automatically shift attention to shape.

Nouns on the MacArthur Communicative Development Inventory

Samuelson and Smith, 1999, provides further supporting evidence for the idea
that early learned nouns present the kinds of regularities that could create a
shape bias. In this study, we examined the statistical regularities presented by
the categories named by the 312 nouns in the animal, vehicle, toy, food and
drink, clothing, body part, small household item, and furniture and room sec-
tions of the MCDI. This parental checklist is a reliable measure of the productive vocabulary of 16- to 30-month-old children. It was developed from extensive studies of parental diaries and in-laboratory testing of children's early
vocabularies (see Fenson et al., 1993). Thus, it is a reasonable proxy for the
typical early nouns that children learning English encounter.

We asked adult subjects to indicate whether each noun on the MCDI named
objects similar in shape, color, or material and whether it referred to solid or
nonsolid things. We also instructed adults in the criteria listed in Table 3.3 and
asked them to place each noun in a syntactic category: 85% agreement among
the adult judges was the criterion for designating a single noun as, for example,
shape based or nonsolid or a count noun.

Figure 3.2 summarizes the key regularities by these measures in terms of

TABLE 3.5. Proportion of Shape-Based
Count Nouns, by Adult Judgment, at Three
Levels of Vocabulary Development

Cumulative Nouns	Proportion of Shape-Based Count Nouns
0–25	.98
26–50	.94
51 plus	.93

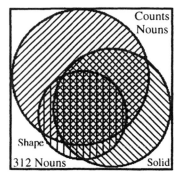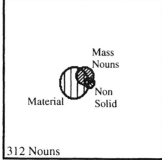

FIGURE 3.2. Venn Diagrams of 312 Nouns. The circles represent the relative number and overlap among nouns on the MCDI that are count nouns, refer to objects of similar shape, and are solid (*at left*) and that are mass nouns, refer to objects of similar material, and are nonsolid (*at right*).

Venn diagrams. In these diagrams, the relative size of each circle represents the relative numbers of nouns of that kind and the size of overlap between intersecting circles represents the numbers of nouns that are jointly of both kinds. The circles on the left depict the relative number of count nouns, names for solid things, and names for categories organized by shape. The circles on the right represent the relative number of mass nouns, names for nonsolid substances, and names for things in categories organized by material. What the figure shows is that many early nouns are count nouns, many refer to solid objects, and many name objects in shape-based categories. Moreover, count nouns, solid things, and shape similarity *go together.* Thus, there are two cues—syntax and solidity—that could cue attention to shape. The circles on the right show that there are many fewer nouns in this corpus that are mass nouns, name nonsolid things, and name categories organized by material. However, nonsolidity, mass-noun syntax, and material-based categories are correlated. This small cluster of nouns is interesting because several studies suggest that children generalize names for nonsolid substances by material, not by shape (see Imai & Gentner, 1997; Soja, 1992), an issue that is discussed later in this chapter.

Summary and Implications

The nouns that children learn early are predominantly count nouns that name solid objects of a particular shape. This fact is important because it means that the statistical regularities needed to *build* a shape bias exist among early nouns. I emphasize the word "build" because building implies a process over time. If the shape bias is a word-learning crane that is itself built out of associative processes, then it must be built one encountered word at a time. For an individual child, the statistical regularities must *emerge* over the course of early word learning. Each noun encountered and acquired will strengthen and weaken associations among clusters of properties. Only when a sufficient number of nouns has been learned will the association strengths that control attention stably reflect the principal regularities.

A key prediction from this associative learning account is this: Children's noun generalizations should *change* as they learn more and more nouns. At first, generalizations of a newly learned noun to new instances should reflect only the grossest regularities. As more nouns are learned, generalizations of novel nouns should reflect subtler statistical truths about how nouns map to categories. The extant evidence, including facts about early noun learning not usually discussed under the rubric of the shape bias, fits this description.

THE DEVELOPMENTAL TREND IN NOVEL-NOUN GENERALIZATION

The associative-learning account provides a unifying explanation of many phenomena in the artificial-noun learning literature—phenomena emerging both before and after the shape bias per se. This section reviews these global changes that occur in noun generalizations with development and their congruence with the idea that, as children learn nouns, they are also learning statistical regularities that then help them learn more nouns.

From Overall Similarity to Shape Similarity

There are more pervasive regularities in early noun vocabularies than those illustrated in Table 3.5 or Figure 3.2, regularities so pervasive, in fact, that it is easy to overlook them. One is that nouns of all kinds (proper, count, and mass) are used to name concrete, that is touchable, stuff—not abstract objects, not relations. Another is that the entities with the same name are *perceptually* similar to each other—in one way or another. Thus, before children know that *count* nouns name things similar in *shape,* we might expect them to know that perceptually similar things have the same name. The extant evidence from children younger than 2 years of age accords with this expectation.

In one relevant study, Waxman and Hall (1993) presented 15- and 21-month-old children with triads of objects. Waxman and Hall named one object, the exemplar, with a new noun and asked the children to indicate which of the two remaining objects had the same name. One test object shared some perceptual features with the exemplar; the other test object shared virtually none. For example, if the named object was a carrot, the test objects would be a tomato (somewhat similar) and a rabbit (not at all similar). That is, the researchers asked the children to choose whether the name applied to something that was somewhat similar to the named object or to something that was not similar at all. Both younger and older children tended to pick the item most similar to the named object, showing that they already knew that nouns span categories of perceptually similar things.

A study by Woodward, Markman, and Fitzsimmons (1994) suggests that even this most rudimentary association—between naming and overall similarity—emerges between 13 and 18 months. In their artificial noun learning task, these researchers, too, presented children with triads containing two perceptually similar objects and one perceptually dissimilar object. For example, on one trial, the child was presented with a single strainer that was named. Then the child was asked to select another object by that name. The two objects that the child could choose between were a second strainer and a clip. Critically, on some trials, the target test object (e.g., the second strainer) was *identical* to the named exemplar; on other trials, it was *perceptually different but similar overall* (differing, for instance, in color). The 13-month-olds succeeded unambiguously in choosing the target when the target was identical to the exemplar, but they chose randomly in three of four experiments when the target differed even slightly from the exemplar. The 18-month-olds, however, succeeded both when the target was identical to and when it was merely similar to the named exemplar. Thus, it seems, the generalization of a just-heard object name to a discriminably different but similar object becomes increasingly robust in the earliest stages of noun learning.

Do children this young know that it is shape similarity in particular that matters for naming solid objects? There is no evidence that they do. The earliest age at which selective attention to shape has been demonstrated is 24 months (see Imai, Gentner, & Uchida, 1994; Landau, Smith, & Jones, 1988; Soja, 1992). Moreover, the results of several studies indicate that the selectivity and certainty of attention to shape in the task of generalizing a novel object name increases substantially between 24 and 36 months of age (Landau, Smith, & Jones, 1988, 1992, 1998; Imai & Gentner, 1997).

Overall, then, there is a developmental progression in the generalization of object names: from generalization to similar objects to generalization to objects specifically like the exemplar in shape. Such progressive refinement of attention in the task of naming is just what is expected of a learner who must discover, one learned word at a time, the statistical regularities between words and categories.

Words Then Count Nouns *Become* Special

The proposal that word-learning cranes are built by the same associative mechanisms that govern learning in other domains implies that words are not intrinsically special in their ability to organize attention to categories. Rather, that specialness is a product of learned associations.

Namy and Waxman (1998; see also chapter 4 in this volume) reported results supporting this idea that words *become* special in their ability to direct children's attention to categories of similar things. In a task nearly identical to that used by Waxman and Hall (1993), Namy and Waxman presented 18- and 26-month-olds with a triad of objects: an exemplar and two choice objects, one perceptually similar to the exemplar and one highly dissimilar to the exemplar. For example, one triad consisted of a van, an airplane, and a whale. The first condition matched one used by Waxman and Hall: the exemplar object was named with a novel name, and, the child was asked, using that name, to select among the two choice objects. It was the second condition that was new: the exemplar was referred to—not with a spoken name—but with a hand gesture, and the child was asked, using the gesture, to select among the two choice objects. The younger children, 18-months-olds, chose by similarity in both conditions. Apparently, for younger children, any associate of an object can work to push attention to similar objects. The older children, in contrast, chose by similarity only in the name condition; they responded randomly when signaled by a gesture to make a choice. These results suggest that words are not special attention cuers initially but become special through their continued and repeated use by others to bring attention to objects. The accrued consequence of these continued experiences is that words become the privileged means by which one directs the attention of another—that is, the privileged way of referring.

My laboratory has collected some preliminary data consistent with this idea. A longitudinal pilot study examined the spontaneous generalizations of gestures and names of 12 children. Half the children were 17 months old and half were 20 months old at the start of the 6-week experiment. During each weekly session, children played with the four pairs of objects illustrated in Figure 3.3. The objects in each pair were always the same shape but differed dramatically in color and material. One object in each pair was the exemplar; one was the test object. During the play period with each pair, the experimenter looked at the exemplar, named it, and made a gesture specific to the exemplar while looking at the exemplar at least eight times. For example, the experimenter expressively put her hands over her head while looking at the "zop" exemplar. She neither named nor gestured while looking at the test object.

Our question was how readily children would begin to use the object name or gesture to refer to objects. Thus our dependent measures were the number of times the children spontaneously named the exemplar and test object and the number of times they spontaneously made the characteristic gesture while looking at the exemplar or the test object. Figure 3.4 shows the mean number of names and gestures offered by the children over the 6 weeks of the experiment.

As the figure shows, the younger children spontaneously produced the experimenter's gestures from the start, and they spontaneously generalized these

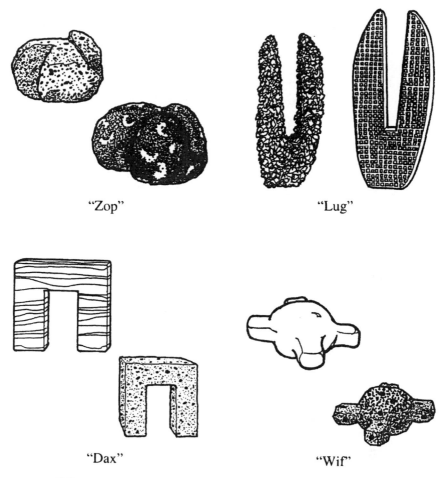

"Zop"   "Lug"

"Dax"   "Wif"

FIGURE 3.3. Stimulus Objects Used in the Name and Gesture Pilot Study.

gestures to the similar test objects. Clearly, gestures are readily linked to objects and readily generalized to similar objects. The production of spontaneous names shows a different course. The younger children were much less likely to produce the spontaneous names, possibly because of the difficulty in *saying* the words. However, by Week 3, all of the youngest children had spontaneously named at least two of the exemplar objects, but at Week 5 only one child had ever spontaneously generalized an exemplar name to a test object. For the youngest children, object names were more closely tied than were gestures to the particular object with which they had been paired.

For the older children, in contrast, words were generalized more often to similar objects than were gestures. The older children could and did make all gestures, mimicking the adult actions from the start, and they generalized these

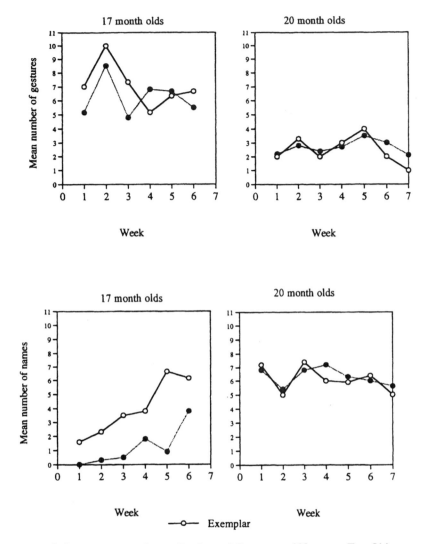

FIGURE 3.4. Spontaneous Generalizations of Gestures and Names to Test Objects (*filled circles*) and to Exemplars (*open circles*).

actions to similar items. However, the older children were more likely to name objects spontaneously than to gesture spontaneously, and they generalized names to new objects as soon as they began producing the names. These results, along with those of Namy and Waxman (1998), suggest that over the course of early word learning—as the act of naming becomes associated with categories of similar items—nouns *become* the privileged way to refer to objects of similar kind.

As children learn even more nouns, they should learn that it is not just any word but a particular kind of word that names objects. And they should learn that it is not just global similarity but shape similarity specifically that is relevant to naming. The evidence suggests that as word learning progresses, count-noun syntax takes precedent in cuing attention to shape. For example, several studies have shown that 2- (and under some conditions 3-) year-old children generalize new words to new objects by shape both when the novel word is presented in a count-noun syntactic frame ("This is a dax") and when it is presented in an adjectival frame ("This is dax one.") However, although older children generalize novel count nouns by shape, they generalize novel adjectives by properties other than shape (see Smith, Jones, & Landau, 1992; Au & Laframboise, 1990; Landau, Smith, & Jones, 1992; see also Waxman, 1994).

In sum, as children learn more and more words, words *become* privileged organizers of attention, and specific linguistic cues—syntactic frames of count nouns as opposed to adjectives—come to increasingly direct attention to specific kinds of properties and similarities. If words gain their power as a result of associations accrued in the course of language learning, the gradual empowerment and differentiation of linguistic cues is just what is expected.

Learning Other Correlations and Other Predictive Cues

If the processes that create the shape bias are general associative mechanisms, then they should create noun-learning cranes other than just the shape bias—as long as there are other statistical regularities among linguistic entities, object properties, and category structures. There is evidence in the literature for at least two additional attentional biases in the context of noun learning.

Solid Things and Nonsolid Stuff. As Figure 3.2 shows, there are statistical regularities peculiar to the naming of nonsolid substances in addition to those relevant to the naming of solid substances. That is, nonsolid substances tend to be named by material rather than shape and by mass nouns rather than count nouns. However, Figure 3.2 also shows that, early in word learning, children tend to know many fewer names for nonsolid than for solid substances. These statistical facts about the structure of early noun vocabularies suggest that (1) children should (given a sufficient number of learned names for nonsolid substances) generalize a newly encountered name for a nonsolid substance to new instances by material, (2) children's attention to material over shape when learning a new name should increase when the name is presented in the context of mass-noun syntax, and (3) children's attention to material in the context of nonsolid substances and mass syntax should emerge later or more weakly than does their attention to shape in the context of a solid object and count syntax.

All three of these predictions have empirical support (see Soja, Carey, &

Spelke, 1991; Soja, 1992; Imai & Gentner, 1997; Gathercole & Min, 1997; Samuelson & Smith, 1999). In one relevant study, Soja (1992) presented 24- and 30-month-old children with solid or nonsolid exemplars named with either a count noun ("This is a mel") or a mass noun ("This is some mel"). The solid exemplars were made from wood or hardened clay; the nonsolid exemplars were made from such substances as hair gel and face cream. Soja found that solidity and count syntax pushed attention to shape and nonsolidity and mass syntax pushed attention to material. Moreover, the effects of solidity and syntax were stronger for 30-month-olds than for 24-month-olds. And, critically, solidity and count syntax were much stronger forces on children's generalizations than were nonsolidity and mass syntax—just as they should be if the strength of the attentional bias in children depends on the strength of the association in the nouns they learn.

Objects with Eyes and Feet.   My colleagues and I (Jones, Smith, and Landau, 1991) hypothesized that artifact and animal categories differ in their organizational structure. Based on our own intuitions, we speculated that textural properties—being feathered or furry—as well as shape similarity were critical in organizing animal categories. We recently confirmed these intuitions by asking adults to judge the similarities among animal artifact categories named by nouns on the MCDI. More specifically, 15 adults judged the categories named by 43 animal and 82 artifact terms (vehicles, toys, small household objects) on the parent checklist. Adults judged animal terms to name objects that were principally rounded rather than angular (84% of the animal names) and to name objects that had a characteristic texture (93% of the animal names). In contrast, adults only infrequently judged the artifact terms to name objects that were rounded (39% of the artifact names) and to name objects with a characteristic texture (33% of artifact names). Adults in this study also judged shape to be relevant to category membership for 68% of the animal categories and 79% of the artifact categories. These regularities suggest that children could learn that animal and artifact categories are organized differently and could therefore know, upon hearing a novel object named, that shape and texture matter if it is an animal but that only shape matters if it is an artifact.

In Jones, Smith, and Landau, 1991, we provided the pertinent evidence. We reasoned that one predictive cue of animacy is having eyes. Thus, children might learn to name objects with eyes by shape and texture but objects without eyes by shape alone. We tested this prediction by presenting 2- and 3-year-old children with the exemplars shown at the top of Figure 3.5. Half the children completed the task with the eyed objects and half with the eyeless objects. In each condition, we named the exemplar with a count noun (e.g., "This is a dax") and asked the children if each test object was also a "dax." Test objects matched the exemplar in shape only, texture only, or shape _and_ texture (they differed

Exemplars with and without Eyes

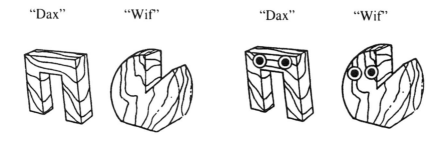

Exemplars with Feet

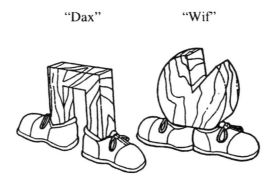

FIGURE 3.5. Exemplars Used to Contrast Children's Noun Generalizations.

from the exemplar in size). Two-year-old children generalized the name to objects having the same shape as the exemplar and ignored texture and size with both eyeless and eyed objects. Three-year-old children, on the other hand, generalized names of objects without eyes to all new objects that matched the exemplar in shape, regardless of texture; as predicted, however, they generalized names of objects with eyes only to new objects that matched the exemplar in both shape and texture. The fact that children know that shape matters in naming eyed and eyeless objects before they know that texture is additionally relevant for eyed objects fits the statistical learning account. Shape is relevant to many of the noun categories these children have learned; shape plus texture is relevant only to a subset of these categories, a subset cued by the presence of eyes.

In Jones and Smith, 1998, we replicated the eye effect using the cue of feet.

If children are statistical learners who gain knowledge of and then use whatever cues are present, then the perceptible property of feet should cue attention to texture just as eyes did; because having feet is correlated with having eyes, it should, as did eyes, predict category membership based on common shape and texture. The exemplars that we used to test this idea are illustrated at the bottom of Figure 3.5. Children's generalizations in this experiment closely replicated those found earlier for objects with eyes. Again, 2-year-olds generalized novel names by shape both when the objects did and did not have feet, but 3-year-olds generalized the novel names by shape when the objects did not have feet and by texture as well as shape when the objects did have feet. Apparently, children learn and use multiple cues to category organization at multiple levels.

Think about what this means: As children learn more and more object names, they will learn more and more about the co-occurrences of naming, object properties, and category structure. All these correlated cues will work to tune attention to properties that have, in the past, been most predictive of category membership *for categories of that kind.* When a child who already knows some nouns hears a new noun used to name a new object, he or she can zoom in on the appropriate features for that kind of object. Because the child can use statistical generalizations about category structure from previously learned categories, he or she does not have to learn by trial and error the relevant properties for each unique category.

The Taxonomic versus the Shape Bias. Because associative learning works continuously, it will build as many context-specific cranes as there are regularities among the categories being learned. This idea offers a reconciliation of two competing views of how and why children are smart learners of nouns. One view, the basis of this chapter, proposes a shape bias. The other view proposes a more conceptually based taxonomic bias (Markman & Hutchinson, 1984; Waxman & Gelman, 1986; Imai, Gentner, & Uchida, 1994; Keil, 1994; Bauer & Mandler, 1989). Typically, the two are seen as competing and opposing proposals. But the findings about eyes and feet suggest a reconciliation in that they show that there is not *just* a shape bias. Different attentional biases emerge with development for different kinds of categories. The shape bias has drawn a lot of attention because it is the first selective attentional bias. But it is first because it reflects the most broadly important property across many kinds of object categories. The eye, foot, and nonsolid substance results show that in other contexts, for other kinds of items, children develop other perceptual biases. Indeed, I bet that if we did the proper experiments, we would find many such "biases," at least among older word learners: attentional shifts to just the right bundles of properties relevant for categorizing vehicles, or machinery, or furniture, or food. This is a reasonable prediction: As children continually learn clusters of correlated cues, they should learn finer-grained statistical regularities specific to specific kinds of categories.

Here, then, is the reconciliation of the taxonomic and shape biases: As these complex, context-sensitive attentional biases develop and multiply, they will instantiate a lot of knowledge about different kinds of categories. If this is so, learned attentional biases may well be the very mechanism through which an understanding of taxonomies is implemented. Children's knowledge of the kinds of things there are in the world and their attention to specific object properties in naming may both be manifestations of learning the same rich associative structures (cf., Markman, 1989).

HOW LEARNING WORDS CHANGES WORD LEARNING

This chapter began with the idea of the shape bias as a crane, a mechanism emergent from ordinary learning processes that then helps the child bypass the trial and error of ordinary learning. Two supporting lines of evidence have been presented this far: (1) the statistical regularities among linguistic entities, object properties, and category structures that are of the kind that could create learning biases and (2) the developmental trend suggests progress as children learn nouns toward increasingly refined attentional biases that reflect increasingly finer-grained statistical regularities in the language. This section presents a third and final line of evidence: the dependence of individual children's generalization of a newly encountered noun on the nouns that those individual children already know. Both studies are reported more fully in Smith, Jones, Landau, Gershkoff-Stowe, and Samuelson, 2000.

A Longitudinal Study

In a longitudinal study, we tracked the language growth of eight children from 15 to 20 months of age. Parents kept diaries of all new words spoken by their child, and the children came to the laboratory every 3 weeks to participate in an artificial noun-generalization task. At the beginning of the study, the children had very few words in their productive vocabulary (fewer than 15). At the end of the study, each child had over 150 words, and for each child more than half of these were specifically count nouns. Thus, if the shape bias is learned from learning words, the children in this study should not show a shape bias at the beginning, because they do not know many words, but they should show selective generalization for solid objects by shape at the end of the study, because by that time they have learned many count nouns—nouns that at this age level overwhelmingly refer to shape-based categories.

The stimuli used in the laboratory task are shown in Figure 3.6. They in-

EXEMPLAR

Mottled Wood

TEST OBJECTS

Shape   Texture   Color

Red Wire Mesh   *Blue Wood*   *Mottled Bean Bag*

FIGURE 3.6. Exemplar and Test Objects used in the Longitudinal Study of the
Emergence of the Shape Bias.

cluded an exemplar object made of wood and three test objects that matched
the exemplar in either color, shape, or texture. The task began when the experimenter put the exemplar and three test objects on the table in front of the
child. The experimenter picked up the exemplar and said, "This is a dax.
Look. This is a dax." Then while still holding the exemplar, the experimenter
held out her other hand, palm up, and said, "Give me a dax. Give me another
dax."

Figure 3.7 shows children's generalizations by shape as a function of the
number of nouns (proper, mass, and count) in their productive vocabulary. As
expected, shape choices did not predominate early in the study, when children
knew few nouns, but did so reliably by the end, when they knew many. More
specifically, *after* all eight children had 50 nouns (and on average 35 count
nouns) in their productive vocabulary, they began to extend the novel word
"dax" systematically to the same-shaped test object. Moreover, by adult judgments, over 90% of these first 35 count nouns referred to categories well organized by shape. This fact supports the proposal that the shape bias is a statistical generalization from already learned object names.

If this shape bias is a crane that lifts noun learning, however, then the shape
bias once formed should alter the course and speed of noun learning. That is,
by the present account, the shape bias is not just an *effect* of noun learning; it
is also a *cause* of which nouns are easily learned in the future. If hearing count-
noun syntax automatically shifts attention to shape, then the acquisition of count
nouns—nouns that in early vocabularies overwhelming refer to shape-based
categories—should accelerate. We sought support for this idea in a training
study.

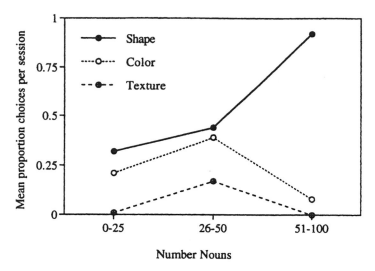

FIGURE 3.7. Choices of the Test Objects as a Function of the Number of Nouns in Children's Spoken Vocabulary.

A Training Study

The strongest possible evidence for the idea that word-learning cranes are built is the ability to build one experimentally. And the strongest possible evidence that the shape bias alters the course of noun learning is the ability to show than an experimentally made shape bias changes how children learn real nouns outside the laboratory. We attempted this powerful test of the associative-learning account by teaching artificial lexical categories that were well organized by shape to children who did not yet know many words. The subjects were eight children who were 17 months of age and who had, on average, 14 count nouns in their productive vocabulary by parent report on the MCDI. These children came to the laboratory once a week for 9 weeks and for 7 of those weeks received extensive training on four different novel categories—all well organized by shape. The top of Figure 3.8 illustrates the training stimuli for one lexical category.

Each lexical category was trained as follows: The experimenter placed the two exemplars for a category on the table and named them—for example, "This is a zup. Here is another zup." As illustrated in Figure 3.8, these two exemplars differed in many ways but were identical in shape. The experimenter and child played with the two objects for 5 minutes, during which time the experimenter repeatedly named the objects—for example, "Put the zup in the box. Can you put the zup in the wagon?" Halfway through a play session with one pair of exemplars, the experimenter placed a nonexemplar for that category (see Figure

Training set

The zup set

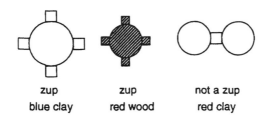

| zup | zup | not a zup |
| blue clay | red wood | red clay |

Test set

Week 8: Trained lexical categories

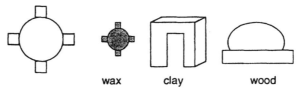

wax　　clay　　wood

Week 9: Novel lexical categories

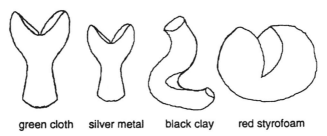

green cloth　silver metal　black clay　red styrofoam

FIGURE 3.8. Training Set and Two Test Sets Used in the Training Study.

3.8) briefly on the table. The experimenter announced that this just introduced object was not a member of the category (e.g., "*That's* not a zup!") and immediately removed it. The nonexemplar matched each exemplar in one nonshape attribute but differed from both exemplars in shape, thus providing the child with evidence as to the kinds of items that are *not* in the lexical category.

For the first 7 weeks, the experimenters trained the children as described above once a week for each of four lexical categories. On Weeks 8 and 9 of the experiment, the children participated in two test sessions that asked them to generalize what they had learned over the first 7 weeks. The first test session, Week 8, measured children's generalizations of the trained lexical categories to new items. The middle section of Figure 3.8 shows the stimuli used to test generalization of the "zup" category. The test began when the experimenter placed one of the trained exemplars on the table along with three new objects, one that matched the exemplar in material, one that matched it in color, and one that matched it in shape. The experimenter picked up the exemplar and said, "This is a zup" and then instructed, "Get me a zup." Given the 7 weeks of training, the exemplar is not a novel object and the label is not a novel name for these children. Thus, if the children have learned that the specifically trained names refer to objects of a particular shape, they should generalize these already learned names to the novel object that is the same as the exemplar in shape.

On Week 9, the experimenters tested the children in a novel-noun generalization task structured in the same way as the generalization task at Week 8. However, as illustrated by the sample stimulus set at the bottom of Figure 3.8, all the objects and names were new. This generalization task thus tests the critical prediction that learning specific categories well organized by shape transforms the act of naming into a contextual cue that automatically shifts attention to shape. If the 7 weeks of intensive training on shape-based categories has caused the linguistic context of naming to cue attention automatically to shape, than these children should form and generalize *new* names on the basis of shape.

This experiment also included eight control children, who were selected at the same time as the children in the trained group. They were 17 months old at the start of the 9-week experiment and had, on average, 16 count nouns in their productive vocabulary. These children, however, did not participate in the 7 weeks of training. Instead they returned to the laboratory for other experiments and for the generalization tasks of Weeks 8 and 9, when they and the children in the trained group were 19 months of age. Since the control children had not received intensive training in shape-based lexical categories and did not know many count nouns, the expectation was that they would not selectively attend to shape in the generalization tasks at either Week 8 or Week 9.

The main results are shown in Figure 3.9. Consider Panel 1 first. At Week 8, when the trained children were asked to generalize the trained names to new objects, they did so on the basis of shape. These children had clearly learned that the words taught to them in the experiment refer to objects of a particular shape. As expected, the control children, for whom this was a *new* word interpretation task, did not systematically attend to shape.

At Week 9, both the trained and control children heard novel objects named by novel nouns. However, as shown in Panel 2, the trained children, but not the control children, systematically generalized these newly learned names to other novel objects by shape. In brief, we taught the trained children four categories organized by shape, but the children learned more than just these categories. They learned to attend to shape when novel rigid objects were named. This generalized attentional shift *is* a learning bias. These children were thereafter biased to induce a shape-based category when a new object was named.

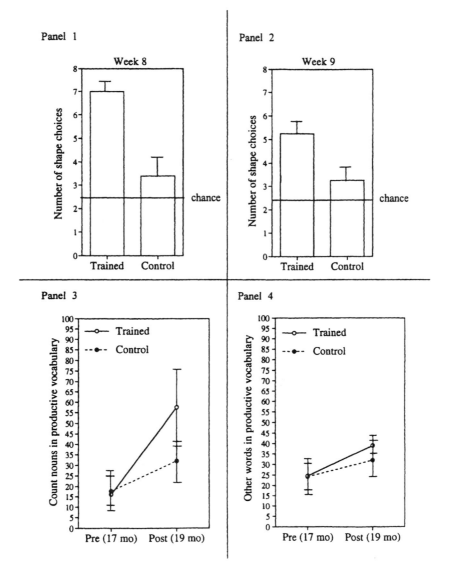

FIGURE 3.9. Results of the Training Study. Panel 1 shows the mean shape choices made by the children in the trained and control conditions at Week 8. Panel 2 shows the mean shape choices made at Week 9. Panel 3 shows the mean number of count nouns in productive vocabulary at Week 1 and Week 8. Panel 4 shows the mean number of words other than count nouns in productive vocabulary at Week 1 and Week 8.

Is this a crane that once formed "lifts" development, allowing it to make faster progress than expected by trial-and-error learning? The answer is yes. This trained bias to link nouns to shape-based categories accelerated object-name learning *outside the laboratory* for the children in the trained group. The parents of the children in both the trained and the control groups were asked to complete the MDCI again at Week 8, indicating all the words in their children's productive vocabulary at that point. The bottom panels of Figure 3.9 show the change in vocabulary from Week 1 to Week 8 for the two groups. The children in the training condition showed a 166% increase in the number of count nouns known. In contrast, children in the control condition showed only a 73% increase in the average number of count nouns. Notice that the training did not affect the rate of acquisition of words that are not count nouns. Thus, the children who were taught names for four artificial categories well organized by shape also learned, outside the laboratory, more names for real categories—categories of the kind typically well organized by shape—than did children who did not receive this training. Learning shape-based lexical categories creates a shape bias, which in turn promotes the rapid learning of object names.

I believe that we have reproduced in the laboratory and accelerated by several months the natural processes through which the shape bias is made. This shape bias is a developmental crane that enables children to induce a shape-based category from hearing a single thing named, and in this way, to often be immediately right about the extension of a category. One might ask: How could learning just four names for artificial categories generate this accelerated learning of real count nouns? After all, children in the control condition also learned object names outside the laboratory during this period—many more than just four—and they developed neither a shape bias nor an accelerated rate of vocabulary growth.

These facts can be explained as follows: First, our training presented unusually transparent shape-based category structures. Although most concrete object categories may be well organized by shape, not all are. Moreover, some real-world object categories that are well organized by shape also exhibit, within the category, similarities of color, size, texture, or movement. By isolating shape similarity in our training set, we made the property that is highly predictive of category membership in the world perfectly predictive in the laboratory. Second, our training *alone* may not have created the shape bias. If we taught children only these four new names and did not allow them to be exposed to any other naming outside of the laboratory, it is possible that there would be no shape bias evident in Week 9 testing. That is, learning in the laboratory and in the world may have worked together to create our results. In the initial weeks, the laboratory training may have created a slightly heightened attention to shape in the context of naming, which may have helped the children acquire several more count nouns outside the laboratory than they would have without the training. Given the statistical properties of early count nouns, this learning is likely to have caused at least a slight strengthening of the link between naming and shape, a link that would be reinforced by the continuing laboratory experience, which in turn would probably promote the learning of several more real count nouns between laboratory sessions, which would strengthen the link between count-noun syntax and shape even more, and so on. In brief, the laboratory created changes internal to the children that may have then changed what they attended to and learned outside the laboratory, causing a snowballing developmental effect several months earlier than the development would have occurred without our intervention. This may be what language learning is like in general: Each advance is a crane that prepares the way—that guides and lifts subsequent learning.

CONCLUSION

Figure 3.10 summarizes several of the developmental experiments reviewed here. Each curve summarizes the degree to which children generalize a novel label exclusively on the basis of shape, as a function of the age of the subjects, the kind of object labeled, and the syntactic frame in which the novel word ap-

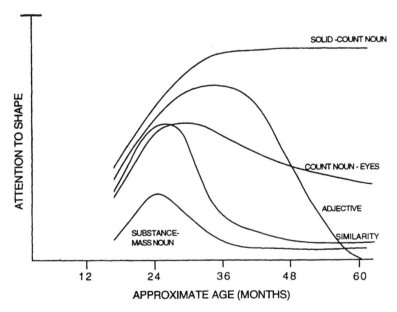

FIGURE 3.10. Curves Summarizing Results Across Many Experiments. The curves show exclusive attention to shape as a function of age and task, syntax, and object properties.

peared. Altogether, the evidence indicates that, with development, the shape bias becomes both stronger and more specific to count nouns and artifacts. Descriptively, attentional biases specific to animates, substances, mass nouns, and adjectives seem to differentiate out of an early bias to attend to the overall similarity of objects and then a bias to attend to shape. By the present account, attention to shape in the context of a count noun differentiates first because it is the most pervasive regularity among the early nouns that children know.

If we considered the increasing evidence from other languages, we would have to draw more curves on the graph in Figure 3.10. A number of recent studies of children learning Korean and Japanese as their first language suggest that these children also generalize object names to new objects by shape but that their shape bias is more restricted to objects of complex shape (Imai & Gentner, 1997) and to rigid objects with nondeformable shapes (Kobayashi, 1997; Samuelson & Smith, 1999) and is more easily challenged by information about object function (Gathercole & Min, 1997) than is the shape bias of children learning English. In brief, how children generalize a newly learned noun depends on the specific language they are learning. These cross-language studies in conjunction with the results of the training experiment strongly indicate that children's attentional biases in the task of learning object names—biases that promote the learning of certain kinds of words and categories—emerge out of the specific word-learning experiences of children.

REFERENCES

Allport, A. (1989). Visual attention. In M. I. Posner (Ed.), *Foundations of cognitive science* (pp. 631–682). Cambridge, MA: MIT Press.

Au, T. K., & Laframboise, D. E. (1990). Acquiring color names via linguistic contrast: The influence of contrasting terms. *Child Development, 61,* 1808–1823.

Bauer, P., & Mandler, J. (1989). Taxonomies and triads: Conceptual organization in one- to two-year-olds. *Cognitive Psychology, 21,* 156–184.

Biederman, I. (1987). Recognition by components: A theory of human image understanding. *Psychological Review, 94,* 115–147.

Clark, A. (1993). *Associative engines: Connectionism, concepts, and representational change.* Cambridge, MA: MIT Press.

Clark, E. V. (1973). What's in a word? On the child's acquisition of semantics in his first language. In T. E. Moore (Ed.), *Cognitive development and the acquisition of language* (pp. 65–110). New York: Academic Press.

Dennett, D. C. (1995). *Darwin's dangerous idea: Evolution and the meaning of life.* New York: Simon & Schuster.

Fenson, L., Dale, P. S., Reznick, S., Thal, D., Bates, E., Hartung, J., Pethick, S., & Reilly, J. (1993). *MacArthur communicative development inventories.* San Diego, CA: Singular.

Gathercole, V. C. M., & Min, H. (1997). Word meaning biases or language-specific effects? Evidence from English, Spanish and Korean. *First Language, 17,* 31–56.

Golinkoff, R. M., Mervis, C. B., & Hirsh-Pasek, K. (1994). Early object labels: The case for a developmental lexical principles framework. *Journal of Child Language, 21,* 125–155.

Imai, M., Gentner, D., & Uchida, N. (1994). Children's theories of word meaning: The role of shape similarity in early acquisition. *Cognitive Development, 9,* 45–76.

Imai, M., & Gentner, D. (1998). A crosslinguistic study of early word meaning: Universal ontology and linguistic influence. *Cognition, 62,* 169–200.

James, W. (1950). *The principles of psychology* (Vol. 1). New York: Dover Publications. (Original work published 1890)

Jones, S., Smith, L., & Landau, B. (1991). Object properties and knowledge in early lexical learning. *Child Development, 62,* 499–516.

Jones, S., & Smith, L. B. (1998). How children name objects with shoes. *Cognitive Development, 13,* 323–334.

Keil, F. (1994). Explanation, association, and the acquisition of word meaning. In L. R. Gleitman & B. Landau (Eds.), *Lexical acquisition* (pp. 169–197). Cambridge, MA: MIT Press.

Kelly, M. H., & Martin, S. (1994). Domain-general abilities applied to domain-specific tasks: Sensitivities to probabilities in perception, cognition and language. In L. R. Gleitman & B. Landau (Eds.), *Lexical acquisition* (pp. 105–141). Cambridge, MA: MIT Press.

Kobayashi, H. (1997). The role of actions in making inferences about the shape and material of solid objects among Japanese 2-year-old children. *Cognition, 63,* 251–269.

Kruschke, J. K. (1992). ALCOVE: An exemplar-based connectionist model of category learning. *Psychological Review, 99,* 22–44.

Landau, B., Smith, L. B., & Jones, S. S. (1988). The importance of shape in early lexical learning. *Cognitive Development, 3,* 299–321.

Landau, B., Smith, L. B., & Jones, S. S. (1992). Syntactic context and the shape bias in children's and adult's lexical learning. *Journal of Memory and Language, 31,* 807–825.

Landau, B., Smith, L. B., & Jones, S. (1998). Object shape, object function, and object name. *Journal of Memory and Language, 38,* 1–27.

Lewicki, P., Hill, T., & Sasak, I. (1989). Self-perpetuating development of encoding biases. *Journal of Experimental Psychology: General, 118,* 323–338.

MacIntosh, N. J. (1965). Selective attention in animal discrimination learning. *Psychological Bulletin, 64,* 125–150.

Macnamara, J. (1982). *Names for things: A study of human learning.* Cambridge, MA: MIT Press.

Markman, E. M. (1989). *Categorization and naming in children: Problems of induction.* Cambridge, MA: MIT Press.

Markman, E. M., & Hutchinson, J. E. (1984). Children's sensitivity to constraints on word meaning: Taxonomic versus thematic relations. *Cognitive Psychology, 16,* 1–27.

Medin, D. L., Altom, M. W., Edelson, S. M., & Freko, D. (1982). Correlated symptoms and simulated medical classifications. *Journal of Experimental Psychology: Learning, Memory, and Cognition, 8,* 37–50.

Medin, D. L., & Wattenmaker, W. D. (1987). Category cohesiveness, theories, and cognitive archeology. In U. Neisser (Ed.), *Concepts and conceptual development: Ecological and intellectual factors in categorization* (pp. 25–62). Cambridge, England: Cambridge University Press.

Mervis, C. B. (1987). Child-basic object categories and lexical development. In U. Neisser (Ed.), *Concepts and conceptual development: Ecological and intellectual factors in categorization.* Cambridge, England: Cambridge University Press.

Mervis, C. B., Mervis, C. A., Johnson, K. E., & Bertrand, J. (1992). Studying early lexical development: The value of the systematic diary method. In C. Rovee-Collier & L. Lippsitt (Eds.), *Advances in infancy research* (Vol. 7, pp. 291–379). Norwood, NJ: Ablex.

Namy, L. L., & Waxman, S. R. (1998). Words and gestures: Infants' interpretations of different forms of symbolic reference. *Child Development, 69,* 295–308.

Pinker, S. (1989). Learnability and cognition: The acquisition of argument structures. Cambridge, MA: MIT Press.

Rescorla, R. A., & Wagner, A. R. (1972). A theory of Pavlovian conditioning: Variations in the effectiveness of reinforcement and nonreinforcement. In A. H. Black & W. F. Prokasy (Eds.), *Classical conditioning II.* New York: Appleton-Century-Crofts.

Rosch, E., & Mervis, C. B. (1975). Family resemblances: Studies in the internal structure of categories. *Cognitive Psychology, 7,* 573–605.

Samuelson, L., & Smith, L. B. (1999). *Statistical regularities among count/mass syntax, solidity, and category structure in early noun vocabularies. Cognition, 73,* 1–33.

Shanks, D. R. (1995). *The psychology of associative learning.* Cambridge, England: Cambridge University Press.

Smith, L. B. (1995). Self-organizing processes in learning to learn words: Development is not induction. In C. A. Nelson (Ed.), *Basic and applied perspectives on learning, cognition, and development: The Minnesota Symposia on Child Psychology* (Vol. 28, pp. 1–32). Mahwah, NJ: Erlbaum.

Smith, L. B., Gershkoff-Stowe, L., & Samuelson, L. (2000). The statisical structure of the first hundred nouns. In preparation.

Smith, L. B., Jones, S., Landau, B., Gershkoff-Stowe, L., & Samuelson, L. (2000). *The origins of the shape bias.* Manuscript submitted for publication.

Smith, L. B., Jones, S. S., & Landau, B. (1992). Count nouns, adjectives, and perceptual properties in children's novel word interpretations. *Developmental Psychology, 28,* 273–286.

Soja, N. (1992). Inferences about the meanings of nouns: The relationship between perception and syntax. *Cognitive Development, 7,* 29–46.

Soja, N. N., Carey, S., & Spelke, E. S. (1991). Ontological categories guide young children's inductions of word meanings: Object terms and substance terms. *Cognition, 38,* 179–211.

Wang, H. (1993). On physicalism and algorithmism. *Philosophia Mathematica, 1,* 97–133.

Waxman, S. R. (1994). The development of an appreciation of specific linkages between linguistic and conceptual organization. In L. R. Gleitman & B. L. Landau (Eds.), *The acquisition of the lexicon* (pp. 229–250). Cambridge, MA: MIT Press.

Waxman, S. R., & Gelman, R. (1986). Preschoolers' use of superordinate relations in classification and language. *Cognitive Development, 1,* 139–156.

Waxman, S. R., & Hall, D. G. (1993). The development of a linkage between count nouns and object categories: Evidence from fifteen- to twenty-one-month-old infants. *Child Development, 64,* 1224–1241.

Woodward, A. L., Markman, E. M., & Fitzsimmons, C. M. (1994). Rapid word learning in 13- and 18-month-olds. *Developmental Psychology, 30,* 553–566.

Younger, B. (1990). Infants' detection of correlations among feature categories. *Child Development, 61,* 614–621.

CHAPTER 4

Constraining the Problem Space in Early Word Learning

Amanda L. Woodward

Quine's famous (1960) "gavagai" example—in which a linguist sees a native point to a rabbit and hears the native say, "Gavagai" just as the rabbit runs by— is well worn in discussions of word learning by now, but it is still apt. Given a new word produced by a speaker in a real-world context, even assuming that the word refers to something in the immediate environment, there are, in principle, indefinitely many ways in which the word could be interpreted. A challenge facing learners, then, is to limit the range of hypotheses to be considered. In this respect, word learning is not unique. Constraining the problem space is a ubiquitous need in acts of cognition. Given the rich array of information available in the world, thinkers need to select elements that are most relevant to the task at hand. This basic problem has been investigated for a wide range of cognitive abilities, including finding solutions to problems (e.g., Holyoak, 1995), deciding which features are central to members of a category (e.g., Medin & Wattenmaker, 1987), and making attributions about the causes of human behavior and other events (e.g., Ahn, Kalish, Medin, & Gelman, 1995; Schwarz, 1995). Multiple sources of constraint contribute to people's success at solving these problems. Knowledge within a domain, properties of human memory and learning, properties of the task, and heuristics are among the many factors that have been found to constrain reasoning.

Like other complex cognitive problems, word learning is multiply constrained. By the time children reach preschool age, they have a well-equipped arsenal to help them narrow the hypothesis space in word learning. For one, children bring to bear their knowledge about language, speakers, and the world. To narrow the range of hypotheses that they consider in word learning, they use the syntactic structure of the sentence surrounding a new word, morphological cues, the meanings of the other words in the sentence, their knowledge about pragmatics, and their knowledge about kinds of objects and events. In addition, children's word learning is constrained by a set of default assumptions that lead them to consider some possible word-referent mappings before they consider others. In preschool-aged children, these sources of constraint interact. No single factor can account for the word-learning success of young children. It is much more likely that each act of learning reflects the interaction of multiple constraints (see chapter 1 in this volume and Woodward & Markman, 1998, for elaborations of this view).

Our goal in this book—to ask how word learning begins—leads us to focus on 1- and 2-year-olds. The 2nd year of life is a time of salient transitions in language development. Babies produce their first words at about 12 months of age, but they generally do not develop large productive repertoires until the vocabulary spurt that often occurs at 18 to 24 months of age. To illustrate, Fenson and his colleagues (1994) found that the productive vocabularies of babies from 12 to 16 months of age grew slowly, with median scores increasing from just under 10 words to 40 words. By 24 months of age, babies produced about 300 words. Based on this evidence it could be concluded that word learning begins in earnest in the second half of the 2nd year of life.

However, if comprehension instead of production is used as an index of learning, word learning seems to be progressing at a good clip long before this time. There are two kinds of evidence for this view: First, observations of babies in everyday contexts have long indicated that by 12 months of age, babies respond appropriately to many of the words they hear (Benedict, 1979; Fenson et al., 1994; Huttenlocher, 1974). Fenson and his colleagues report parental estimates showing that babies understand between 50 and 100 words at 12 months, an age when they produce fewer than 10 words. Second, by 13 months of age, babies can acquire a new word in comprehension based on relatively brief exposure. In an experiment investigating this ability, my collaborators and I introduced 13- and 18-month-old infants to a novel word as the name for a novel object (Woodward, Markman, & Fitzsimmons, 1994). We called the baby's attention to the object and then labeled it nine times. Following training, we tested comprehension of the word using a multiple-choice procedure. Because we embedded the training and testing procedures in naturalistic interaction, there was a concern that the experimenter could inadvertently influence the baby's performance—for example, by creating a preference for the labeled object during training or by giving subtle cues during testing. To guard against the first possibility, we introduced a distracter item during training and then assessed babies' preferences for the target versus the distracter item on preference control trials. These control trials never revealed a preference for the object that had been labeled during training. To guard against the second possibility, we used different experimenters to administer the training and testing procedures. The tester did not know which object had been assigned as the target for any given baby. The results of several studies indicated that when the testing conditions were not demanding, babies at both ages chose the correct object at rates greater than chance. We then tested another group of 13-month-olds, this time imposing a 24-hour delay between training and testing. Babies once again chose the target object at above-chance rates. This early rapid word learning has been replicated using similar procedures (Woodward & Hoyne, 1999), and other researchers have reported similar findings using different procedures (Bird & Chapman, 1998; Schafer & Plunkett, 1998; Stager & Werker, 1997; Werker, Cohen, Lloyd, Casasolo, & Stager, 1998).

Thus, even the youngest word learners do not seem to ponder all of the possible interpretations of a new word. Instead, even in unfamiliar experimental contexts, babies arrive at an interpretation of a new word relatively quickly. In this chapter I will consider how this process occurs. Given the multiple constraints at work for older word learners, my goal is to explore the range of constraints that may be at work for babies. In the last 5–10 years, there has been an explosion in research on early word learning. Although the literature provides many pieces of the puzzle, important gaps remain. Several assumptions frame my review of the current literature. First, I assume that babies, like older children, are active learners who draw on the sources of constraint that are available to them in learning. These may include both knowledge-based constraints and default assumptions. Second, I assume that babies know less about people, language, and the world than older learners do. Thus, a critical question is how and when babies acquire the breadth of knowledge that constrains word learning in older children. Third, I assume that the default assumptions evident in older children have a developmental history and that these assumptions may therefore be undergoing change in the youngest word learners. Thus, it is also critical to ask when and how these constraints develop. In short, I consider the possible sources of constraint that babies have when they first learn words, how these differ from those of older learners, and where they come from. I begin with a review of the evidence for default assumptions in very early word learning.

DEFAULT ASSUMPTIONS

By the time children are in preschool, they have acquired a set of default assumptions that lead them to favor some interpretations of new words over others. In particular, children assume that new words name objects as wholes rather than as their parts or properties (this is the whole-object assumption or principle of object scope; see Golinkoff, Mervis, & Hirsh-Pasek, 1994; Markman, 1989), that novel names extend to members of a kind (this is the taxonomic assumption, noun-category bias, or principle of categorical scope; see (Golinkoff, Mervis, & Hirsh-Pasek, 1994; Markman, 1989; Markman & Hutchinson, 1984; Waxman, 1991, 1994), and that objects have only one category label (this is the mutual-exclusivity assumption; see Markman, 1989; Markman & Wachtel, 1988; Merriman & Bowman, 1989; for related formulations, see E. V. Clark,

1987, 1993; Mervis & Bertrand, 1994; Mervis, Golinkoff, & Bertrand, 1994). These assumptions operate as defaults—given counterevidence, they can be overridden (Markman, 1989, 1992; Merriman & Bowman; Woodward & Markman, 1991). Strong evidence for these assumptions in children and adults comes from many different laboratories (for reviews, see Golinkoff, Mervis, & Hirsh-Pasek; Markman, 1989; Merriman & Bowman; Woodward & Markman, 1998).

That these constraints are distinct from other sources of constraint is evident in their interactions with them. To illustrate, the social context of sharing attention on a set of objects is not sufficient to lead children to focus on categories of objects rather than on other aspects of the situation. If the objects are pictures of two dogs and a bone, for example, young children are likely to focus on the thematic relation between the dogs and the bone. Introducing a new label shifts children's attention to object categories. Given a new label, such as "dax," in reference to one of the dogs, preschoolers extend "dax" to the other dog and not to the bone (Markman & Hutchinson, 1984). Even a seemingly clear pragmatic act, pointing at an object while uttering a novel word, is interpreted differently by children based on their default assumptions. To illustrate, Markman and Wachtel (1988) introduced children to novel substance terms, for example, pointing to an object and saying, "See this? It's chrome." When the referent object was unfamiliar, such as a pair of tongs, children ignored grammatical form class and interpreted "chrome" as the name for the object as a whole. When the object was familiar, such as a cup, children honored the mutual-exclusivity assumption, concluding that "chrome" was not a second name for the object as a whole. Hall, Waxman, and Hurwitz (1993) found that in the latter situation, preschool-aged children were likely to interpret "chrome" as a property term.

In recent years, there has been active debate about how best to characterize these assumptions. One level of argument concerns their exact definition. Is it more accurate to describe children's word learning as being guided by a taxonomic assumption (Markman, 1989; Markman & Hutchinson, 1984) or by a noun-category bias (Waxman, 1991, 1994)? Is mutual exclusivity (Markman, 1989; Markman & Wachtel, 1988; Merriman & Bowman, 1989) the correct formulation; or do children instead have a novel-name nameless-category assumption (Golinkoff, Mervis, & Hirsh-Pasek, 1994; Mervis & Bertrand, 1994), a bias to fill lexical gaps (E. V. Clark, 1993; Merriman & Bowman, 1989), or the principle of contrast (E. V. Clark, 1987, 1993)? Clarifying these issues is important for understanding the nature of these constraints. To some extent, the correct formulation may be a function of the age of the learner. For example, the noun-category bias formulation seems to work well for preschool-aged children, who often (but not always) attend to form class when deciding how to extend a word, but it works less well for very young word learners who seem not to distinguish between nouns and other classes of words (Waxman & Markow, 1995).

A second level of debate concerns the source of these assumptions. Some researchers have proposed that the assumptions emerge from basic properties of human cognition (Gentner, 1982; Gentner & Boroditsky, in press; Imai & Gentner, 1997; Markman, 1989, 1992). Other theorists have proposed that one or more of these assumptions are based on the child's knowledge about statistical regularities in parental speech. These issues come to the fore when considering word learning in its earliest stages. Are these default assumptions evident in very early word learning, and, if so, which account of their origins is most accurate?

Links between Words and Objects

Preschool-aged children have a well-documented propensity to interpret novel words as the name for an object as a whole rather than for one of its parts or properties (e.g., Golinkoff, Mervis, & Pasek, 1994; Hall, Waxman, & Hurwitz, 1993; Imai & Gentner, 1997; Landau, Smith, & Jones, 1988; Markman, 1989; Markman & Wachtel, 1988). This bias is strong enough that children often misinterpret property terms as object labels, even when there are syntactic cues indicating that the word is not a noun (Hall, 1991; Markman & Wachtel). Two-year-olds also have this propensity. When an experimenter shows 2-year-olds a new object and tells them, "This is my dax," for example, the children extend the name "dax" to objects of the same kind as the original but not to objects made of the same substance (Imai & Gentner, 1997; Soja, Carey, & Spelke, 1991) or to parts of the object (Kobayashi, 1998; Markman & Wasow, described in Woodward & Markman, 1998; Mervis, Golinkoff, & Bertrand, 1994). Like older children, 2-year-olds often interpret a novel word as an object label even when they are given form-class cues indicating that the word is a mass or property term—for example, when the experimenter says, "This is some dax" or "This is a daxish one" (Hall, Waxman, & Hurwitz, 1993; Soja, 1992). Markman (1989, 1992) proposed that the link between words and whole objects may be privileged because object categories are conceptually richer than are part or property categories and because children tend to process new stimuli holistically rather than analytically.

In addition to a bias to interpret names for entities at a particular level of analysis—objects as wholes rather than their parts or properties—there may be a second kind of object assumption at work in early word learning: the bias to interpret new words as object labels rather than as terms for other aspects of a situation, such as relations or actions. This possibility derives from observations made by Gentner (1982; Gentner & Boroditsky, in press), who proposed that object concepts are more cohesive than are relational concepts and objects are more readily extracted as perceptual units than are actions. That is, object-sized units are "natural partitions" of information. As evidence for this proposal, Gentner has presented studies of adults' memory for nouns and verbs as well as crosslinguistic analyses of lexicalization patterns for object and action terms. The prediction that follows from these observations is that, because word learning requires mapping linguistic units onto conceptual units, this mapping should occur most easily when the conceptual units are readily extracted and conceptually cohesive—that is, for object terms.

This prediction has generated a lot of heat. Several researchers have been quick to point out that, from the first, babies acquire words for actions, properties, and routines as well as for objects (Bloom, Tinker, & Margulis, 1993; Nelson, Hampson, & Shaw, 1993; Tomasello, 1995). However, the product of learning, the end-state lexicon, may not perfectly reflect the processes by which learning occurred (Woodward & Markman, 1991, 1998). If the object bias is a default assumption, given additional evidence such as pragmatic or syntactic cues, babies may well acquire many nonobject terms. A better source of evidence for or against word-learning assumptions would come from studies of the process of learning. If they exist, default assumptions should be evident in babies' first approaches to new words.

Only a few studies have taken this approach in testing the natural-partitions hypothesis. In one, Schwartz and Leonard (1984) provided 1- to 1½-year-olds with extensive exposure to eight new object labels and eight new action words and then assessed how readily babies learned the words. Based on production, babies learned more object words than action words. A different approach is to tap babies' interpretations of new words in ambiguous contexts, in which the word might name an action or an object. Several researchers report anecdotes indicating that, in ambiguous labeling contexts, 1-year-olds sometimes misinterpret new words as object labels—for example, interpreting the word "hot" as the name for a coffee mug (e.g., Macnamara, 1982; Waxman, 1991). Two preliminary studies have taken an experimental approach to this question. Echols (1991) introduced 14-month-olds to novel objects undergoing distinct kinds of motion in a habituation paradigm. She found that when babies heard words, it drew their attention to the identity of the object rather than to the kind of motion that the object underwent. In a study with 18- and 24-month-olds, I tested whether hearing a new label would lead babies to attend more to objects or to salient entities that were not objects (Woodward, 1993). Babies saw two video displays presented simultaneously, one showing an object and the other showing a substance undergoing motion (e.g., blue dye diffusion through water). In order to test whether labels enhance attention to what babies are already interested in or promote attention specifically to objects, I designed the substance displays to be more interesting than the objects. Overall, infants preferred to watch the substance displays. When they heard a new label, however,

18-month-olds shifted attention to the object, looking for a longer time at the object on these trials than they did when there was speech but no new label. Twenty-four-month-olds did not show this time difference, but their production of the novel words suggested that they had linked them with the object displays.

In sum, there is evidence for two kinds of object assumption in the word learning of 1- and 2-year-olds. However, there are important gaps in the empirical record. The "objects as wholes" assumption has not been investigated in babies under age 2; on the other hand, evidence for the natural-partitions hypothesis has come mainly from babies under age 2. In addition, for each of these assumptions, the developmental process by which novel words come to draw attention to objects is not known. The findings of my (1993) study indicate that by the time babies reach 18 months of age, novel words per se focus infants' attention on objects. Echols's (1991) work with 14-month-olds contrasted labeling utterances with no speech. Thus, it is possible that, initially, any speech draws infants' attention to objects. Echols found a developmental difference in the effects of speech: For 9-month-olds, speech drew attention to elements that were constant across trials, for both objects and motions. For 14-month-olds, however, speech drew attention to objects even when motion was constant across trials and objects were not. Further research is required to confirm and extend these findings.

The question of developmental origins has been considered from another vantage point. As described so far, the object assumption has been conceptualized as being a product of basic aspects of human cognition: Babies interpret words as naming objects as wholes because this level of analysis is most readily apparent to them and because this level of analysis provides a rich packaging of information (Markman, 1989, 1992); babies interpret words as naming objects rather than actions or relations because objects are more coherent perceptual and conceptual units (Gentner, 1982). An alternative has been suggested: The whole-object assumption is a strategy acquired based on probabilistic regularities in parental speech, in particular in middle-class American parental speech that stresses nouns over other classes of words (Gathercole & Min, 1997; Gopnik & Choi, 1995; Tardif, 1996; cf. chapter 3 in this volume). This suggestion was the impetus behind a number of crosslinguistic studies of parents' speech and babies' early vocabulary growth. The studies explored languages such as Japanese and Korean, because these languages have several features that might lead to a lesser emphasis on nouns in parental speech. For one, these languages are verb final, and the final position in an utterance has been argued to be salient to language learners. In addition, these languages allow for nominal ellipsis—that is, leaving out nouns that are part of the shared communicative context. The first question is whether these linguistic differences lead to parental speech that stresses object terms less than does parental speech in middle-class American homes. The answer seems to be yes (Au, Dapretto, & Song, 1994; Fernald & Morikawa, 1993; Gopnik & Choi, 1995; Tardif, 1996).

This observation leads to the question of whether these differences in parental speech lead to different kinds of word-learning biases in babies. The studies provide remarkably mixed answers to this question. As a proxy for measuring the object bias, most researchers have used babies' productive lexicons, asking how many nouns or object labels as compared to other word types babies produce. Some researchers report that babies from different language communities do not differ in the proportion of nouns in their productive lexicons and that babies are noun-dominant across languages (Au, Dapretto, & Song, 1994; Caselli et al., 1995; Fernald & Morikawa, 1993; Gentner & Boroditsky, in press). However, others report that babies acquiring languages such as Korean or Mandarin have fewer nouns or object labels in production than do babies acquiring English (Gopnik & Choi, 1995; Tardif, 1996). Gentner and Boroditsky note that this difference in findings corresponds to a difference in methodology: studies reporting a noun advantage across languages use checklists to assess vocabulary, whereas studies reporting fewer nouns in some languages sample babies' speech from taped naturalistic interactions. There are reasons to believe that both methods are biased (see Gentner & Boroditsky for a discussion).

This methodological problem aside, there is a deeper problem in interpreting these findings vis-à-vis the object bias. As I argued earlier, a child's endstate lexicon may be an unreliable index of the process by which learning occurred. For this reason, using babies' productive lexicons as a proxy for word-learning biases is a flawed approach. Clearer evidence would come from crosslinguistic studies in which babies' interpretations of ambiguous terms were assessed. Imai and Gentner (1997) conducted such a study with English and Japanese speakers ranging in age from 2 years to adulthood. They drew on Soja, Carey, & Spelke's (1991) methodology to ask whether people would interpret a new word as naming an object as a whole or naming the substance of which the object was made. For complex objects (e.g., a citrus reamer) and nonsolid substances (e.g., hand lotion), Japanese and English speakers agreed. Even the 2-year-olds construed the new words as naming objects for the former and substances for the latter. The two groups differed, however, in how they treated simple solid objects (e.g., a kidney-shaped piece of wax). For these, English speakers extended the new word to items with the same overall shape, that is to objects of like kind. Japanese speakers, in contrast, were agnostic—they interpreted the term as naming the substance half the time and the object half the time (see Gathercole & Min, 1997, for similar evidence from Korean-speaking children). Imai and Gentner proposed that there is a continuum of individuation. Some entities (people and complex objects) stand out as salient units, and others (nonsolid substances) do not. Items such as chunks of wax fall somewhere between these two. Thus, there is evidence for both crosslinguistic similarity in and language-specific influences on word learning. For highly individuable entities, speakers of dissimilar languages agree that names refer to objects as wholes. This evidence is consistent with the conclusion that the object bias derives from properties of cognition that do not vary across language groups. However, there is room for language experience to influence interpretations of new words, specifically for items in the middle of the continuum.

Extending Names to Members of a Kind

In many learning contexts, babies generalize to whole situations. After visiting the doctor for a vaccination, for example, a baby may fear anything that reminds him or her of that visit, including not only hypodermic needles but also waiting rooms, people wearing white clothing, and stethoscopes. Even in the realm of communication, generalization to thematic associates may occur. Petitto (1988) described infants' prelinguistic gestures as sometimes extending to thematically related items; for example, some babies used the same gesture to communicate about jars and the act of opening jars. Babies also notice taxonomic relations in and out of word-learning contexts (Mandler & McDonough, 1993; Oakes, Madole, & Cohen, 1991; Quinn, 1987; Waxman & Markow, 1995). For word learning, of course, it is critical to attend to taxonomic relations. Names for objects and actions extend to members of a kind, not to thematic associates.

Early theories of language acquisition proposed that babies' first words were "complexive" in nature—that they were associated with whole situations rather than with a particular class of referents (Piaget, 1962; Vygotsky, 1962). According to these accounts, a child's use of a word such as "cookie" might extend to cookies; objects shaped like cookies; and items associated with cookies, such as cookie jars, kitchens, and grandmothers. Huttenlocher and Smiley (1987) analyzed the spontaneous word use of 1- to 2-year-olds to see whether this was the case. They found that babies' use of object labels was almost always an extension to items within a basic level or superordinate category. When babies used a noun in the absence of an appropriate referent, there were clear indications that they were requesting absent objects or commenting on relationships between objects rather than extending the word thematically.

Waxman and Hall (1993) explored babies' novel-name extensions in an experimental context. They introduced 16-month-olds to triads in which two items were taxonomically related and two were thematically related—for example, a cup, another cup, and a doll. Babies were introduced to both the taxonomic relation (the two cups) and the thematic relation (that the doll could "drink" from the cup). After this introduction, in one condition, the experimenter labeled the first cup, saying, "This is a dax." Then the experimenter showed the baby the other cup and the doll and asked the baby to find another dax. In the control condition, the experimenter showed the baby the first cup and then the other cup and the doll and instructed him or her to "find another one." Babies who heard a new label selected the taxonomic match most of the time. In contrast, in the absence of a label, babies selected the taxonomic match only about half of the time (see also Markman, 1994, for further evidence from 1-year-olds, and Waxman & Kosowski, 1990, for evidence from 2-year-olds). Thus, in a receptive word-learning task as well as in their uses of nouns, 1-year-olds, like older children, do not interpret new terms as extending to thematically related items. Moreover, Hall (1991) found that, as is the case for the whole-object assumption, 2-year-olds sometimes overlook form-class cues in interpreting a novel term as a category label. When babies were introduced to a novel stuffed animal and told, "This is Zav," they extended "Zav" to other animals, treating it as a common noun rather than as a proper noun. Babies even produced "zav" as a count noun, saying, for example, "There are two zavs."

Words highlight categorical relations for babies still earlier, at 12 months of age. Waxman and Markow (1995) found that novel words directed babies' attention to categorical relations that they would not otherwise notice. When experimenters gave babies members of a basic-level category to play with, one after the other (e.g., a red toy car, a blue toy car, etc.), babies habituated to the category, exploring later items for a shorter time than they explored prior ones. Then, when babies were shown an out-of-category member such as an airplane they dishabituated, attending to this object for a longer time. Waxman and Markow found that 12-month-olds did not habituate spontaneously for superordinate sets. However, when the experimenter labeled each object as she handed it to the baby, babies habituated to items of the same category and dishabituated to items from outside the category. This occurred only when the items were members of the same category. When infants were handed random objects (e.g., a dinosaur, a clown, and a pipe), labeling did not lead to "categorization." Moreover, it was the presence of a novel word per se that led babies to categorize. When there were no labels, the experimenter talked about the toys and engaged in joint attention with the baby, and these behaviors alone did not boost categorization.

By the time a child reaches 12 months of age, then, the effect of new words can be distinguished from general effects of speech and social engagement. The former, but not the latter, leads babies to pay special attention to categorical relations. Even so, speech sounds are affectively charged from the beginning of life, and speech may serve to regulate infants' attention (Baldwin & Markman, 1989; Fernald, 1992). The specific link between words and categories that is evident in 12-month-olds may emerge, in part, from this more general effect of speech on infants' attention. In keeping with this possibility, Balaban and Waxman (1997) reported that, for 9-month-olds, speech sounds in general, rather than novel words per se, enhance attention to stimuli in a categorization task. Balaban and Waxman familiarized infants with pictures of items from within a basic-level kind (e.g., dinosaurs) and then showed them a new exemplar of that category or an item from another category (e.g., a bird). When the pictures were accompanied by recorded words or by recorded speech that had been low-pass filtered so that no individual words were identifiable, infants showed more attention to the item from the new category than they did when the pictures were accompanied by recorded tones (but see Roberts & Jacob, 1991).

Markman (1992) proposed that the specific link between words and taxonomic categories is related to using taxonomic relations as a basis for inductive inference. Just as babies assume that items of like kind share important properties (Baldwin, Markman, & Melartin, 1993; Gelman & Coley, 1991), they may also assume that items of like kind have the same name. Under this account, babies' appreciation of the link between words and categories would be dependent on their prelinguistic category knowledge. In contrast, Smith (see chapter 3 in this volume) has suggested that infants learn to extend labels to items with the same overall shape (and thus, generally, of the same kind) based on regularities in parents' speech. If this is correct, then babies bring little if any category knowledge to word learning. There are many unresolved questions about the state of category knowledge in infants. Nevertheless, it is clear that prelinguistic infants form categories for both unfamiliar and familiar objects (Mandler & McDonough, 1993; Quinn, 1987; Quinn, Eimas, & Rosenkrantz, 1993). Moreover, Mandler and her colleagues have argued that prelinguistic infants' categories are not based only on perceptual regularities; they also reflect knowledge about important conceptual distinctions (e.g., Mandler & McDonough, 1993, 1996). This knowledge provides a basis for inductive projection (Mandler & McDonough, 1996) and could also provide a basis for extending newly learned words.

Mutual Exclusivity

Preschool-aged children have the default assumption that items will have only one name (Markman, 1989; Markman & Wachtel, 1988; Merriman & Bowman, 1989). This mutual-exclusivity assumption could contribute to word learning in several ways. For one, it could make word learning harder when the child encounters a second name for an item with a known name. In this case, mutual exclusivity might lead children to reject the second label. Merriman and Bowman called this the "rejection effect." In other situations, mutual exclusivity could facilitate word learning. It could help the learner to rule out familiar objects in the case where a novel object is named. Merriman and Bowman called this the "disambiguation effect." It could also help to override the whole-object assumption in learning a part or property term. Moreover, if the child erroneously overextended a new term—for example, calling sheep "goats," mutual exclusivity could lead him or her to correct the extension of the term "goat" once "sheep" was learned. This is an example of two effects described by Merriman and Bowman: the "restriction" effect (the extension of "goat" has been restricted) and the "correction" effect (for sheep, the correct term has been substituted for "goat"). In different contexts, all of these effects appear in preschool-aged children (e.g., see Markman & Wachtel; Merriman & Bowman). Investigations of mutual exclusivity in 1- and 2-year-olds vary in terms of which of the effects they explore.

A number of studies provide evidence for disambiguation in 1½- and 2-year-olds. When experimenters present babies with a familiar object (e.g., a spoon) and an unfamiliar object (e.g., a honey dipper) and ask them about a novel label (e.g., "Can you get the dax?"), babies select the novel object (Golinkoff, Hirsh-Pasek, Bailey, & Wenger, 1992; Merriman & Marazita, 1995; Mervis & Bertrand, 1994). Several researchers have pointed out that the disambiguation effect could result from biases other than mutual exclusivity. If babies had a bias to fill lexical gaps (E. V. Clark, 1987, 1993; Merriman & Bowman, 1989), then they would also select the unfamiliar object as the referent of the new word. Another possible constraint on word learning, the novel-name nameless-category principle (Golinkoff, Mervis, & Hirsh-Pasek, 1994), which would lead children to link new names with object categories for which they have no name, could also explain the disambiguation effect. A different procedure, such as the one used in a study reported by Markman (1994; see also Woodward & Markman, 1998), is necessary to distinguish between these possibilities. Experimenters gave 16- and 19-month-olds a familiar object (e.g., a spoon). Then they asked babies to "Get the mido." Babies responded by looking around for another object, apparently not considering the spoon to be a possible "mido." Since there was no novel object in the situation, there was not a lexical gap or nameless category. Rather, babies assumed that the familiar item was not also called a "mido."

While this is an example of infants attempting to disambiguate, it is also an example of infants rejecting the spoon as a likely referent for "mido." Rejection of new labels given in reference to items with known names has also been tested by assessing babies' propensity to accept second labels. Two-year-olds can learn multiple category labels for the same item, seeming to interpret the words as synonyms, overlapping terms, or hierarchically related terms (Banigan & Mervis, 1988; E. V. Clark, 1997; Mervis, Golinkoff & Bertrand, 1994; Waxman & Senghas, 1992). This fact has been taken as evidence against mutual exclusivity (e.g., E. V. Clark, 1993, 1997; Golinkoff, Mervis, & Hirsh-Pasek, 1994; Mervis, Golinkoff, & Bertrand). However, Liittschwager and Markman (1994) pointed out that the critical question is whether second labels are harder to learn than first labels. Because mutual exclusivity is proposed to be a default assumption, learners will be able to acquire terms that violate it. Like other default assumptions, mutual exclusivity should be evident in the process of word learning. Liittschwager and Markman tested this by attempting to teach 16- and 24-month-olds first versus second labels. In one condition, they introduced babies to a novel label for an object that was unfamiliar (e.g., a honey dipper). In this case the novel name was a first label. In a second condition, they introduced a novel label for an object for which babies would have a familiar name (e.g., a toy unicorn that babies would call a "horse"). In this case, the novel name was a second label. Babies' comprehension of the new labels was assessed by a multiple-choice procedure. The 16-month-olds learned the first labels but not the second labels. In contrast, the 24-month-olds learned both the first and the second labels. Liittschwager and Markman reasoned that the context of labeling provided evidence that might run counter to mutual exclusivity (the experimenter clearly indicated the toy while labeling) and that 24-month-olds might be able to draw on this evidence to override the default assumption. If so, then increasing the demands of the learning task might make it harder for 24-month-olds to override mutual exclusivity. With this in mind, Liittschwager and Markman next introduced 24-month-olds to two new first or second labels rather than to one. In this case, the 24-month-olds learned the first labels but not the second labels. Thus, although 24-month-olds were able to learn second labels when the task was not demanding, for both 16- and 24-month-olds, learning second labels was harder than learning first labels.

If babies had the mutual-exclusivity assumption, then they might respond to certain instances of second-label learning by restricting or correcting the meanings of previously learned words (see Merriman & Bowman, 1989, for a discussion of the conditions under which children will respond to a new word by restricting an old term versus by rejecting the new term). Merriman and Stevenson (1997) investigated this effect in 24-month-olds. They showed babies sets containing a typical familiar item (e.g., a car), two atypical items from the category, and one item from outside the category (e.g,. a bicycle). In the context of a storybook, one of the atypical items was given a novel name—for example, "jegger." Then Merriman and Stevenson showed babies the full set of items and asked them to identify all the cars and all the jeggers. The question was whether hearing the first atypical car called a "jegger" would decrease babies' likelihood of identifying that item as a "car." This is what Merriman and Stevenson found. Compared to the other atypical car, babies were less likely to select the jegger when asked to indicate all the cars. Thus, accepting the new word led babies to restrict the range of the familiar term "car."

In summary, recent studies provide evidence for several effects of mutual exclusivity in the word learning of babies 2 years of age and younger. As orig-

inally formulated by Markman (1989; Markman & Wachtel, 1988), mutual exclusivity pertains to object labels; however, other researchers have suggested
that learners may assume mutual exclusivity within other semantic domains—
for example, for verbs and spatial terms (Merriman, Evey-Burkey, Marazita, &
Jarvis, 196; Regier, 1997; cf. Golinkoff, Hirsh-Pasek, Mervis, Frawley, &
Parillo, 1995). Markman (1992) noted that mutual exclusivity is similar to a
number of other phenomena including the one-to-one principle, the essential-
ist bias in categorization, and blocking and overshadowing in classical conditioning. Based on this observation, she suggested that mutual exclusivity may
be a particular case of a more general tendency to systematize information in
learning. In an alternative formulation, E. V. Clark (1987, 1993) has stressed
the role of pragmatic and linguistic knowledge in children's resistance to multiple labels for the same object. In the section "Knowledge-Based Constraints,"
I consider these factors.

Conclusion

There is a good deal of evidence for the whole-object, taxonomic, and mutual-
exclusivity assumptions in 2-year-old word learners. The evidence in children
under age 2 is less plentiful. Nevertheless, there are strong indications that 1-
year-olds' word learning is constrained by default assumptions such as those at
work in older learners. Twelve- to 18-month-olds seek out object-sized units in
word learning. Twelve-month-olds respond to new words by attending to taxonomic categories, and even the earliest words that babies produce seem to be
category terms. A bit later, by 16 months of age, babies show evidence of mutual exclusivity by rejecting second labels for familiar objects.

Even so, as for older children, these default assumptions are insufficient
to account for the full range of words that are learned from the start of vocabulary acquisition (Bloom, Tinker, & Margulis, 1993; Nelson, 1988; Nelson,
Hampson, & Shaw, 1993). From the first, babies acquire words other than object labels (e.g., event terms, social greetings, and spatial terms), words that do
not extend to members of a category (e.g., proper nouns and performatives such
as "peekaboo," and multiple labels for the same object (Banigan & Mervis,
1988; E. V. Clark, 1997; Mervis, Golinkoff, & Bertrand, 1994; Waxman &
Senghas, 1992). In older learners, the child's knowledge about language and
language users provides a strong source of constraint in word learning. This
knowledge can help to explain the breadth of older children's vocabularies
(e.g., Anglin, 1993). One question, then, is what kinds of knowledge interact
with default assumptions in very young word learners? To answer this question, I focus on knowledge that undergoes important developments during a
baby's 2nd year of life: knowledge about acts of communication and the language system.

KNOWLEDGE-BASED CONSTRAINTS

Knowledge about Communication

Because, in the word of the infant, words are actions, infants most likely draw on their understanding of human action in making sense of words. For mature language users, interpreting utterances involves understanding intentional action and knowledge states in themselves and in their interlocutors. Adults use behavioral evidence to infer what conversational partners know and what their intentions in using language are; that is, we use folk "theories of mind" in making sense of language acts (E. V. Clark, 1997; H. Clark, 1992; but see Keysar, Barr, & Horton, 1998, for exceptions).

To what extent does this knowledge play a role in early word learning? The work of Akhtar, Tomasello, and Baldwin, among others (for reviews, see chapter 5 in this volume; Baldwin, 1995; Baldwin & Tomasello, 1998; Tomasello, 1995), has documented that, for 18- to 24-month-olds, behavioral cues to referential intent influence children's interpretations of new words. For example, 18-month-olds will learn the link between a new word and a toy when the person who utters the word looks toward the toy and indicates it by pointing but will not do so when such behaviors are absent or when the behaviors specify another object (e.g., Baldwin, 1991; Baldwin et al., 1996; Moore, Angelopoulos, & Bennett, 1999). One issue that has arisen is whether these effects are best characterized as based in the baby's knowledge or the adult's highlighting of objects (Moore, Angelopoulos, & Bennett; Samuelson & Smith, 1998). Much evidence from the work of Akhtar, Tomasello, Baldwin, and others indicates that, by the time babies reach 18 to 24 months of age, highlighting alone is insufficient to explain the role of communicative cues in word learning. Babies' interpretations of novel words seem to be a function neither of simply attending to an object while a word is uttered (Baldwin, 1991; Baldwin, et al.) nor seeing the object or action immediately after hearing a word (Baldwin, 1991; Tomasello & Barton, 1994), and babies can correctly interpret a new word even when they never see the referent during or after the time that word is uttered (Akhtar & Tomasello, 1996). The conclusion supported by these findings is that 18- to 24-month-old babies filter their word learning through their understanding of human action and, more specifically, communication.

It might be tempting to conclude from these findings that by 18–24 months, babies understand communication in much the same way that adults do. However, given the well-documented deficits in preschool-aged children's theories of mind (see, e.g., Astington, Harris, & Olson, 1988) and in the pragmatic skills of toddlers and young children (see Shatz, 1983, for a review), it seems very likely that the knowledge that 18- to 24-month-olds have about communication differs significantly from that of adults. Therefore, it is important to specify the ways in which toddlers' reasoning is and is not like that of adults (see chapter 5 in this volume; Baldwin & Moses, 1996; Baldwin & Tomasello, 1998; and Moore, Angelopoulos, & Bennett, 1999, for preliminary considerations of this issue). Current evidence suggests two ways in which the knowledge of 18- to 24-month-olds is similar to later knowledge: by this age, babies seem to have precursors to later understandings of intention and attention, both of which are critical to reasoning about communication.

Evidence for the first of these similarities comes from a number of studies. Fourteen-month-olds distinguish between purposeful and apparently accidental actions when imitating: They are more likely to imitate the former than the latter (Carpenter, Akhtar, & Tomasello, 1998). Somewhat older babies, 18-month-olds, can use behavioral cues to infer the goal of a novel action: When they see an actor apparently fail to complete an intended action, babies at this age infer the intended act and imitate it rather than the actual motions of the actor's hands (Meltzoff, 1995). By age 18–24 months, babies use their notions of purposeful action in word learning. Tomasello and Barton (1994) found that 24-month-olds interpreted new verbs as naming acts that are done purposefully rather than those that are portrayed as accidental. Moreover, 18- and 24-month-olds use other behavioral indicators of a satisfied or frustrated intention to inform their interpretation of a new word (Akhtar & Tomasello, 1996; Tomasello & Barton).

Eighteen- to 24-month-olds also seem to understand some aspects of attention. Infants attend the direction of another person's gaze from quite early in life (Scaife & Bruner, 1975), but not until later, at 12–18 months, is there evidence that infants understand something about the role of eyes in perceptual experience (Lempers, Flavell, & Flavell, 1977). The work of Baldwin (1991, 1995) clearly indicates that 18-month-olds understand the relevance of this behavior for language use. Eighteen-month-olds interpret words as naming objects looked at by the speaker, even when baby and speaker attend to different objects. By 2 years of age, babies understand an additional aspect of attention: O'Neill (1996) reported evidence that 2-year-olds have a nascent understanding of the link between seeing and knowing. Babies in her study were more likely to give their mothers detailed information about a recent event if the mothers were out of the room or had their eyes covered during the event than if the mothers had observed it with them. In addition, a study by Akhtar, Carpenter, & Tomasello (1996) suggests that 2-year-olds can go one step further: They keep track of what others have and have not seen and infer that speakers will remark on items that are new to them. In the study, this inference enabled babies to determine which of several objects had been named by an experimenter (but see Samuelson & Smith, 1998, for an alternative interpretation).

A recent study by Moore, Angelopoulos, & Bennett (1999) indicates another potential development in babies' reasoning about shared attention between the ages of 18 and 24 months. In their study, 18-month-old babies used a speaker's line of regard to determine which of two objects she was referring to. Even when one of the objects moved around and made noise, if the speaker looked at the baby but not at either of the objects, 18-month-olds did not think the new word named the object. In contrast, 24-month-olds assumed that the speaker was referring to the salient object. Older, but not younger babies, therefore, may reason that if there is a very salient item, people nearby will notice it and re-mark on it. Adults make a similar assumption. At a fireworks display, we do not need to monitor the gaze of our interlocutor to make an intelligent guess about the subject of his or her "oohs" and "aahs."

Does knowledge about communication play a role in word learning at the beginning—that is, for infants between 12 and 18 months of age? Although there has not been nearly as much research at this age as there has been at older ages, two preliminary findings indicate that some form of social knowledge is used by 12- to 13-month-olds when they encounter new words. First, Baldwin and Tomasello (1998) reported a study in which 12-month-olds were introduced to a new word under one of two conditions: In one condition, there was a sin-gle novel object in front of the baby. In the other, there were two novel objects. Infants were much more likely to check the speaker's line of regard in the lat-ter condition than in the former. That is, when faced with a potentially am-biguous labeling event, 12-month-olds seemed to seek to resolve the ambigu-ity by checking the speaker's behavior.

A second study, recently completed in my laboratory, indicates that 13-month-olds not only seek out information about line of regard and pointing but also use this information in word learning. In this study, 13-month-olds were introduced to a new object label as they jointly attended to an object with an experimenter. The label was produced by a second experimenter. For half the babies, the second experimenter looked at and pointed toward the object that the baby was attending to (the joint-attention condition). For example, the ex-perimenter would say, "Wow, the gombie!" For the other half, the experimenter looked at a video screen, never at the toy the baby attended to, and produced the same utterance (the discrepant-attention condition). The video screen showed the camera's view of the interaction, so that the speaker could time her utterances to coincide with the baby's attention to the object. Thus, in both con-ditions, babies had their attention directed to an object by the first experimenter, and then they heard a word. Only in the joint-attention condition, however, were there clear behavioral cues linking the speaker to the target object.

After training, my collaborators and I tested comprehension using a multi-ple-choice procedure. An experimenter showed babies a tray containing the tar-get toy and a second novel object while asking them, "Get the gombie." This portion of the procedure was administered by a third experimenter who did not know which object had been paired with the label or whether the baby was assigned to the joint- or discrepant-attention condition. In the joint-attention condition, babies selected the previously labeled object at above-chance rates. In the discrepant-attention condition, in contrast, babies chose randomly. Thus, hearing the label as they attended to the object was not sufficient for infants in this condition to learn the relation between the word and the object.

One possible explanation for this difference in learning is that the joint- and discrepant-attention training procedures manipulated babies' attention in different ways. Perhaps babies in the joint-attention condition had their attention focused more effectively on the object than did the infants in the discrepant-attention condition. To evaluate this possibility, we are currently coding babies' patterns of visual attention from the videotapes. This coding is partially completed (14 of the 20 babies in each group have been coded). The preliminary data indicate that babies in the two training conditions did not differ in terms of the amount of time they looked at the target object, the amount of time they looked at the speaker, or the number of times they looked at the target at the exact moment the label was produced. Thus, at this point, it does not seem that the differences in learning resulted from differences in attentional highlighting during training. Instead, it may be that infants' construal of the speaker's actions matters for word learning.

In sum, there is evidence that for 13-month-olds, as for older babies, behavioral cues to communicative intent impact on word learning and that this impact may not reduce to attentional highlighting. There are at least two possible explanations for this finding. The first is that the knowledge that has been demonstrated in 18- to 24-month-olds is present much earlier in life, by 13 months of age. The second possibility is that, in word learning, infants initially attend to behaviors such as gazing and pointing based on a less-elaborated understanding of the link between speaker and referent. The evidence favors the second possibility. Hirsch-Pasek, Golinkoff, and Hollich (chapter 6, this volume), for example, report that under more stringent testing conditions, 12-month-olds engaged in word learning seem not to attend to an adult's gaze. In addition, several studies have found that 12-month-olds are more limited than are 18- to 24-month-olds in their production and comprehension of nonverbal communicative behaviors (e.g., Butterworth & Grover, 1988; Lempers, Flavell, & Flavell, 1977). How, then, might younger 1-year-olds understand the connection between speaker and referent? By 6 months of age, infants construe some actions in terms of the relationship between actor and object (Woodward, 1998), and recent work in my laboratory indicates that, by 12 months of age, babies interpret pointing and gazing in this way. Early word learning could build on this understanding. Babies may use behaviors by adults, such as gazing, touching, and pointing, to interpret utterances—like other actions—in terms of the objects to which the speaker is connected, without yet understanding that words communicate mentally represented information. This would mean that, without having a full-fledged understanding of the way that words relate to ideas, babies understand something about reference—that words are "about" or directed toward objects. The relationship between knowledge about communication and word learning may well be bidirectional. Baldwin and Moses (1996) have proposed that learning words and interpreting the language behavior of others leads babies to acquire the insight that other people have knowledge states. If so, this insight would in turn have a powerful effect on babies' ability to make sense of language.

Knowledge about Word Forms

Beyond understanding that other people have intentions and attention, mature language users understand the particular way that linguistic symbols— words—are used to fulfill communicative intent. This is not a simple extension from general reasoning about intentional action; it requires understanding some facts about the linguistic system. Words are independent from their referents in form. Their meaning rests not in an inherent relationship between the form and its referent but rather in the fact that speakers of a language agree on their meanings; that is, words are conventionally set. Words function as symbols in a system in which a change in a single componential unit, a phoneme, signals difference in meaning. In these respects, words differ from nonverbal communicative acts such as gestures.

E. V. Clark (1987, 1993) has proposed that knowledge about these aspects of the language system provides a source of constraint in word learning. Specifically, she suggests that language learners are guided by the assumptions that people use particular word forms because they have agreed-upon meanings (the principle of conventionality) and that if someone uses a form that is not conventionally appropriate for a familiar item, he or she must intend to mean something else (the principle of contrast). These principles would result in learners' assuming that every difference in form indicated some difference in meaning. Given a new word—"carnivore" for a dog, for example—a child would reason that "carnivore" must mean something other than "dog." These assumptions could also contribute to children's learning about morphology and syntax; learners would be motivated to find the difference in meaning implied by different forms such as "dogs" versus "dog" or "walked" versus "walk." Thus, understanding the conventional and contrastive nature of linguistic symbols could serve as a powerful tool in language acquisition.

Whether this specific formulation is correct for young children has been debated. The evidence for these principles in babies is that they avoid having two labels for the same object (E. V. Clark, 1987, 1993). As discussed earlier, this evidence is also consistent with the stronger mutual-exclusivity assumption (the assumption that objects have only one label). In fact—as several re-searchers have pointed out—by themselves, the principles of contrast and con-ventionality are insufficient to explain children's resistance to second labels (Golinkoff, Mervis, & Hirsh-Pasek, 1994; Markman, 1989). If children had the principle of contrast, then a second label (e.g., for a dog) could be readily ac-cepted as a hierarchically related term ("animal"), overlapping term ("pet"), or less-formal term ("pooch"), among other possibilities, so long as the meaning of the second term differed in some way from that of "dog." To explain the ob-servation that children resist second labels, E. V. Clark (1987, 1993) proposed that children have additional biases to favor terms at a single level of analysis and terms that do not overlap in meaning (but see E. V. Clark, 1997, for argu-ments against this view). This cluster of assumptions yields predictions similar to that of mutual exclusivity.

Setting aside for the moment the question of whether mutual exclusivity or contrast is the correct formulation, we can ask whether 1- and 2-year-olds have the kinds of knowledge just described—that is, do they understand the formal properties of linguistic symbols? Early in infancy, babies have the perceptual prerequisites to identify the class of forms that is conventionally used to name and to note differences between particular word forms. Infants distinguish speech from other kinds of sounds (Balaban & Waxman, 1997) and can dis-criminate phonetic contrasts between different speech sounds (for a review, see Goodman & Nusbaum, 1994). However, recent findings indicate that it takes babies some time to determine the relevance of these perceptual differences to word meaning.

The most basic convention is that we use some forms—spoken words—and not others as linguistic symbols. Long before babies learn what words mean, they respond to speech as a special kind of signal. Speech is salient and affec-tively charged for infants, and it serves to regulate infants' attention and mood (Balaban & Waxman, 1997; Baldwin & Markman, 1989; Fernald, 1992). Nevertheless, babies do not seem to begin word learning with the strong ex-pectation that names will be in the form of spoken words. In several recent stud-ies, younger 1-year-olds have been found to accept a range of signals in situa-tions that older learners reserve for spoken words (Namy, 1998; Namy & Waxman, 1998; Woodward & Hoyne, 1999; chapter 3 in this volume). In our 1999 study, Hoyne and I introduced 13-month-old infants to novel signals that were embedded in labeling routines: A researcher would call the baby's atten-tion and point to a toy saying, "Look" and would then produce a new sound (e.g., a siren whistle) while indicating the toy. That is, the experimenter ac-companied the sound with behavioral cues to referential intent. We measured babies' learning of the relation between the sound and the toy by using a mul-tiple-choice procedure. A second researcher placed the target object and another novel object in a tray and asked the baby to "get one," as the researcher produced the sound. For comparison, a second group of 13-month-olds was introduced to words. Thirteen-month-olds who heard sounds responded just as did those who heard words—that is, they chose the object that had been "labeled" with the sound during training. We found no evidence that babies were more resistant to the sounds than to the words. Babies responded to test questions as often and as quickly in the sound condition as in the word condition. Moreover, as was the case for words, babies generalized the sound labels to an item that differed in color from the training object. We next examined whether older babies, 20-month-olds, would accept the sound labels. Given the same training with sounds, 20-month-olds responded randomly on test trials. That is, the older babies did not seem to consider the novel sounds as potential labels, even though the sounds were accompanied by gazing and pointing.

Namy and Waxman (1998) reported a similar pattern of findings with somewhat older babies. In their studies, 18-month-olds but not 24-month-olds accepted novel gestural labels for objects. Moreover, 18-month-olds generalized these labels to items of like kind (see also Acredolo & Goodwyn, 1988). In subsequent work Namy (1998) found this pattern for sound and pictogram labels. In all of these studies, younger 1-year-olds treated novel signals as if they were labels. They readily learned the specific links between particular signals and particular objects, generalized the labels to an appropriate range of taxonomically related referents, and responded readily to the signal when it was embedded in communicative routines. In other words, babies seem to understand something about the functions of names before they have strong expectations about the forms that will serve these functions.

At the same time that babies are honing their expectations about the limits of the class of word forms, they are refining their expectations about meaningful differences between words. Even for a newborn, minimal pairs such as "bih"/"dih" are readily discriminable. However, Stager and Werker (1997) found that 14-month-olds do not exploit phonemic differences between minimal pairs when they are learning to link word forms with pictures. In their first study, Stager and Werker habituated infants to two word/picture pairings. One picture was shown as the babies heard "bih"; another was shown as they heard "dih." Then, in test, on some trials there was a mismatch—for example, "dih" was played with the picture that had been paired with "bih" during habituation. Fourteen-month-olds did not respond to this mismatch. Next, Stager and Werker administered a simpler test: They habituated infants to a single word/ object pairing and then played a recording of a mismatching word in test. In this study, too, fourteen-month-olds failed to respond to the change in word (see Bird & Chapman, 1998, for further evidence). Strikingly, 8-month-old infants succeeded at this task, looking for a longer period of time on mismatch trials. Stager and Werker proposed that 8-month-olds solved the task by making a perceptual distinction and that 14-month-olds failed by approaching it as a word-learning task. Fourteen-month-olds succeeded at noticing the difference between "bih" and "dih" when they were not learning a picture/word correspondence, and they succeeded at distinguishing words that differed globally ("lif" versus "neem") in a word-learning task (see Bird & Chapman; Schafer & Plunkett, 1998; Werker, Cohen, Lloyd, Casasolo, & Stager, for further evidence). Werker (1994) has reported unpublished findings indicating that, by 19 months of age, babies can learn that minimally different words have different referents. Thus, in the first half of the 2nd year, babies are homing in on the level of phonetic detail that is relevant for word meaning.

By 2 years of age, then, babies have the wherewithal to understand contrast between conventionally set linguistic symbols. They have the expectation that some forms—spoken words—serve as names for things, and other forms do not. Moreover, based on Werker's (1994) data, by this age, babies seem to have determined the level at which forms within the system differ from one another. Before age 2, babies' understanding of the formal properties of names is surprisingly limited. Nevertheless, babies as young as 16 months old note global differences between word forms and, based on these differences, reject second labels. This ability could result from the cognitive factors described by Markman (1992). Babies may seek to simplify the word-learning problem by assuming that each object has only one name—that is, via the mutual-exclusivity assumption. This kind of simplification assumption does not require that babies understand much about the linguistic system. Even so, mutual exclusivity would be limited in significant ways by babies' knowledge about word forms.

Knowledge about Syntax

Once children understand that linguistic forms constitute a special class of actions, they can learn about the combinatorial properties of this system. How children acquire syntax is strongly debated, but regardless of how they go about it, once they do, they have an important source of knowledge to bring to bear in word learning. By the time they reach elementary school, children can use a range of syntactic information in word learning, including count- versus mass-noun syntax, articles specifying count- versus proper-noun status, syntactic and morphological cues to adjective versus noun status, the argument structure of a sentence, and aspects of derivational morphology (e.g., Anglin, 1993; E. V. Clark, 1993; Fisher, Hall, Rakowitz, & Gleitman, 1994).

Children have access to some syntactic cues to meaning by the time they are 2 years old. Macnamara's (1982) pioneering work suggested that by 18 months of age, babies use the presence or absence of an article in front of a noun to inform their interpretations of common versus proper nouns. Subsequent studies, which included important controls absent in the original work, established this ability in 2-year-olds (Gelman and Taylor, 1984; Hall, 1991). Two-year-olds also distinguish between novel count nouns (e.g., the "daxin") and novel adjectives (e.g., a "daxish" one) (Waxman & Kosowski, 1990; Waxman & Markow, 1998). In addition, E. V. Clark (1993) described evidence from children's coinage of new terms that indicates that, by 2 years of age, babies draw on another aspect of English morphology in vocabulary acquisition: They have learned the rules for compound formation.

Gleitman, Naigles, Fisher, and their colleagues (Fisher, Hall, Rakowitz, & Gleitman, 1994; Gleitman, 1990; Naigles, 1990, 1996) have argued that syntactic frames provide a particularly important source of constraint for verb learning. Because verbs have relational meanings, syntactic cues such as the number and arrangement of arguments in a sentence give information about a verb's meaning. Naigles (1990) established that 2-year-olds use this cue. Based on whether a novel verb occurred in a transitive or intransitive sentence frame, babies interpreted the verb as naming a causative or noncausative action (for further evidence, see Hirsh-Pasek & Golinkoff, 1996). Naigles (1996) found that 2-½-year-olds also attend to a verb's occurrence in multiple sentence contexts and use this information to make inferences about the verb's meaning.

There is little evidence about whether babies draw on syntactic information in word learning before 2 years of age, and the evidence that exists suggests that they do not. In one of the few studies addressing this question, Hirsh-Pasek and Golinkoff (1996) reported that unlike 24-month-olds, the 19-month-olds they tested showed no attention to argument structure in verb learning. Based on babies' spontaneous production of newly learned verbs, Olguin and Tomasello (1993) have argued that babies' first action terms are learned without an understanding of the grammatical aspects of verbs. Before babies use syntactic frames in learning verbs, they may be able to use form-class cues to distinguish between nouns and other kinds of words. Waxman and Markow (1998) recently reported that 21-month-old infants use syntactic cues to distinguish adjectives from nouns. Given a novel adjective (e.g., "This is a citron one"), babies extended the new word to items that shared a salient property—color or texture. Given a novel noun (e.g., "This is a citron"), babies extended the word to members of a kind, even if they differed in color or texture. The lower limit for this ability is not yet known, though it seems to be absent in 12-month-olds (Waxman & Markow, 1995).

Conclusion

The evidence confirms that, as is the case for older word learners, toddlers draw on multiple sources of evidence in making sense of new words. By the time babies are 2 years old, they understand some aspects of intention, knowledge, and communication; they know about the conventional forms of names and how they vary; and they understand some aspects of syntax. Moreover, there is empirical confirmation that 2-year-olds use each of these kinds of knowledge in word learning. We know less about this type of knowledge in babies before this age. There is preliminary evidence that, by 12–13 months of age, babies understand words as being about their referents: Babies at this age attend to behaviors such as looking and pointing when interpreting new words. Other aspects of understanding reference—for example, knowing that words communicate ideas or information (mental entities)—may not emerge until 2 years of age or later. Moreover, although younger 1-year-olds understand something about the functions of names, the evidence suggests that they have strongly delimited neither the class of forms that serve this function nor the level of perceptual detail that signals a difference in meaning.

Because what babies know about acts of communication and language figures intimately into the process of word learning, this portion of the chapter has focused on that knowledge. In fact, understanding the referential, conventional, and syntactic nature of words is what makes a word/object mapping an act of word learning. Consideration of the development of these systems of knowledge provides a new look at a very old question. There has long been debate about whether the words learned by young 1-year-olds are "true" words or are, instead, learned without an understanding of their status as linguistic symbols (for various points of view on this question, see Huttenlocher & Smiley, 1987; Lock, 1980; McShane, 1979; Oviatt, 1980; Piaget, 1962; Vygotsky, 1962; Werker, Cohen, Lloyd, Casasolo, & Stager, 1998). Early theorists proposed that the transition from "proto" to "true" words occurred via a sudden insight or via radical qualitative changes in conceptual structure argued to occur at the time of the productive vocabulary spurt. However, based on the work just reviewed, my argument is, instead, that the difference between early and later word learning can be described in more quantitative terms: How much and what kind of knowledge does the baby bring to bear in word learning?

The findings reviewed in this section raise the question of how knowledge about language and communication interacts with default assumptions. On one hand, knowledge about the communicative nature of words seems to be a prerequisite for default assumptions about word meanings. In order for assumptions about the scope and extension of new words to make sense, babies must understand, in at least some limited way, that words are about objects and events (see Golinkoff, Mervis, & Hirsh-Pasek, 1994). On the other hand, when babies first start learning words, they seem to lack an understanding of some critical features of linguistic symbols, and the roots of default assumptions are evident at this early point in development. So, 12- to 18-month-olds have the whole-object and taxonomic assumptions, yet babies at this age do not have strong expectations about the forms of names. They are likely to accept other kinds of signals that are given in labeling contexts with behavioral cues to referential intent. Therefore, for younger 1-year-olds, gestural labels or other signals might elicit the same kinds of shifts in focus (to objects or to taxonomic relationships) as do words. There is preliminary evidence for this: Both Namy and Waxman (1998) and Hoyne and I (Woodward & Hoyne, 1999) found that younger 1-year-olds readily extend gesture or sound labels, like words, to members of like kind.

Changing knowledge about word forms would have a profound effect on mutual exclusivity. For one, to the extent that 1-year-olds have not delimited spoken words as a special class, gestural forms might interfere with word forms. Acredolo and Goodwyn's (1988) work on early gestural labels provides preliminary evidence on this question. They documented that 1-year-olds can learn a range of novel gestural labels. In this study, when babies acquired the words for these items, they stopped using the gestures. This is reminiscent of babies' correction or restriction of a known label in response to their learning a new word.

In addition, the level or detail of babies' representations of word forms imposes a limit on mutual exclusivity. If babies cannot determine that two word forms differ, they cannot use the difference in form to make inferences about meaning. The evidence for mutual exclusivity in 16-month-olds involves words that differ globally in form (e.g., "horse" and "mido"); thus, it is compatible with Stager and Werker's (1997) findings concerning the level of perceptual detail to which infants are sensitive in word-learning tasks. The prediction that mutual-exclusivity effects will vary as a function of increasing sensitivity to differences in form is yet to be tested. Keeping track of differences in form may continue to challenge older babies: Merriman and Marazita (1995) reported that manipulations that boost phonemic processing in 2-year-olds enhance the disambiguation effect. It is possible that vocabulary growth contributes to babies' increasing precision in distinguishing between word forms. Mervis and Bertrand (1994) reported that in a sample of 16- to 20-month-olds, the disambiguation effect varied as a function of productive vocabulary size. Babies with more words in production showed the disambiguation effect, whereas those with smaller vocabularies did not.

SUMMING UP

My goal in this chapter was to survey the word-learning landscape for 1- to 2-year-olds. When a very young learner hears a new word, how does he or she make sense of it? The first conclusion that emerges is that, even for young 1-year-olds, there are important features of the landscape. Twelve- to 18-month-old babies use aspects of a speaker's behavior to interpret new words. They seem to understand words not as undifferentiated associates of items in the world but as actions that are directed at or "about" objects. Moreover, young 1-year-olds show evidence of the whole-object, taxonomic, and mutual-exclusivity assumptions. They favor object-label interpretations, extend new words readily to members of like kind but not to thematic associates, and avoid having two labels for the same object. This is a powerful set of tools to get language learning off the ground, and it helps to explain how 12- to 14-month-old infants readily learn words in brief laboratory sessions.

The second conclusion is that, as a result of (in large part) rapidly developing knowledge about language and communication, the landscape changes considerably by the time babies are 2 years old. By 2 to 2½ years of age, babies understand acts of communication as involving the transmission of information. They can make subtle inferences about shared experiences and shared information. These abilities provide the means for making inferences about new terms across a range of situations. By age 2, babies have honed their expectations about the forms of words and have an understanding of the combinatorial system that gives rise to different words. This knowledge adds power to the ability to use the form of a new word to make inferences about its meaning. Finally, by age 2 or just before, babies have begun to understand words as syntactic units and to use this information in interpreting new words.

From the beginning, then, word learning is multiply constrained. Even young 1-year-olds draw on both default assumptions and behavioral cues in word learning. The developing ability of babies to make sense of behaviors such as looking, pointing, and speaking plays a central role in their interpretations of new words, just as does their predisposition to interpret words as naming object-sized units and extending to members of a kind. Any account proposing that a single factor is responsible for early word learning will be lopsided at best. Because word learning in the wild most likely involves multiple constraints, it may not be a clear reflection of any one of them. Experiments are useful for clarifying the role of individual constraints on word learning, but they do not always shed light on the ways in which multiple constraints converge in natural contexts.

In this chapter I have distinguished between default assumptions, which are hypothesized to be based in aspects of the baby as learner and perceiver, and knowledge-based constraints, which are the product of learning in a particular domain. How well this distinction can be maintained is yet to be seen. Several proposals about default assumptions characterize them as knowledge based, deriving solely from knowledge about regularities in parental word use or about the pragmatics of communication. Although these accounts seem inaccurate in their strongest forms, Imai and Gentner's (1997) findings suggest that regularities in input can modulate cognitively based word-learning biases. Moreover, domain-specific knowledge contributes importantly to the deployment of word-learning constraints—for example, in informing understanding of taxonomic categories or providing a basis for distinguishing between different word forms.

As I hope this chapter illustrates, understanding the development of word learning requires tracking several distinct streams that ultimately converge on the problem. Knowledge about human action, communication, and language are part of the story. Each of these systems of knowledge, though related, has its own developmental history. In addition, predispositions to see objects as salient units, to organize important information in terms of taxonomic categories, and to simplify complex learning problems contribute to the development of default assumptions. Accounts of how each of these sources of constraint develops and is recruited in word learning will, by necessity be different. All of these disparate factors come together in the minds of word-learning children and babies.

All of these sources of constraint in 1- and 2-year-olds may seem implausible. After all, babies know little and are limited in their cognitive abilities. Word learning must be quite special to recruit so many resources so early in life. But consider that 2-year-olds and younger babies are making progress at other kinds of complex cognitive tasks as well—for example, determining the bases for category membership (Gelman & Coley, 1991; Mandler & McDonough, 1993, 1996), solving increasingly complex means-ends problems (Diamond, 1991; Frye, 1991), and understanding the causes of events (Oakes & Cohen, 1990; Shultz, 1982). Like adults, 1- and 2-year-olds succeed at limiting the problem space across many contexts. In this respect, early word learning is not unique, but neither is it any less impressive.

ACKNOWLEDGMENTS

Preparation of this chapter was supported in part by a grant from the Robert R. McCormick Tribune Foundation.

REFERENCES

Acredolo, L., & Goodwyn, S. (1988). Symbolic gestures in normal infants. *Child Development, 59,* 450–466.

Ahn, W., Kalish, C. W., Medin, D. L., & Gelman, S. A. (1995). The role of covariation versus mechanism information in causal attribution. *Cognition, 54,* 299–352.

Akhtar, N., Carpenter, M., & Tomasello, M. (1996). The role of discourse novelty in early word learning. *Child Development, 67,* 635–645.

Akhtar, N., & Tomasello, M. (1996). Twenty-four-month-old children learn words for absent objects and actions. *British Journal of Developmental Psychology, 14,* 79–93.

Anglin, J. M. (1993). Vocabulary development: A morphological analysis. *Monographs of the Society for Research in Child Development, 58* (10, Serial No. 238).

Astington, J. W., Harris, P. L., & Olson, D. R. (Eds.). (1988). *Developing theories of mind.* Cambridge, England: Cambridge University Press.

Au, T. K., Dapretto, M., & Song, Y. (1994). Input versus constraints: Early word acquisition in Korean and English. *Journal of Memory and Language, 3,* 567–582.

Balaban, M. T., & Waxman, S. R. (1997). Do words facilitate object categorization in 9-month-old infants? *Journal of Experimental Child Psychology, 64,* 3–26.

Baldwin, D. A. (1991). Infants' contribution to the achievement of joint reference. *Child Development, 62,* 875–890.

Baldwin, D. A. (1995). Understanding the link between joint attention and language. In C. Moore & P. J. Dunham (Eds.), *Joint attention: Its origins and role in development* (pp. 131–158). Hillsdale, NJ: Erlbaum.

Baldwin, D. A., & Markman, E. M. (1989). Establishing word-object relations: A first step. *Child Development, 60,* 381–398.

Baldwin, D. A., Markman, E. M., Bill, B., Desjardins, R. N., Irwin, J. M., & Tidball, G. (1996). Infants' reliance on a social criterion for establishing word-object relations. *Child Development, 67,* 3135–3153.

Baldwin, D. A., Markman, E. M., & Melartin, R. L. (1993). Infants' ability to draw inferences about nonobvious object properties: Evidence from exploratory play. *Child Development, 64,* 711–728.

Baldwin, D. A., & Moses, L. M. (1996). The ontogeny of social information gathering. *Child Development, 67,* 1915–1939.

Baldwin, D. A., & Tomasello, M. (1998). Word learning: A window on early pragmatic understanding. In E. V. Clark (Ed.), *Proceedings of the 29th Annual Child Language Research Forum* (pp. 3–23). Stanford, CA: Center for the Study of Language and Information.

Banigan, R. L., & Mervis, C. B. (1988). Role of adult input in young children's category evolution: II. An experimental study. *Journal of Child Language, 15,* 493–504.

Benedict, H. (1979). Early lexical development: Comprehension and production. *Journal of Child Language, 6,* 183–200.

Bird, E. K., & Chapman, R. S. (1998). Partial representations and phonological selectivity in the comprehension of 13- to 16-month-olds. *First Language, 18,* 105–127.

Bloom, L., Tinker, E., & Margulis, C. (1993). The words children learn: Evidence against a noun bias in early vocabularies. *Cognitive Development, 8,* 431–450.

Butterworth, G., & Grover, L. (1988). The origins of referential communication in human infancy. In L. Weiskrantz (Ed.), *Thought without Language* (pp. 5–24). Oxford, England: Clarendon Press.

Carpenter, M., Akhtar, N., & Tomasello, M. (1998). Fourteen- through eighteen month old infants differentially imitate intentional and accidental actions. *Infant Behavior and Development, 21,* 315–330.

Caselli, M. C., Bates, E., Casadio, P., Fenson, J., Fenson, L., Sanderl, S., & Weir, J. (1995). A cross-linguistic study of early lexical development. *Cognitive Development, 10,* 159–199.

Clark, E. V. (1987). The principle of contrast: A constraint on acquisition. In B.

MacWhinney (Ed.), *Mechanisms of language acquisition: The 20th Annual Carnegie Symposium on Cognition* (pp. 1–34). Hillsdale, NJ: Erlbaum.

Clark, E. V. (1993). *The lexicon in acquisition.* Cambridge, England: Cambridge University Press.

Clark, E. V. (1997). Conceptual perspective and lexical choice in acquisition. *Cognition, 64,* 1–37.

Clark, H. (1992). *Arenas of language use.* Chicago: University of Chicago Press.

Diamond, A. (1991). Neuropsychological insights into the meaning of object concept development. In S. Carey & R. Gelman (Eds.), *The epigenesis of mind* (pp. 67 110). Hillsdale, NJ: Erlbaum.

Echols, C. (1991). *Infants' attention to objects and consistency in linguistic and non-linguistic contexts.* Paper presented at the Biennial Meetings of the Society for Research in Child Development, Seattle, WA.

Fenson, L., Dale, P. S., Reznick, J. S., Bates, E., Thal, D. J., & Pethick, S. J. (1994). Variability in early communicative development. *Monographs of the Society for Research in Child Development, 59* (5, Serial No. 242).

Fernald, A. (1992). Human maternal vocalizations to infants as biologically relevant signals: An evolutionary perspective. In J. H. Barkow, L. Cosmides, & J. Tooby (Eds.), *The adapted mind: Evolutionary psychology and the generation of culture* (pp. 391–428). Oxford, England: Oxford University Press.

Fernald, A., & Morikawa, H. (1993). Common themes and cultural variation in Japanese and American mothers' speech to infants. *Child Development, 64,* 637–656.

Fisher, C., Hall, D. G., Rakowitz, S., & Gleitman, L. (1994). When it is better to receive than to give: Syntactic and conceptual constraints on vocabulary growth. *Lingua, 92,* 333–375.

Frye, D. (1991). The origins of intention in infancy. In D. Frye & C. Moore (Ed.), *Children's theories of mind: Mental states and social understanding.* Hillsdale, NJ: Erlbaum.

Gathercole, V. C. M., & Min, H. (1997). Word meaning biases or language-specific effects? Evidence from English, Spanish and Korean. *First Language, 17,* 31–56.

Gelman, S. A., & Coley, J. D. (1991). The importance of knowing a dodo is a bird: Categories and inferences in 2-year-old children. *Developmental Psychology, 26,* 796–804.

Gelman, S., & Taylor, M. (1984). How two-year-old children interpret proper and common names for unfamiliar objects. *Child Development, 55,* 1535–1540.

Gentner, D. (1982). Why nouns are learned before verbs: Linguistic relativity versus natural partitioning. In S. Kuczaj (Ed.), *Language development: Vol. 2. Language, thought, and culture* (pp. 301–333). Hillsdale, NJ: Erlbaum.

Gentner, D., & Boroditsky, L. (in press). Individuation, relativity, and early word learning. In M. Bowerman & S. Levinson (Eds.), *Language acquisition and conceptual development.* Cambridge, England: Cambridge University Press.

Gleitman, L. R. (1990). The structural sources of verb meanings. *Language Acquisition, 1,* 3–55.

Golinkoff, R. M., Hirsh-Pasek, K., Bailey, L. M., & Wenger, N. R. (1992). Young children and adults use lexical principles to learn new nouns. *Developmental Psychology, 28,* 99–108.

Golinkoff, R. M., Hirsh-Pasek, K., Mervis, C. B., Frawley, W. B., & Parillo, M. (1995). Lexical principles can be extended to the acquisition of verbs. In M. Tomasello & W. E. Merriman (Eds.), *Beyond names for things: Young children's acquisition of verbs* (pp. 185–222). Hillsdale, NJ: Erlbaum.

Golinkoff, R. M., Mervis, C. B., & Hirsh-Pasek, K. (1994). Early object labels: The case for a developmental lexical principles framework. *Journal of Child Language, 21,* 125–155.

Goodman, J. C., & Nusbaum, H. C. (Eds.). (1994). *The development of speech perception.* Cambridge, MA: MIT Press.

Gopnik, A., & Choi, S. (1995). Names, relational words, and cognitive development in English and Korean speakers: Nouns are not always learned before verbs. In M. Tomasello & W. E. Merriman (Eds.), *Beyond names for things: Young children's acquisition of verbs* (pp. 63–80). Hillsdale, NJ: Erlbaum.

Hall, D. G. (1991). Acquiring proper names for familiar and unfamiliar objects: Two-year-olds' word learning biases. *Child Development, 62,* 1142–1154.

Hall, D. G., Waxman, S. R., & Hurwitz, W. M. (1993). How two- and four-year-old children interpret adjectives and count nouns. *Child Development, 64,* 1651–1664.

Hirsh-Pasek, K., & Golinkoff, R. M. (1996). *The origins of grammar: Evidence from early language comprehension.* Cambridge, MA: MIT Press.

Holyoak, K. J. (1995). Problem solving. In E. E. Smith & D. N. Osherson (Eds.), *An invitation to cognitive science: Thinking* (pp. 267–296). Cambridge, MA: MIT Press.

Huttenlocher, J. (1974). The origins of language comprehension. In R. Solso (Ed.), *Theories in cognitive psychology* (pp. 331–368). Hillsdale, NJ: Erlbaum.

Huttenlocher, J., & Smiley, P. (1987). Early word meanings: The case of object names. *Cognitive Psychology, 19,* 63–89.

Imai, M., & Gentner, D. (1997). A crosslinguistic study of early word meaning: Universal ontology and linguistic influence. *Cognition, 62,* 169–200.

Keysar, B., Barr, D. J., & Horton, W. S. (1998). The egocentric basis of language use: Insights from a processing approach. *Current Directions in Psychological Science, 7,* 46–50.

Kobayashi, H. (1998). How 2-year-olds learn novel part names of unfamiliar objects. *Cognition, 68,* B41–B51.

Landau, B., Smith, L. B., & Jones, S. S. (1988). The importance of shape in early lexical learning. *Cognitive Development, 3,* 299–321.

Lempers, J. D., Flavell, E. R., & Flavell, J. H. (1977). The development in very young children of tacit knowledge concerning visual perception. *Genetic Psychology Monographs, 95,* 3–53.

Liittschwager, J. C., & Markman, E. M. (1994). Sixteen- and 24-month-olds' use of mutual exclusivity as a default assumption in second label learning. *Developmental Psychology, 30,* 955–968.

Lock, A. (1980). *The guided reinvention of language.* London: Academic Press.

Macnamara, J. (1982). *Names for things: A study of human learning.* Cambridge, MA: MIT Press.

Mandler, J. M., & McDonough, L. (1993). Concept formation in infancy. *Cognitive Development, 8,* 291–318.

Mandler, J. M., & McDonough, L. (1996). Drinking and driving don't mix: Inductive generalization in infancy. *Cognition, 59,* 307–335.

Markman, E. M. (1989). *Categorization and naming in children: Problems of induction.* Cambridge, MA: MIT Press.

Markman, E. M. (1992). Constraints on word learning: Speculations about their nature, origins, and domain specificity. In M. R. Gunnar & M. P. Maratsos (Eds.), *Modularity and constraints in language and cognition: The Minnesota Symposia on Child Psychology* (Vol. 25, pp. 59–101). Hillsdale, NJ: Erlbaum.

Markman, E. M. (1994). Constraints on word meaning in early language acquisition. *Lingua, 92,* 199–227.

Markman, E. M., & Hutchinson, J. E. (1984). Children's sensitivity to constraints on word meaning: Taxonomic versus thematic relations. *Cognitive Psychology, 16,* 1–27.

Markman, E. M., & Wachtel, G. F. (1988). Children's use of mutual exclusivity to constrain the meaning of words. *Cognitive Psychology, 20,* 121–157.

McShane, J. (1979). The development of naming. *Linguistics, 17,* 79–905.

Medin, D. L., & Wattenmaker, W. D. (1987). Category cohesiveness, theories, and cognitive archeology. In U. Neisser (Ed.), *Concepts and conceptual development: Ecological and intellectual factors in categorization* (pp. 25–62). Cambridge, England: Cambridge University Press.

Meltzoff, A. M. (1995). Understanding the intentions of others: Re-enactment of intended acts by 18-month-old children. *Developmental Psychology, 31,* 838–850.

Merriman, W. E., & Bowman, L. L. (1989). The mutual exclusivity bias in children's word learning. *Monographs of the Society for Research in Child Development, 54*(3–4) (Serial No. 220).

Merriman, W. E., Evey-Burkey, J. A., Marazita, J. M., & Jarvis, L. H. (1996). Young two-year-olds' tendency to map novel verbs onto novel actions. *Journal of Experimental Child Psychology, 63,* 466–498.

Merriman, W. E., & Marazita, J. M. (1995). The effect of hearing similar-sounding novel words on young 2-year-olds' disambiguation of novel noun reference. *Developmental Psychology, 31,* 973–984.

Merriman, W. E., & Stevenson, C. M. (1997). Restricting a familiar name in response to learning a new one: Evidence for the mutual exclusivity bias in young two-year-olds. *Child Development, 68,* 211–228.

Mervis, C. B., & Bertrand, J. (1994). Acquisition of the novel name-nameless category (N3C) principle. *Child Development, 65,* 1646–1663.

Mervis, C. B., Golinkoff, R. M., & Bertrand, J. (1994). Two-year-olds readily learn multiple labels for the same basic-level category. *Child Development, 65,* 1163–1177.

Moore, C., Angelopoulos, M., & Bennett, P. (1999). Word learning in the context of referential and salience cues. *Developmental Psychology, 35,* 60–68.

Naigles, L. (1990). Children use syntax to learn verb meanings. *Journal of Child Language, 17,* 357–374.

Naigles, L. R. (1996). The use of multiple frames in verb learning via syntactic bootstrapping. *Cognition, 58,* 221–251.

Namy, L. (1998). *What's in a name when it isn't a word?* Unpublished manuscript.

Namy, L. L., & Waxman, S. R. (1998). Words and gestures: Infants' interpretations of different forms of symbolic reference. *Child Development, 69,* 295–308.

Nelson, K. (1988). Constraints on word learning? *Cognitive Development, 3,* 221–246.

Nelson, K., Hampson, J., & Shaw, L. K. (1993). Nouns in early lexicons: Evidence, explanations and implications. *Journal of Child Language, 20,* 61–84.

Oakes, L. M., & Cohen, L. B. (1990). Infant perception of a causal event. *Cognitive Development, 5,* 193–207.

Oakes, L. M., Madole, K. L., & Cohen, L. B. (1991). Infants' object examining: Habituation and categorization. *Cognitive Development, 6,* 377–392.

Olguin, R., & Tomasello, M. (1993). Twenty-five-month-old children do not have a grammatical category of verb. *Cognitive Development, 8,* 245–272.

O'Neill, D. K. (1996). Two-year-old children's sensitivity to a parent's knowledge state when making requests. *Child Development, 67,* 659–677.

Oviatt, S. L. (1980). The emerging ability to comprehend language: An experimental approach. *Child Development, 51,* 97–106.

Petitto, L. A. (1988). "Language" in the prelinguistic child. In F. S. Kessel (Ed.), *The development of language and language researchers* (pp. 187–221). Hillsdale, NJ: Erlbaum.

Piaget, J. (1962). *Play, dreams and imitation in childhood* (C. Gattegno & F. M. Hodgson, Trans.). New York: W. W. Norton.

Quine, W. V. O. (1960). *Word and object.* Cambridge, MA: MIT Press.

Quinn, P. (1987). The categorical representation of visual pattern information by young infants. *Cognition, 27,* 145–179.

Quinn, P. C., Eimas, P. D., & Rosenkrantz, S. L. (1993). Evidence for representations of perceptually similar natural categories by 3-month-old and 4-month-old infants. *Perception, 22,* 463–475.

Regier, T. (1997). Constraints on the learning of spatial terms: A computational investigation. *Psychology of Learning and Motivation, 36,* 171–217.

Roberts, K., & Jacob, M. (1991). Linguistic versus attentional influences on nonlinguistic categorization in 15-month-old infants. *Cognitive Development, 6,* 355–375.

Samuelson, L. R., & Smith, L. B. (1998). Memory and attention make smart word learning: An alternative account of Akhtar, Carpenter and Tomasello. *Child Development, 69,* 94–104.

Scaife, M., & Bruner, J. S. (1975). The capacity for joint visual attention in the infant. *Nature, 253,* 265–266.

Schafer, G., & Plunkett, K. (1998). Rapid word learning by 15-month-olds under tightly controlled conditions. *Child Development, 69,* 309–320.

Schwartz, R. B., & Leonard, L. B. (1984). Words, objects, and actions in early lexical acquisition. *Journal of Speech and Hearing Research, 27,* 117–127.

Schwarz, N. (1995). Social cognition: Information accessibility and use in social judgment. In E. E. Smith & D. N. Osherson (Eds.), *An invitation to cognitive science: Thinking* (pp. 345–376). Cambridge, MA: MIT Press.

Shatz, M. (1983). Communication. In J. H. Flavell & E. M. Markman (Eds.), *Handbook of child psychology: Vol. 3. Cognitive development* (pp. 841–889). New York: John Wiley & Sons.

Shultz, T. R. (1982). Rules of causal attribution. *Monographs of the Society for Research in Child Development, 47* (1) (Serial No. 194).

Soja, N. N. (1992). Inferences about the meanings of nouns: The relationship between perception and syntax. *Cognitive Development, 7,* 29–45.

Soja, N. N., Carey, S., & Spelke, E. S. (1991). Ontological categories guide young children's inductions of word meaning: Object terms and substance terms. *Cognition, 38,* 179–211.

Stager, C. L., & Werker, J. F. (1997). Infants listen for more phonetic detail in speech perception than in word-learning tasks. *Nature, 388* (24), 381–382.

Tardif, T. (1996). Nouns are not always learned before verbs: Evidence from Mandarin speakers' early vocabularies. *Developmental Psychology, 32,* 492–504.

Tomasello, M. (1995). Pragmatic contexts for early verb learning. In M. Tomasello & W. E. Merriman (Eds.), *Beyond names for things: Young children's acquisition of verbs* (pp. 115–146). Hillsdale, NJ: Erlbaum.

Tomasello, M., & Barton, M. (1994). Learning words in non-ostensive contexts. *Developmental Psychology, 30,* 639–650.

Vygotsky, L. S. (1962). *Thought and language.* Cambridge, MA: MIT Press.

Waxman, S. R. (1991). Convergences between semantic and conceptual organization in the preschool years. In J. P. Byrnes & S. A. Gelman (Eds.), *Perspectives on language and cognition: Interrelations in development* (pp. 107–145). Cambridge, England: Cambridge University Press.

Waxman, S. R. (1994). The development of an appreciation of specific linkages between linguistic and conceptual organization. *Lingua, 92,* 229–257.

Waxman, S. R., & Hall, D. G. (1993). The development of a linkage between count nouns and object categories: Evidence from fifteen- to twenty-one-month-old infants. *Child Development, 64,* 1224–1241.

Waxman, S. R., & Kosowski, T. D. (1990). Nouns mark category relations: Toddlers' and preschoolers' word-learning biases. *Child Development, 61,* 1461–1473.

Waxman, S. R., & Markow, D. B. (1995). Words as invitations to form categories: Evidence from 12- to 13-month-old infants. *Cognitive Psychology, 29,* 257–302.

Waxman, S. R., & Markow, D. B. (1998). Object properties and object kind: Twenty-one-month-old infants' extension of novel adjectives. *Child Development, 69,* 1313–1329.

Waxman, S. R., & Senghas, A. (1992). Relations among word meanings in early lexical development. *Developmental Psychology, 28,* 862–873.

Werker, J., Cohen, L. B., Lloyd, V. L., Casasola, M., & Stager, C. L. (1998). Acquisition of word-object associations by 14-month-olds. *Developmental Psychology, 34,* 1289–1309.

Werker, J. F. (1994). Cross-language speech perception: Developmental change does not involve loss. In J. C. Goodman & H. C. Nusbaum (Eds.), *The development of speech perception: The transition from sounds to spoken words* (pp. 93–120). Cambridge, MA: MIT Press.

Woodward, A. L. (1993). The effect of labeling on children's attention to objects. In E. V. Clark (Ed.), *Proceedings of the 24th Annual Child Language Research Forum* (pp. 35–47). Stanford, CA: Center for the Study of Language and Information.

Woodward, A. L. (1998). Infant selectivity encode the goal object of an actor's reach. *Cognition, 69,* 1–34.

Woodward, A. L., & Hoyne, K. L. (1999). Infants' learning about words and sounds in relation to objects. *Child Development, 70,* 65–72.

Woodward, A. L., & Markman, E. M. (1991). Constraints on learning as default assumptions: Comments on Merriman and Bowman's "The mutual exclusivity bias in children's word learning." *Developmental Review, 11,* 137–163.

Woodward, A. L., & Markman, E. M. (1998). Early word learning. In D. Kuhn & R. S. Siegler (Eds.), *Handbook of child psychology: Vol. 2. Cognition, perception, and language* (pp. 371–420). New York: John Wiley & Sons.

Woodward, A. L., Markman, E. M., & Fitzsimmons, C. M. (1994). Rapid word learning in 13- and 18-month-olds. *Developmental Psychology, 30,* 553–566.

CHAPTER 5

The Social Nature of Words and Word Learning

Nameera Akhtar
Michael Tomasello

Language is a social art. In acquiring it we have to depend entirely on intersubjectively available cues as to what to say and when. (Preface to W. V. O. Quine, *Word and Object*, p. ix)

Word learning has often been portrayed as a classic example of an induction problem: When faced with a novel word, how does a child (or an adult, for that matter) determine the meaning or referent of that word? Logically, there seem to be innumerable possibilities, even in the relatively straightforward case of ostension—the situation in which a speaker points to an object and utters a single word. Is the speaker labeling the entire object, commenting on one of its properties, or labeling the action that the object is engaged in? How does the listener decide? The scenario becomes even more complicated when we consider the fact that young children in the beginning stages of language acquisition are often faced with situations that involve *multiple* objects and actions for which they do not yet have names. How do they decide which of several possible referents the speaker intends to label with a new word that is used in the presence of several nameless objects, actions, and attributes?

There are currently three major approaches to these central questions in research on early word learning. One approach emphasizes the logical problem of referential indeterminacy and posits the existence of word-learning constraints or principles as a solution to the problem (Golinkoff, Mervis, & Hirsh-Pasek, 1994; Markman, 1992; Woodward & Markman, 1998; chapters 4 and 6 in this volume). Another approach asserts that general processes of association and learning are sufficient to account for early lexical acquisition (Smith, Jones, & Landau, 1996; chapter 3 in this volume). What is common to these two approaches, however, is a relative neglect of the social dimensions of word learning.

In contrast, our approach—known as the social-pragmatic approach (Akhtar & Tomasello, 1998; Bruner, 1983; Nelson, 1985; Tomasello, 1992b; 1995)—

emphasizes the social-communicative dimension of language learning as primary. This theoretical approach involves a somewhat different way of conceptualizing the nature of word learning: In brief, our view is that when a child hears a speaker use an unfamiliar term, the child must use his or her understanding of the communicative situation to focus his or her attention on the same entity (object, attribute, action) on which the speaker is focused. That is, in order to understand what an adult is referring to with a novel term, the child must enter into a state of joint focus with the adult. According to this account, when children learn new words, their objective is not to establish the abstract "meanings" of the words themselves but, in a more general sense, the goal is to understand what their social partner wants to call their attention to.

While we believe that social-pragmatic processes constitute the foundation of word learning, we recognize that other processes play important roles as well. For example, infants and children also (1) segment the speech stream to extract individual words (Jusczyk, 1997); (2) retain in memory the sequences of phonemes that occur together most frequently (Jusczyk & Hohne, 1997; Saffran, Aslin, & Newport, 1996); (3) employ general skills of attention and memory to engage in cross-situational learning, enabling them to use multiple models of the same word to make inferences about word meanings over time (Akhtar & Montague, 1999); (4) use known words to "contrast" with new words to help "constrain" their referential extensions (Clark, 1990); (5) use the surrounding syntactic context to help infer word meanings (Gleitman, 1990); and (6) induce other principles of word learning via generalizations about individual word-learning instances (Golinkoff, Mervis, & Hirsh-Pasek, 1994). These skills—though all are important (and some are undoubtedly essential)—are, in our view, ancillary to the fundamental social-communicative process.

We begin our presentation of the social-pragmatic approach to early word learning with a theoretical analysis of the essentially intersubjective nature of communicative symbols. We contrast our view with the positions of the lexical principles and associative theorists, and then we explore the implications of our analysis for the processes that are involved in learning words. Finally, we provide a brief review of recent studies conducted within the social-pragmatic framework. Because the vast majority of research has examined children's acquisition of object labels and verbs, both our theoretical analysis and our review of studies that highlight children's use of social-pragmatic skills in word learning concentrate on these word types.

THE INTERSUBJECTIVE NATURE OF WORDS

The social-pragmatic approach emphasizes the inherently social nature of language and language learning (see Akhtar & Tomasello, 1998; Tomasello, in press). Lois Bloom captures the essence of this approach most succinctly in her statement that children learn language "*in* and *for* conversations" (1997, p. 348, italics added); that is, language learning is intrinsically social in that it is acquired (1) in interactions with others and (2) for the purpose of communicating with others. These two incontrovertible facts have led us to emphasize the child's developing social-cognitive abilities and the critical role these abilities play in the child's acquisition of language. This emphasis does not, however, involve discounting the significant roles played by the child's general cognitive and affective development or the influence of language that has already been learned on subsequent learning (see Bloom for a review). Our aim is simply to illuminate the social dimension of communicative symbols (i.e., words) and to highlight the social-cognitive processes involved in lexical acquisition.

Human language differs from other forms of communication in that it involves the use of symbols to represent different meanings or intents. One crucial difference between communicative *symbols* and other communicative *signals* is that symbols are *decontextualized* communicative acts that are used to stand for or represent a given communicative intention (Bates, 1979; Werner & Kaplan, 1963); that is, communicative symbols can be used to refer to something that is not currently present. Another significant and unique characteristic of communicative symbols is their *reciprocal* intersubjective nature (in Saussurean terminology, the bidirectionality of the sign); for example, someone who uses the word "dog" to refer to a furry, four-footed pet presumably would understand someone else's use of that same symbol. Indeed, the very definition of a *conventional* communicative act is that both the speaker and the listener simultaneously appreciate its communicative significance from each other's perspective; that is, in a sense, one who produces such an act comprehends it from the listener's perspective as he or she produces it (Mead, 1934; Savage-Rumbaugh, 1990). Words are therefore inherently intersubjective in that they serve as conventional and symbolic communicative acts that individuals both understand themselves and understand that others understand.

Not all early communicative behaviors are reciprocal in this way. Prelinguistic infants use a number of intentional gestures that are most likely ritualized from other behaviors; for example, the "hands-up" gesture as a request to be picked up may be a ritualization of the infant's trying to pull his or her way up to the parent's arms (Tomasello, 1996). Because there is no evidence that prelinguistic infants comprehend these early gestures when produced by another, they cannot be viewed as true communicative symbols. The same has been said of some of children's early attempts at language. It is possible that a proportion of children's early words may be learned through some form of conditioning; for example, the child mimics an adult sound (word), and the adult reliably responds in some interesting way, so the child continues to produce that sound in anticipation of the adult's response. These so-called context-bound words or presymbolic forms are often characterized as being devoid of communicative intent and as constituting merely associated parts of a given activity context rather than as true communicative symbols (Barrett, 1989; Bates, 1979).

Because many of our fellow contributors to this volume seem to endorse the view that early word learning involves the formation of pure associations between objects and labels (see chapters 1, 3, and 6), the relation of early words to context is worth exploring further. Many researchers in lexical acquisition either implicitly or explicitly accept the word-to-world mapping metaphor, which essentially depicts word learning as the formation of associations between the words children hear and the entities they perceive.[1] It is somewhat ironic that this metaphor is so widespread when it seems, in essence, to be a recapitulation of Skinner's (1957) long since discredited view that language can be reduced to correlations between speech and objective external stimulus conditions. We believe that this mechanistic view of word learning derives in part from a tendency to focus exclusively on the acquisition of object labels and in part from inattention to the socially constructed contexts of language learning and language use.

Because objects present enduring percepts to the language-learning child, and adults (at least middle-class Western ones) tend to label objects when children are attending to them (Tomasello & Farrar, 1986), the idea that children may readily form simple associations between their perceptions of objects and object labels seems reasonable.[2] Most actions, however, are transient, and the fact that children learn verbs for transitory actions may represent a problem for the associative perspective, especially since adults do not tend to label actions as they are occurring.[3] More often they use verbs to request and comment on actions before or after the referent actions have taken place (Tomasello & Kruger, 1992)—that is, when there is no relevant percept available to associate with the verb.

One might argue that verbs are acquired relatively late in development and that their acquisition may rely on special processes that are not operational until after many object labels have been acquired through purely associative processes. This is possible but is not consistent with the fact that children learning languages such as Korean (Choi & Gopnik, 1995; Gopnik & Choi, 1995) and Mandarin Chinese (Tardif, 1996) acquire verbs quite early in development. Furthermore, relational words such as "no" and "gone," which also are not associated with any stable percept, are found in the early vocabularies of English-learning toddlers, who appear to use them in appropriate, contextually flexible ways from the start (Gopnik, 1988). Our view is that children are not merely forming associations between words and referents; rather, whether they are learning verbs or object labels, they are engaged in an essentially social interaction with a speaker, and their goal is to determine what the speaker means to call their attention to. Thus, children generally hear their first verbs in contexts that are replete with information about the intentions of their social partners (Tomasello, 1992a). As a result, they can use their event knowledge (Akhtar & Tomasello, 1996; Nelson, 1986) and other social-pragmatic cues (Tomasello & Akhtar, 1995) to determine the referential intentions of others who use verbs in situations where no salient action is currently taking place. In general, evidence that very young children learn all kinds of words that are not labels for objects (Ninio, 1993b; Tomasello, 1992a; chapter 2 in this volume) makes it rather difficult to support the contention that early words are the result of simple paired associations between words and their referents.

To support their view, those who maintain that children's earliest words are simple paired associates of some situation or event generally cite one of the two following characteristics of children's early word production: (1) initially underextended use of object labels (Barrett, 1989) and (2) the "pure performative" (rather than referential) function of much of children's earliest word use (e.g., "Bye" and "Thank you" [Greenfield & Smith, 1976]). In both cases, the claim often made is that the child's early use of a word is, in a sense, elicited by selected features of the overt physical situation in which that word is initially encountered. Thus, according to the associative perspective, children initially neither use words to express their communicative intentions nor interpret the words used by others as intentional communicative acts. Rather, this perspective sees early word use as a form of conditioned response to certain stimulus conditions. Although not all authors of the associative perspective interpret underextensions and performatives in these precise terms, the view that early words are nothing more than paired associations between vocalizations and some context or set of stimulus conditions leads directly to this interpretation.

As Ninio (1993a) has persuasively argued, however, the fact that some of children's early words are used in somewhat restricted contexts does not lead to the inevitable conclusion that words are merely paired associates of those contexts. Consider, for example, a child who uses the word "nose" only when someone touches his or her nose and says, "What's that?" Certainly the child's use of the term differs from adult usage, but this does not mean that is without communicative intent. Perhaps the word is, from the child's perspective, simply what one says to take one's turn in a game of labeling various body parts; that is, the word may be viewed as a performative that means, in essence, "I am taking my turn." This interpretation regards the child's utterance as a meaningful social behavior that emerges from his or her desire to interact with and communicate with another person. In this respect, it is important to note that adults, too, use performative utterances in very specific situations, such as chess moves, conversation-opening greetings, and so forth. If we consider these to be legitimate communicative acts on the part of adults, we cannot apply a double standard and view them as something entirely different when used by young children. Of course, adults' use of performatives is interpreted in the context of their flexible use of other terms. In this regard, it is worth noting that naturalistic studies of very early word learning have shown that, although a substantial proportion of first words seem to be context-bound, many are classified as contextually flexible from the start (Harris, Barrett, Jones, & Brookes, 1988). At this point, then, there does not seem to be any data-based reason for favoring either the associative interpretation or the communicative interpretation of early speech. Indeed, it is quite possible that the use of some early words starts off as more purely associative in character, and some are used, from the beginning, with communicative intent. However, any assertion that language use begins as somewhat mindless conditioned responses and eventually turns into intentional communicative behavior has the burden of describing and explaining when, how, and why the transformation takes place.

At this point, it is important to clarify that we are certainly not claiming that associative processes play no role in word learning—indeed, we recognize that they must. Our contention is, however, that they *alone* cannot account for word learning. As Baldwin (1995, p. 140) has pointed out, words co-occur with more than just the specific entities that they are used to refer to; it is therefore unclear "how a pure covariation detector could ever sort out which co-occurrences are worth attending to, which carry meaning, and which do not" (see also Zukow-Goldring & Ferko, 1994). The fact that children rarely attach words to inappropriate referents that co-occur with the words suggests that mere proximity or temporal contiguity of word and referent is not what drives word learning. Rather, children learn novel words by attending to what is most *relevant* in the communicative context in which they hear a given word used (chapter 2 in this volume); that is, they attend to what the adult is most likely to be referring to, given the immediately preceding context.

Baldwin and her colleagues (1996) have shown that 18- to 20-month-old children learn a novel word only when there is some indication of referential intent on the part of the speaker. In two studies, children in one condition heard a new object label uttered by an adult who was looking at what the children were holding. Children in another condition heard the label uttered by a speaker who was out of view. The children learned the word only when the speaker displayed signs of attending to the toy that they were attending to; mere coupling of a word and object did not lead to word learning. This finding fits with several other studies that demonstrate that temporal contiguity (or simple covariation) between word and referent is not sufficient for word learning to take place (Akhtar & Tomasello, 1996; Baldwin, 1993a, 1993b; Tomasello & Barton, 1994).

In a recent study, however, Schafer and Plunkett (1998) claimed to have demonstrated that 15-month-old children can learn a word on the basis of a few pairings of an isolated auditory label and an image of a novel object. The experimenters showed infants images of two novel objects and paired each with the auditory presentation of a novel word. To assess comprehension of the new words, during a subsequent test phase, they examined the amount of time that children looked at each new image when three different isolated labels were presented. The auditory label sometimes matched one of the images and sometimes did not. The main comparison of interest was whether children would look longer at matching images. Schafer and Plunkett found a significant difference in the overall amount of time that children looked at matching versus nonmatching targets. However, more detailed analyses revealed that there were no significant differences in looking behavior when each test label was compared with the control label (the word that had not previously been paired with any image), which indicated that the infants did not really learn either of the two novel labels. Even if significant learning *had* been demonstrated, a clear conclusion could not be drawn that the infants had acquired "words" during this procedure. *Showing that infants are sensitive to covariation or correlation between two manipulated variables does not mean that they have learned a word.* Imagine for a moment that these researchers had paired different auditory tones (rather than new phoneme sequences) with the different images. Would demonstrating that these tones became associated with these images then lead to the conclusion that the tones functioned as "words"? Indeed, this very technique (pairing tones and images versus wordlike stimuli and images) has been used to study infants' categorization abilities (e.g., Roberts, 1995), with no assumption that the infants' ability to use the paired associates to form categories implies that they have learned "words" that "map onto" those categories.

Defining what counts as a "word" is a problem that has vexed philosophers for many years (Premack, 1990; Williams, 1994). Rather than attempt to solve it here, we point out simply that for different purposes different definitions will suffice; for example, for a computer programmer, a word is simply a sequence of letters with spaces on either side of it. Bloom (1998, p. 309) has convincingly argued that, to study language learning effectively, "we need to look at what language does and why children acquire language." In our view, what language does is provide a conventional and generative code for communicating with others, and this is why children acquire it: to express themselves and to understand others. Consequently, if our purpose is to try to explain how children come to use conventional symbols to communicate with others (this is, after all, what words do and why children acquire them), then a sound-referent pair that is neither used nor comprehended as a communicative symbol (i.e., in interactions with others) cannot be granted the status of a word. Of course, it remains to be seen whether a "word" learned in Schafer and Plunkett's (1998) procedure would be used or comprehended by 15-month-olds in subsequent communicative interactions with another human being.[4] Our prediction is that it would not.

SOCIAL PRAGMATICS AND THE PROBLEM
OF REFERENTIAL INDETERMINACY

In response to the general question "How do children decide what an adult is most likely labeling with a new word?" some theorists have proposed that children might approach the word-learning task with built-in *constraints* on the hypotheses they will entertain. Markman (1992), for example, described these constraints as default probabilistic assumptions about what a novel word is most likely to refer to. One example of such a constraint is the whole-object assumption, which states that young children who hear a new word will assume that the word refers to an object and not to an attribute or part of an object. One important point to note is that these assumptions have been clearly described as a priori constraints. They are intended to get word learning off the ground, so to speak, as this quote from Woodward and Markman (1998, p. 380) illustrates: "Constraints on word learning [are] . . . most useful to very young learners, who are in need of an entering wedge into vocabulary acquisition."

The lexical-principles approach described by Golinkoff, Mervis, & Hirsch-Pasek (1994) differs significantly from previous constraints approaches, because it views principles as the *products* of development. Lexical principles do not operate from the start; they are a posteriori heuristics or strategies that children use to narrow the possibilities in word-learning situations: "Principles are intelligent strategies that [restrict] the search space by heightening certain hypotheses over others. . . . The principles are themselves by-products of cognitive and linguistic development" (Golinkoff, Mervis, & Hirsh-Pasek, p. 128). Viewed this way—as *products* of language learning—lexical principles can be considered *generalizations* that young children form about how people tend to use language. We are in complete agreement with the proponents of lexical principles on this point—that in the process of language learning, children most likely form some generalizations about language use. However, there is an important difference between the lexical-principles and social-pragmatic approaches in how they deal with the problem of referential indeterminacy: How do children determine which aspect of a given situation is being referred to when they hear a new word?

In their attempt to combine the lexical-principles and social-pragmatic approaches, the authors of chapter 6 in this volume claim that a principle such as the principle of object scope may tell the child what ontological category (e.g., objects) is being labeled, but social cues such as gaze direction may provide the more specific information about which individual object within that category is being labeled. Our view differs somewhat from theirs in that we see the entire process of word learning as much more social than this account implies. Indeed, we contend that children can use social-pragmatic cues as well as their knowledge of routine events to determine to which ontological category a speaker is referring.

In one study (Tomasello & Akhtar, 1995, Study 1), we examined whether 2-year-olds' attention to novelty would help them determine to which ontological category a given word might belong. There were two experimental groups. In both groups, children heard a new word modeled as a one-word utterance ("Modi!") just as a nameless target object was performing a nameless target action. However, the speaker's behavior prior to the language model differed from one group to the other. In the new-action group, the speaker performed various familiar actions on the target object, making the nameless action the novel element in the discourse context when the language model was presented. In the new-object group, the speaker performed the target action on various familiar objects, making the target object the novel element in the discourse context when the language model was presented. Results showed that the children learned the word for whichever element was new to the discourse context at the time of the language model. That is, most children in the new-action condition interpreted "modi" as an action label, whereas most children in the new-object condition interpreted "modi" as an object label.

These findings suggest that instead of being biased to attend to objects when they hear novel words (as indicated by the whole-object assumption), young children attend to what is most relevant to a speaker's referential intentions. Because speakers tend to comment on novelty, it follows that children will attend to the newest element in the discourse context. Although it is possible that the children attended to the novel element simply because their attentional systems are attracted to novelty, the results of a second study (Tomasello & Akhtar, 1995, Study 2) suggest that 2-year-olds are indeed sensitive to adults' referential intentions. In this study, too, children heard a new word in the context of a nameless object and a nameless action. In each of two conditions, an adult requested that the child perform the nameless action with the nameless object. In this case, children had to determine, from the adult's nonverbal behaviors (gaze alternation between the action prop and the child versus gaze alternation between the object and the child) whether the single word the adult used was an object label or an imperative verb. Again, children were more likely to interpret the word as an object label in the object-focus condition and more likely to interpret it as a verb in the action-focus condition.

Both studies indicate that children are sensitive to the referential intentions of adults and suggest that referential indeterminacy may not be as intractable a problem for young children as some philosophers and psychologists contend. In this regard, it is important to note that much of children's early language tends to be learned in the context of routine (i.e., repetitive) social interactions (Bruner, 1983; Ninio & Bruner, 1978; Snow & Goldfield, 1983). Some of these routine situations are universal (e.g., nursing and feeding infants), whereas others may be culturally specific. Peters and Boggs (1986), who have analyzed adult-child routines from a variety of cultural groups, have found interesting parallels in the structures of some of these routines across cultures. Moreover, they speculate that the existence of some routines is inevitable in social groups and that the existence of cultural differences in the particulars does not preclude the existence of important universal characteristics.

The major implication for social-pragmatic theories of language acquisition is that routines provide a sort of scaffold for early word learning in that "they create, with no need of a conventional language whatsoever, a shared referential context within which the language of the adult makes sense to the prelinguistic child" (Tomasello, 1992b, p. 70). When children develop a nonlinguistic understanding of some of the situations they experience regularly, they are able to anticipate the subsequent steps within a given routine. And the ability to readily understand the situation and what will follow allows them to focus their attentional and cognitive resources on the language used by others within the routine (Akhtar & Tomasello, 1996; Nelson, 1986). Therefore, sharing an understanding with their social partners about the overall goal of the activity (e.g., diapering or feeding) may allow infants to comprehend some of the language used within the activity. Applying this logic to Quine's (1960) famous "gavagai!" example, if, before hearing the speaker say the word "gavagai" as the rabbit ran past, the linguist understood that he and his informant were going hunting for food, the linguist would be far less likely to interpret the word as a color term or as a name for a part of the rabbit than as a name for the rabbit itself or as some action relevant to hunting.

The upshot of all this is that the problem of referential indeterminacy simply may not apply to children's early language learning. It is important to note that Quine (1960) actually posed the problem as a philosophical question with respect to the indeterminacy of *radical* translation between languages. What he meant by "radical" was that the linguist knew nothing of the customs and habits of the people whose language he was trying to acquire; that is, there was no "shared culture" between them (p. 28). This is not the case with young children acquiring a first language. As the epigraph at the beginning of this chapter indicates, Quine was well aware of the intersubjective nature of language. And he made it clear that his problem of "radical translation" was meant to apply to a situation that was stripped of intersubjective cues to the informant's communicative intent. The main point is this: If children understand (nonlinguistically) something about the speaker's focus of attention, they do not need linguistic constraints or principles to comprehend a novel piece of language. Children can achieve this understanding in at least two ways: (1) by participating in routine structured interactions as previously described and (2) by actively discerning various cues to a speaker's attentional focus.

PROCESSES INVOLVED IN ACQUIRING RECIPROCAL COMMUNICATIVE SYMBOLS

Infants begin life as social creatures, but by the end of their 1st year, a significant change in the quality of their social interactions has occurred (Trevarthen & Hubley, 1978). In the 1st few months of life, infants engage in dyadic (often face-to-face) interactions with adults, but between 9 and 12 months of age babies become capable of triadic interactions: interactions with another person *about* some third entity (person, object, or event). Engaging in triadic interactions requires the ability to coordinate attention to the speaker as well as to a topic, and, as Tomasello (1992b, 1995) has argued, this ability plays a foundational role in infants' early word-learning attempts.[5]

The key social-cognitive ability that underlies triadic interactions (which include social referencing, gaze following, as well as word learning) is the capacity to view other humans as intentional agents with attentional states that can be manipulated and shared (Tomasello, Kruger, & Ratner, 1993). There is now considerable evidence that infants perceive the actions of others as goal directed (e.g., Gergely, Nadasdy, Csibra, & Biro, 1995; Meltzoff, 1995). Presumably, infants also perceive others' verbalizations (which are essentially vocal actions) as intentional. And in the same way that infants try to understand what adults intend to accomplish with their actions, infants try to figure out what adults intend (or what they are attending to) when they use novel words. In using a given word, a speaker means to call attention to some entity for which that word is a conventional symbol. Therefore, in order to understand a new word, the child must enter into a state of joint focus with the speaker (Akhtar & Tomasello, 1998). In some situations, an adult can aid the child by commenting on something that is already at the child's focus of attention (Dunham, Dunham, & Curwin, 1993; Tomasello & Farrar, 1986). However, children actively monitor the attentional states of their social partners (Baldwin & Tomasello, 1998) and do not err in situations in which they hear a novel word while their attention is on something different from what the speaker is labeling (Baldwin, 1991, 1993a, 1993b). Rather, they look up from what they are attending to and attempt to determine the focus of the adult's attention.

According to the social-pragmatic perspective, children learn to understand words by actively inferring a speaker's attentional focus (using a variety of social and contextual cues), and they learn to produce words by engaging in what Tomasello, Kruger, & Ratner (1993) call "imitative learning." Imitative learning broadly defined involves acquiring a novel behavior by replicating both the precise form and function of that behavior. It is obvious that in the case of word learning, the child must acquire the (conventional) form used by an adult speaker and, to use words appropriately, must understand something of how they function in communicative contexts. Thus, most words are, almost by definition, reciprocal communicative symbols from the start, because they are acquired by the child appreciating the communicative function of the word from both the speaker's and his or her own perspective.

It is possible, however, that children will use some words without initially understanding their communicative function; that is, they may simply mimic the sounds they have heard others produce. In our view, such productions would not be classified as "words," because they are not used communicatively. It is possible, however, for these uses to subsequently become true words; children may eventually note that others use this form intentionally to draw attention to a specific entity, and they may thereafter assume this usage themselves. That is, subsequent imitative learning can transform the mimicked sound to a reciprocal communicative symbol.

Imitative learning therefore requires not only that the child understand the adult's communicative intention in using a new piece of language but also that the child use this same piece of language when he or she has the same communicative intention. In other words, in comprehending a new word the child comes to understand that the adult is using the word to encourage him or her to focus attention on one specific aspect of the current communicative context. To learn to produce the word him- or herself (in appropriate communicative situations), the child must in some sense identify with the adult's intention in order to make the transition to cases in which the child has the same communicative intention—that is, the intention to encourage another person to focus on the same referent. The early linguistic symbols that children learn via this process of imitative learning are thus reciprocal and intersubjective by their very nature. Learning to use conventional symbols in the way that others use them relies on both children's ability to perceive and understand the behavior of others intentionally and the tendency of children to identify with others (Meltzoff & Gopnik, 1993) so that they can express similar intentions in similar circumstances in the future. Understanding other individuals as intentional agents, and the intersubjectivity that this presupposes, is thus the key social-cognitive skill necessary for children's early ability to acquire conventional words in the service of communication.

It is important to clarify that we do not claim that young children never make errors in learning words. We claim, instead, that they understand the fact that adults *have* intentions (or goal-directed behaviors), and they *try* to read these intentions, though they may not always be successful in this effort. Young children are just at the start of a lifelong process of learning about specific intentions in specific situations. As with other cognitive skills, reading intentions improves with practice. Our view is that, before infants learn how to recognize more specific or subtle intentions, they learn to understand that a speaker *intends* for them to *attend* to something. It is understanding this particular intention that, we maintain, plays a fundamental role in early word learning. Evidence that 1-year-olds recognize adults' intentions for them to attend to entities in the environment comes from cross-sectional and longitudinal studies of gaze following (Corkum & Moore, 1995) and point following (Carpenter, Nagell, & Tomasello, 1998). All of these skills—gaze following, point following, and word learning—involve an understanding of adults' intentions for infants to attend to outside entities (rather than to the adults themselves). It is important to note that all three of these abilities emerge in a synchronized fashion around the end of the infant's 1st year of life (see Carpenter, Nagell, & Tomasello for a detailed analysis of the developmental patterns of emergence of point following, language comprehension, and language production).

We argue that it is significant that these three developmental achievements are intercorrelated and emerge together. It is important to pay attention to the age of emergence of language comprehension (usually 8–9 months) and language production (usually 12–13 months). Why is it that language emerges when it does? On what other cognitive and social-cognitive achievements does it depend? What is the associative theorists' explanation for the fact that infants are able to make arbitrary associations (Rovee-Collier & Gerhardstein, 1997) from a very early age but they are not able to comprehend language until many months later? Similarly, is there a principled reason for why "constraints" or lexical principles might kick in when they do? In our view, language is a behavior that depends on the ability to establish joint attention with more knowledgeable members of the culture; this is why it emerges in a synchronized fashion with other joint-attention behaviors (point and gaze following).

In summary, the social-pragmatic perspective on word learning maintains that, when a child hears a speaker use an unfamiliar term, he or she must attend to that which the speaker is attending to; that is, in order to understand what the speaker is referring to with a novel term, the child must enter into a state of joint focus with the speaker. The child's goal in language-learning situations is not so much to learn the disembodied "meanings of words" but to come to an understanding of what the speaker is calling his or her attention to. Sometimes, when a particular object or characteristic of the context is especially salient (or if it is made salient by the person with whom the child is interacting), their attention will be drawn to the same entity automatically. In other situations, children may have to actively search for cues to the adult's referential intent. We believe that by the middle to end of children's 2nd year of life, they are very actively engaged in this process and are able to employ their attentional resources strategically to determine an adult's referential intent in a given word-learning situation. Recent research indicates that children are able to use a variety of referential cues to accomplish this in different word-learning situations, as the following studies show.

DETERMINING REFERENTIAL INTENT
IN WORD-LEARNING SITUATIONS

One obvious example of a referential cue that children use is gaze direction. People tend to label what they are looking at. And from a very early age, children seem to be sensitive to this cue. Dare Baldwin (1993a, 1993b) has shown that children as young as 19 months tend to follow an adult's gaze to determine which of two objects the adult is labeling. In Baldwin's experimental setup, a child participant plays with one novel object while an adult plays with another. The adult looks down at the object and labels it while the child is focused on his or her own object. In this situation, children look up to see what the adult is looking at and then learn the label for that object.

Moore, Angelopoulos, and Bennett (1999) have recently shown that children do this even under conditions where the object *not* being referred to is made extremely salient. These researchers came up with a dramatic way of pitting gaze direction and salience against each other. In their study, an experimenter looked at and labeled one toy at the same time that *another* toy was made more salient by being lit up. The salience captured the children's attention (they looked over at the toy that was lit up), but in a subsequent comprehension test, the 24-month-old subjects consistently chose the object that the adult had been looking at rather than the one that was made perceptually salient by being lit up. This suggests that, at least by the time children reach 24 months of age, gaze direction wins out over salience in this type of word-learning situation (see also chapter 6 in this volume).

Children can also learn words in many social situations in which gaze direction is not informative. We conducted one study in which the object being labeled was new only to the speaker, not to the child (Akhtar, Carpenter, & Tomasello, 1996, Study 2). In this experiment, each child first played with three nameless objects with two experimenters and a parent. Then one experimenter and the parent left the room while the child played with a fourth nameless object (the target). The adults then returned and exclaimed over the contents of a box containing all four objects. One adult held the box and looked at the child while uttering the novel word: "There's a gazzer in there!" Gaze direction was not informative in this situation, because the four objects were crowded in the box. We hypothesized that if 2-year-olds are sensitive to what the adults did and did not experience, and if they know (in some implicit way) that speakers tend to comment on what is new to them, then they should still be able to determine to which of the four objects the speaker was referring. Our results showed that the majority of the children learned the word for the object that the adults had not played with, indicating their sensitivity to the fact that adults tend to label or comment on that which is new (see Samuelson & Smith, 1998, for an alternative explanation).

One important point to note is that the majority of word-learning studies with toddlers use explicit labeling contexts—situations in which the adult's intention is to label an object or action for the child. But a true demonstration of the *active* role that young children play in word learning would show that they can learn words in situations where they are not even being addressed; that is, it would show that young children can learn new words by tuning in to the conversations of others. There is some evidence that children in other cultures may have to learn language through this type of "eavesdropping" (see Lieven, 1994, for a review). In these cultures, infants do not seem to be addressed directly by adults, at least not to the degree that they are in middle-class Western cultures. These children tend to experience less one-on-one "language teaching" interaction than their counterparts in industrialized societies. Consequently, children growing up in these cultures must develop skills of tuning in to what others around them are talking about.

We believe that this skill is also necessary in middle-class Western cultures. In fact, all children in all cultures probably learn some words (maybe even the majority of their words) through observing their use by others (Bloom, Margulis, Tinker, & Fujita, 1996; Oshima-Takane, 1988; Oshima-Takane, Goodz, & Deverensky, 1996). From our perspective, this means that children must be attending to the communicative intentions of people who are not even interacting with them. Akhtar, Jipson, and Callanan (in press) recently tested this overhearing hypothesis. In this study, children were exposed to a novel object label and a novel verb. Half of the children heard these words as they were interacting with an adult experimenter; the other half only observed the adult interacting with another adult. Thus, half of the children were directly addressed, and half simply *overheard* the new words in conversations between two adults. The data indicate that 2-year-olds did not seem to have any problem learning the words in the overhearing context. We believe that these findings, along with many other studies (Akhtar & Tomasello, 1996; Tomasello & Akhtar, 1995) that we have reviewed elsewhere (Akhtar & Tomasello, 1998; Tomasello, in press), support the hypothesis that young children are quite actively involved in determining the referential intentions of mature language users.

It is important to draw attention to two points. The first is that in almost all studies of novel word learning, children are presented with one and only one naming context, whereas in their everyday interactions they are often exposed to the same word in multiple syntactic and pragmatic contexts. As Gleitman (1990) and Fisher (1994) and their colleagues have proposed, hearing a new verb in multiple syntactic frames may help the child to narrow down its possible meaning. Akhtar and Montague (1999) have shown that hearing a novel word used across different situations can aid a child in determining to which aspect of the communicative situation the speaker is referring. The importance of this "cross-situational learning" (Siskind, 1996) is best illustrated by considering the situation in which a child hears a new adjective. If the child hears the word "red" only once, he or she may not understand to what aspect of the situation the speaker is referring. But if this same child later encounters multiple different objects called "red," accomplishing the task of determining what the speaker means by "red" becomes much more feasible. So, keeping in mind what element remains consistent across naming contexts also helps children learn words.

The second point is that it is important to remember that all of these different cues that are separated for the purposes of experimental control generally tend to act in concert in the child's experience. Given children's apparent sensitivity to multiple probabilistic cues to referential intent and the convergence of these cues in the child's experience, we believe that the young child's task of learning words is not as intractable an induction task as often believed.

CONCLUSION

We are in agreement with theorists who stress the important role played by general cognitive and perceptual processes in word learning. And we agree with the proponents of lexical principles that, in the process of acquiring language, children form generalizations about how people use words that aid them in learning more words. But, in our opinion, neither of these approaches pays sufficient attention to the *social* nature of early word learning. We believe that a deeper appreciation of the variety of social-cognitive skills that young children bring to the task of discerning another's referential intent can be gained by starting from an analysis of the inherently intersubjective nature of language.

NOTES

1. Although she does not discuss the mapping metaphor specifically, Smith (1997) provides an interesting discussion of the influence of metaphors on the methods used to assess children's word learning.

2. Although learning object labels may appear to involve straightforward "mapping" of word to referent, our view is that it also requires the social-cognitive ability to tune in to speakers' referential intentions (Akhtar & Tomasello, 1998).

3. Verbs are also often viewed as more cognitively complex than object labels in that they often "package" many different kinds of information about a given action or event (Tomasello, 1992a)—for example, manner, instrument, perspective (but see Clark, 1997, on children's use of different object labels to provide different perspectives on the same object).

4. It is interesting to note that Schafer and Plunkett also included sets of "real-word" trials (wherein the images of a shoe and a cup were paired with their labels) "to alert infants to the idea that ostensive naming was occurring" (p. 313). On some level, then,

these researchers seem to appreciate that perception of referential intent is an essential part of learning object labels.

5. One important question that is beyond the scope of this chapter is what underlies infants' emerging ability to coordinate attention to speaker and topic (see Acredolo and Goodwyn, 1997, for a list of possible contributing factors).

REFERENCES

Acredolo, L., & Goodwyn, S. (1997). Furthering our understanding of what humans understand. *Human Development, 40,* 25–31.

Akhtar, N., Carpenter, M., & Tomasello, M. (1996). The role of discourse novelty in early word learning. *Child Development, 67,* 635–645.

Akhtar, N., Jipson, J., & Callanan, M. (in press). Learning words through overhearing. *Child Development.*

Akhtar, N., & Montague, L. J. (1999). Lexical acquisition: The role of cross-situational learning. *First Language, 19,* 347–358.

Akhtar, N., & Tomasello, M. (1996). Twenty-four-month-old children learn words for absent objects and actions. *British Journal of Developmental Psychology, 14,* 79–93.

Akhtar, N., & Tomasello, M. (1998). Intersubjectivity in early language learning and use. In S. Braten (Ed.), *Intersubjective communication and emotion in early ontogeny* (pp. 316–335). Cambridge, England: Cambridge University Press.

Baldwin, D. A. (1991). Infants' contribution to the achievement of joint reference. *Child Development, 62,* 875–890.

Baldwin, D. A. (1993a). Early referential understanding: Infants' ability to recognize referential acts for what they are. *Developmental Psychology, 29,* 832–843.

Baldwin, D. A. (1993b). Infants' ability to consult the speaker for clues to word reference. *Journal of Child Language, 20,* 395–418.

Baldwin, D. A. (1995). Understanding the link between joint attention and language. In C. Moore & P. J. Dunham (Eds.), *Joint attention: Its origins and role in development* (pp. 131–158). Hillsdale, NJ: Erlbaum.

Baldwin, D. A., Markman, E. M., Bill, B., Desjardins, R. N., Irwin, J. M., & Tidball, G. (1996). Infants' reliance on a social criterion for establishing word-object relations. *Child Development, 67,* 3135–3153.

Baldwin, D. A., & Tomasello, M. (1998). Word learning: A window on early pragmatic understanding. In E. Clark (Ed.), *Proceedings of the 29th Annual Child Language Research Forum* (pp. 3–23). Stanford, CA: Center for the Study of Language and Information.

Barrett, M. (1989). Early language development. In A. Slater & G. Bremner (Eds.), *Infant development* (pp. 211–241). Hove, England: Erlbaum.

Bates, E. (1979). *The emergence of symbols: Cognition and communication in infancy.* New York: Academic Press.

Bloom, L. (1998). Language acquisition in its development context. In D. Kuhn & R. S. Siegler (Eds.), *Handbook of child psychology: Vol. 2. Cognition, perception, and language* (pp. 309–370). New York: John Wiley & Sons.

Bloom, L., Margulis, C., Tinker, E., & Fujita, N. (1996). Early conversations and word learning: Contributions from child and adult. *Child Development, 67,* 3154–3175.

Bruner, J. (1983). *Child's talk: Learning to use language.* New York: W. W. Norton.

Carpenter, M., Nagell, K., & Tomasello, M. (1998). Social cognition, joint attention, and communicative competence from 9 to 15 months of age. *Monographs of the Society for Research in Child Development, 63* (4):176 (Serial No. 255).

Choi, S., & Gopnik, A. (1995). Early acquisition of verbs in Korean: A cross-linguistic study. *Journal of Child Language, 22,* 497–529.

Clark, E. V. (1990). On the pragmatics of contrast. *Journal of Child Language, 17,* 417–431.

Clark, E. V. (1997). Conceptual perspective and lexical choice in acquisition. *Cognition, 64,* 1–37.

Corkum, V., & Moore, C. (1995). Development of joint visual attention in infants. In C. Moore & P. J. Dunham (Eds.), *Joint attention: Its origins and role in development* (pp. 61–83). Hillsdale, NJ: Erlbaum.

Dunham, P. J., Dunham, F., & Curwin, A. (1993). Joint-attentional states and lexical acquisition at 18 months. *Developmental Psychology, 29,* 827–831.

Fisher, C. (1994). Structure and meaning in the verb lexicon: Input for a syntax-aided verb learning procedure. *Language and Cognitive Processes, 9,* 473–517.

Gergely, G., Nadasdy, Z., Csibra, G., & Biro, S. (1995). Taking the intentional stance at 12 months of age. *Cognition, 56,* 165–193.

Gleitman, L. R. (1990). The structural sources of verb meanings. *Language Acquisition, 1,* 3–55.

Golinkoff, R. M., Mervis, C. B., & Hirsh-Pasek, K. (1994). Early object labels: The case for a developmental lexical principles framework. *Journal of Child Language, 21,* 125–155.

Gopnik, A. (1988). Three types of early word: The emergence of social words, names and cognitive-relational words in the one-word stage and their relation to cognitive development. *First Language, 8,* 49–69.

Gopnik, A., & Choi, S. (1995). Names, relational words, and cognitive development in English and Korean speakers: Nouns are not always learned before verbs. In M. Tomasello & W. E. Merriman (Eds.), *Beyond names for things: Young children's acquisition of verbs* (pp. 63–80). Hillsdale, NJ: Erlbaum.

Greenfield, P. M., & Smith, J. H. (1976). *The structure of communication in early language development.* New York: Academic Press.

Harris, M., Barrett, M., Jones, D., & Brookes, S. (1988). Linguistic input and early word meaning. *Journal of Child Language, 15,* 77–94.

Jusczyk, P. W. (1997). *The discovery of spoken language.* Cambridge, MA: MIT Press.

Jusczyk, P. W., & Hohne, E. A. (1997). Infants' memory for spoken words. *Science, 277* (5334), 1984–1986.

Lieven, E. V. M. (1994). Crosslinguistic and crosscultural aspects of language addressed to children. In C. Gallaway & B. J. Richards (Eds.), *Input and interaction in language acquisition* (pp. 56–73). Cambridge, England: Cambridge University Press.

Markman, E. M. (1992). Constraints on word learning: Speculations about their nature, origins, and domain specificity. In M. R. Gunnar & M. P. Maratsos (Eds.), *Modularity and constraints in language and cognition: The Minnesota Symposia on Child Psychology* (Vol. 25, pp. 59–101). Hillsdale, NJ: Erlbaum.

Mead, G. H. (1934). *Mind, self, and society.* Chicago: University of Chicago Press.

Meltzoff, A. N. (1995). Understanding the intentions of others: Re-enactment of intended acts by 18-month-old children. *Developmental Psychology, 31,* 838–850.

Meltzoff, A. N., & Gopnik, A. (1993). The role of imitation in understanding persons and developing a theory of mind. In S. Baron-Cohen, H. Tager-Flusberg, & D. J. Cohen (Eds.), *Understanding other minds: Perspectives from autism* (pp. 335–366). Oxford, England: Oxford University Press.

Moore, C., Angelopoulos, M., & Bennett, P. (1999). Word learning in the context of referential and salience cues. *Developmental Psychology, 35,* 60–68.

Nelson, K. (1985). *Making sense: The acquisition of shared meaning.* Orlando, FL: Academic Press.

Nelson, K. (1986). *Event knowledge: Structure and function in development.* Hillsdale, NJ: Erlbaum.

Ninio, A. (1993a). Is early speech situational? An examination of some current theories about the relation of early utterances to the context. In D. J. Messer & G. J. Turner (Eds.), *Critical influences on child language acquisition and development* (pp. 23–39). New York: St. Martin's Press.

Ninio, A. (1993b). On the fringes of the system: Children's acquisition of syntactically isolated forms at the onset of speech. *First Language, 13,* 291–313.

Ninio, A., & Bruner, J. S. (1978). The achievement and antecedents of labeling. *Journal of Child Language, 5,* 1–15.

Oshima-Takane, Y. (1988). Children learn from speech not addressed to them: The case of personal pronouns. *Journal of Child Language, 15,* 95–108.

Oshima-Takane, Y., Goodz, E., & Deverensky, J. L. (1996). Birth order effects on early language development: Do secondborn children learn from overheard speech? *Child Development, 67,* 621–634.

Peters, A. M., & Boggs, S. T. (1986). Interactional routines as cultural influences upon language acquisition. In B. B. Schieffelin & E. Ochs (Eds.), *Language socialization across cultures* (pp. 80–96). New York: Cambridge University Press.

Premack, D. (1990). Words: What are they, and do animals have them? *Cognition, 37,* 197–212.

Quine, W. V. O. (1960). *Word and object.* Cambridge, MA: MIT Press.

Roberts, K. (1995). Categorical responding in 15-month-olds: Influence of the noun-category bias and the covariation between visual fixation and auditory input. *Cognitive Development, 10,* 21–41.

Rovee-Collier, C., & Gerhardstein, P. (1997). The development of infant memory. In N. Cowan (Ed.), *The development of memory in childhood: Studies in developmental psychology* (pp. 5–39). Hove, England: Psychology Press.

Saffran, J. R., Aslin, R. N., & Newport, E. L. (1996). Statistical learning by 8-month-old infants. *Science, 274* (5294), 1926–1928.

Samuelson, L. R., & Smith, L. B. (1998). Memory and attention make smart word learning: An alternative account of Akhtar, Carpenter, and Tomasello. *Child Development, 69,* 94–104.

Savage-Rumbaugh, S. (1990). Language as a cause-effect communication system. *Philosophical Psychology, 3,* 55–76.

Schafer, G., & Plunkett, K. (1998). Rapid word learning by fifteen-month-olds under tightly controlled conditions. *Child Development, 69,* 309–320.

Siskind, J. M. (1996). A computational study of cross-situational techniques for learning word-to-meaning mappings. *Cognition, 61,* 39–91.

Skinner, B. F. (1957). *Verbal behavior.* Englewood Cliffs, NJ: Prentice-Hall.

Smith, L. B. (1997). Metaphors and methods: Variability and the study of word learning. In E. Amsel & K. A. Renninger (Eds.), *Change and development: Issues of theory, method, and application* (pp. 153–172). Mahwah, NJ: Erlbaum.

Smith, L. B., Jones, S. S., & Landau, B. (1996). Naming in young children: A dumb attentional mechanism? *Cognition, 60,* 143–171.

Snow, C. E., & Goldfield, B. A. (1983). Turn the page please: Situation-specific language acquisition. *Journal of Child Language, 10,* 551–569.

Tardif, T. (1996). Nouns are not always learned before verbs: Evidence from Mandarin speakers' early vocabularies. *Developmental Psychology, 32,* 492–504.

Tomasello, M. (1992a). *First verbs: A case study of early grammatical development.* New York: Cambridge University Press.

Tomasello, M. (1992b). The social bases of language acquisition. *Social Development, 1,* 67–87.

Tomasello, M. (1995). Joint attention as social cognition. In C. Moore & P. J. Dunham (Eds.), *Joint attention: Its origins and role in development* (pp. 103–130). Hillsdale, NJ: Erlbaum.

Tomasello, M. (1996). The cultural roots of language. In B. M. Velichkovsky & D. M. Rumbaugh (Eds.), *Communicating meaning: The evolution and development of language* (pp. 275–307). Mahwah, NJ: Erlbaum.

Tomasello, M. (in press). Perceiving intentions and learning words in the second year of life. In M. Bowerman & S. Levinson (Eds.), *Language acquisition and conceptual development.* Cambridge, England: Cambridge University Press.

Tomasello, M., & Akhtar, N. (1995). Two-year-olds use pragmatic cues to differentiate reference to objects and actions. *Cognitive Development, 10,* 201–224.

Tomasello, M., & Barton, M. (1994). Learning words in non-ostensive contexts. *Developmental Psychology, 30,* 639–650.

Tomasello, M., & Farrar, J. (1986). Joint attention and early language. *Child Development, 57,* 1454–1463.

Tomasello, M., & Kruger, A. C. (1992). Acquiring verbs in ostensive and nonostensive contexts. *Journal of Child Language, 19,* 311–333.

Tomasello, M., Kruger, A. C., & Ratner, H. H. (1993). Cultural learning. *Behavioral and Brain Sciences, 16,* 495–552.

Trevarthen, C., & Hubley, P. (1978). Secondary intersubjectivity: Confidence, confiding, and acts of meaning in the first year. In A. Lock (Ed.), *Action, gesture, and symbol: The emergence of language* (pp. 183–229). London: Academic Press.

Werner, H., & Kaplan, B. (1963). *Symbol formation.* New York: John Wiley & Sons.

Williams, E. (1994). Some remarks on lexical knowledge. *Lingua, 92,* 7–34.

Woodward, A. L., & Markman, E. M. (1998). Early word learning. In D. Kuhn & R. S.

Siegler (Eds.), *Handbook of child psychology: Vol. 2. Cognition, perception, and language* (pp. 371–420). New York: John Wiley & Sons.

Zukow-Goldring, P., & Ferko, K. R. (1994). An ecological approach to the emergence of the lexicon: Socializing attention. In V. John-Steiner, C. D. Panofsky, & L. W. Smith (Eds.), *Sociocultural approaches to language and literacy* (pp. 170–190). New York: Cambridge University Press.

CHAPTER 6

An Emergentist Coalition Model for Word Learning

Mapping Words to Objects Is a Product of the Interaction of Multiple Cues

Kathy Hirsh-Pasek
Roberta Michnick Golinkoff
George Hollich

Twelve-month-old David has 3 words in his productive vocabulary: "dog," "daddy," and "kiss." He understands about 30 words. At this point in his development, word learning is slow and laborious as he acquires an average of 1 or 2 new words a week. By 24 months of age, David will be a veteran word learner, a virtual vacuum cleaner for words (as Pinker, 1994, put it), with 300 words in his productive vocabulary. David will be able to learn as many as 9 new words a day by some estimates, surprising his parents and caregivers and leading to claims of precocity and genius. But David is no genius; he is simply human.

The challenge for developmental psychology is to understand how children break the language barrier with their first words and turn into master word learners within a year's time. This chapter takes on this challenge by presenting a new theory of lexical development and a new method that allows us to study word learning as the child moves from novice to expert. We begin with an introduction to the word-learning problem and a brief overview of the major theories that have been posited to account for the phenomenon. Then we present our theory—the emergentist coalition model of word learning—an approach that unites these disparate theories. Finally, we offer some experimental evidence gathered by means of the new Interactive Intermodal Preferential Looking Paradigm. This hybrid approach addresses the fundamental challenge of word learning within a developmental framework and embraces the complexity of the word-learning process.

THE WORD-LEARNING PROBLEM

To illustrate the problem of word learning, we begin with a homespun example. Imagine that your friend Anne is invited to someone's house for a brunch. She is standing in the kitchen, chatting with her host as items are being brought out to the table. Her host says, "Could you get the foccacia?" What is foccacia? Her host is involved in several different conversations, so Anne does not want to interrupt and ask. What does she do? First, Anne probably looks to see where her host is looking and perhaps gesturing. Since her host is gesturing vaguely in the direction of the refrigerator (although her host is looking into the sink), Anne has her first clue. She opens the refrigerator door and peers in. What is she looking for? Anne is not even sure. Without realizing it, Anne is looking for something that is unfamiliar, something for which she does not already have a name. Anne sees a plastic bag filled with slices of fat, bumpy bread. Ah ha! This must be the foccacia.

We have all experienced such episodes. Adults have sophisticated strategies for learning new names, strategies that we become vaguely aware of only when something goes wrong. For example, Anne assumed that the word "foccacia" referred to some object in the world. To discover the referent of the word, she eagerly grasped onto the nonverbal cues her host offered. When asked to get more foccacia, she also assumed that the word applied to a similar-looking bread covered with spices. Finally, she assumed that "foccacia" referred to an object—in this case, the bread—and not just the spices on top. In short, Anne used both special and cognitive information to derive the meaning of the novel term.

Current theories of word learning have been polarized by emphasizing only one of these word-learning strategies to the exclusion of the others. Much of this polarization occurred in response to a philosophical conundrum introduced by Willard Quine (1960). This now all-too-familiar example involves a linguist in a foreign land who sees a rabbit scurrying by. At exactly the moment that the rabbit runs by, a native points to the rabbit and says "Gavagai." What is the linguist to think that "gavagai" refers to? Does it refer to the rabbit as a whole, or to the rabbit's ears, or to the rabbit's hopping, or even to the marks that the rabbit leaves in the soil? According to Quine, the world offers an infinite number of possible word-to-world mappings. Theories of word learning can be defined largely by whether they embrace the Quinean conundrum as a foundational assumption or reject it. Theories that posit constraints or principles adopt Quine's view of the problem space. Theories that emphasize social input or associative learning consider Quine's example largely irrelevant to the problem of word learning. Each of these families of theories has staked out an important place in the literature.

The Constraints/Principles Theories

If Quine is to be taken seriously, the problem of word-to-world mapping is underdetermined, and the human mind must be equipped with constraints or principles that narrow the search space. Thus, this family of theories posits that the child approaches word learning with a bias to make certain assumptions over others in determining what a word might mean. Domain-specific constraints theories have been proposed for a number of cognitive-development domains. In discussing children's burgeoning knowledge of numbers, for example, Gelman and Greeno (1989, p. 130) wrote:

> If we grant learners some domain-specific principles, we provide them with a way to define the range of relevant inputs, the ones that support learning about that domain. Because principles embody constraints on the kinds of input that can be processed as data that are relevant to that domain, they therefore can direct attention to those aspects of the environment that need to be selected and attended to.

Similar statements have appeared in the literature on spatial development (Newcombe & Huttenlocher, in press) and object perception (Spelke, 1990). The general thrust of the constraints/principles position is to make a daunting task manageable by restricting the number of hypotheses the learner need entertain to arrive at a representation of a domain.

In the area of word learning, a substantial body of evidence has accumulated to support the constraints position. Markman's (1989) principle of mutual exclusivity, for example, states that children assume that an object can have only one name. The consequence of this principle is that an unfamiliar name will label an unfamiliar object rather than an object that has already been named. Golinkoff, Hirsh-Pasek, Bailey, and Wenger (1992), among others (e.g., Evey & Merriman, 1998), have shown that, when presented with a set of familiar and unfamiliar objects, 28-month-olds will assume that a novel label maps to an unnamed object. These findings support not only Markman's mutual-exclusivity principle but also a more flexible principle (the novel-name nameless-category assumption, or N3C) suggested by Golinkoff, Mervis, and Hirsh-Pasek (1994). Similarly, Clark (1983) held that children operate with a principle called "conventionality," which requires that we use the word that our linguistic community uses in order to be understood. Mervis (see Golinkoff, Mervis, & Hirsh-Pasek) provided numerous diary entries, which showed that children abandon their idiosyncratic terms in favor of the standard terms (e.g., in time, "pops" becomes "pacifier").

Constraints/principles theories have flourished. Over the past 15 years, there has been a proliferation of principles including Waxman and Kosowski's (1990) noun-category bias, Markman's (1989) mutual exclusivity (see also Merriman & Bowman, 1989), Markman and Hutchinson's (1984) taxonomic assumption, and Clark's (1983) pragmatic constraint of contrast. In the face of a growing number of proposed constraints, Golinkoff, Mervis, and Hirsh-Pasek (1994) posited a set of six principles, some new and some already in the literature. The authors claimed that these principles were necessary and sufficient to account for how children get word learning off the ground and for how they become "vacuum cleaners for words" (Pinker, 1994). The Golinkoff, Mervis, and Hirsh-Pasek framework offered a developmental model in which the principles of word learning were organized on two tiers that captured the changing character of word learning. Fundamental to this framework was the idea that the principles themselves undergo change with development and are an emergent product of the combination of word-learning experience and some inborn biases.

The first tier (as seen in Figure 6.1) represents the principles that are foundational to word learning—that is, word learning could not begin without them. For example, it is hard to imagine word learning without the central principle of reference: Reference allows a word to symbolize, or stand for, an object, action, or event. Furthermore, words have a status different from that of other sounds associated with objects, such as the beep of the microwave or the ring of the telephone. These sounds, which occur when the object is present, embody a "goes with" relationship to the object. Words function differently from sounds in that they have a "stands for" relationship to what they label. Words do not need to occur contemporaneously with or be spatially coterminous with the objects, actions, and events they represent. Rather, words stand for their referents, even in contexts far removed from original usage and even when the referents are not present. Returning to our original example, Anne first assumed that the word "foccacia" mapped to some referent in the world.

Second, Anne used the principle of extendability. When her host asked her to get more foccacia, Anne assumed that similar-looking brown bread on a shelf in the refrigerator was in the same category. That is, Anne knew that most words, instead of referring to a single exemplar as do proper nouns, refer to categories of objects (see also Waxman & Kosowski's [1990] noun-category bias; Markman and Hutchinson's [1984] taxonomic assumption; and Golinkoff, Mervis, and Hirsh-Pasek's [1994] categorical-scope principle). Thus, when we call a dog "dog," we are really using "dog" generically to refer to a class of similar animals. It could be otherwise: Each word *could* label only the original exemplar, as is the case when we call our own dog "Fido." However, memory would soon be exceeded if each object, event, and action in the world had its own unique label. Probably by the end of the 1st year of life, children have reached at least a primitive realization that words label more than just the original exemplar. However, they may at first be unsure about the basis for object-label extension (Dromi, 1987).

Third, using the principle that we call "object scope," Anne probably assumed that the word "foccacia" referred to an *object*. Object scope has two

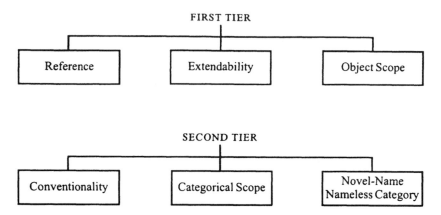

FIGURE 6.1. Two Tiers of the Golinkoff, Mervis, and Hirsh-Pasek (1994) Developmental Lexical Principles Model.

parts: Words refer to objects over actions or events, and words refer to whole objects over part of or an attribute of an object (Markman & Wachtel [1988] posited a similar principle called "whole object").

These first three principles—reference, extendability, and object scope—are sufficient to get the infant's word learning started. None of these require much linguistic sophistication. Yet they are essential to the word-learning process. They merely allow the young child to learn words in a laborious, one-at-a-time fashion, nowhere near approaching the rapid word learning that occurs after the vocabulary spurt. Since the character of word learning changes around the time of the vocabulary spurt, it is obvious that these three principles alone cannot account for the word-learning process. Therefore, reference, extendability, and object scope occupy what Golinkoff, Mervis, and Hirsh-Pasek (1994) have referred to as the first tier of their word-learning model, and they evolve into more sophisticated word-learning principles, which define the second tier.

The first-tier principle of reference evolves into the pragmatic principle of conventionality (Clark, 1983). Whereas reference states that consistent phonological forms (words) map to entities in the environment (via the children's representations of those entities), the principle of conventionality makes it clear that, for communication to proceed successfully, the consistent phonological forms should match those used by others in the environment. If young children are to be understood outside the family circle, they must abandon their invented, literally in-house words in favor of terms that are used more widely.

Similarly, the first-tier principle of extendability allows the young child to apply newly learned words to nonidentical exemplars that share perceptual similarity, or thematic relationships, or taxonomic relationships with the original referents. Extendability evolves into the second-tier principle called "categorical scope," which refines extendability by removing doubts about the basis for extension. The principle of categorical scope states that words label taxonomic categories, first at the basic level and only later at the superordinate level (Golinkoff, Shuff-Bailey, Olguin, & Ruan, 1995). Thus, upon hearing "foccacia" requested again, Anne knew that, instead of assuming that "foccacia" meant "the bag it came in" (a thematic relationship), she should look for something that resembled the foccacia and was probably the same kind of object.

Finally, whereas the first-tier principle of object scope allows the child to map new terms to objects (as opposed to actions)—and to *whole* objects at that—the second-tier principle of novel-name nameless category (N3C) causes the child to search out a nameless object referent as soon as a new word is heard. Thus, for example, Anne assumed that, when she heard the new word "foccacia," it should map to an *unnamed* object category rather than to a food for which Anne already knew the name. Markman's (1989) principle of mutual exclusivity (see also Merriman & Bowman, 1989) is similar to N3C, though N3C does *not* presuppose that children *avoid* having two names for objects (Mervis, Golinkoff, & Bertrand, 1994).

Taking a broad view of word learning in the first 2 years of life, it became apparent to Golinkoff, Mervis, and Hirsh-Pasek (1994) that young children have important insights about word learning that were not being captured by existing principles in the literature. The two-tiered model of lexical principles is a way of explaining how word learning begins and how it might change during development. Nested in this framework by Golinkoff, Mervis, and Hirsh-Pasek is a powerful developmental solution to the Quinean dilemma. Solutions proposed by constraints/principles theorists rest within the mind of the child rather than in a benevolent social environment.

The Social-Pragmatic Theorists

In stark contrast to the constraints/principles view, the social-pragmatic theorists emphasize how children, embedded in a social nexus, are guided by expert word learners as they embark upon the word-learning task. In this context, Quine's problem fizzles away, because environmental input removes the ambiguity of the word-learning situation. As Nelson (1988, pp. 240–241) wrote:

> The typical way children acquire words . . . is almost completely opposite of the Quinean paradigm. Children do not try and guess what it is that the adult intends to refer to; rather . . . it is the adult who guesses what the child is focused on and then supplies the appropriate word.

Bloom (1993) similarly concludes that adults talk about objects, actions, and events that children are already focused on, thereby producing language that is

relevant to the child's interest. Children do not have to wade through alternative interpretations of a word; the correct interpretation is already the focus of
their attention.

There is considerable evidence that children are capable of using social
cues in the service or word learning. In one representative study, for example,
Baldwin (1993) reported that children would not attach a label to an unnamed
object if the speaker did not appear to be referring to the object, even if the object was interesting, even if the object appeared at the same time the label was
uttered, and even if the speaker was touching the object (albeit in an apparently nonreferential manner). Thus, a child might hear an adult say, as the adult
looked into a bucket, "There's a modi in here." Even if the adult first pulled
out an object from a *different* bucket, and only later pulled out the object from
the original bucket, the child would nonetheless attach the label to the second,
not the first, object that he or she saw. Similarly, Tomasello and Barton (1994;
see also Tomasello, Strosberg, & Akhtar, 1996) showed that 18- and 24-
month-olds can use the intention of the experimenter to attach a label to a
novel object or action. Tomasello and Barton had an experimenter pretend to
look for a "toma." As each new toy was revealed, the experimenter scowled
and put it back in its hiding place as if to say, "This is not a toma." Amazingly,
18-month-olds read the social cues and selected the correct toy as the "toma."
In another study, Akhtar and Tomasello (1996) showed that 24-month-old children can mine the social context to attach a new label to a hidden object instead of to new objects that they are shown. Furthermore, Baldwin and her colleagues (1996) showed that children can evaluate whether an adult who utters
a label in great excitement ("It's a toma!") intended to label the object in the
children's presence or something else. Eighteen-month-olds are not fooled
into forming a link between a label that a woman talking on the telephone utters just at the moment that they are focused on a novel toy. Thus, by 19 months
of age, children are sensitive to very subtle social cues when attaching a label
to a referent.

In sum, in the social pragmatic view, children are seen as skilled apprentices
to expert word learner participating in a structured social world. Language
comes as part of the package of being a human social animal. As Nelson (1996,
p. 137) wrote:

> It is suggested here that the general problem for the language learning child is not
> greatly different from that of any speaker and listener—it is to interpret the utterance
> of another within the *context of the activity* [italics added], as represented within the
> listener's current cognitive environment.

On this view, Quine's linguist differs from real children in that children are im-
mersed in rich social contexts that serve to delimit the possible mappings be-

tween words and their referents by providing a master teacher or a guide for the word learner.

The constraints/principles and the social-pragmatic theories of word learning are the most common positions presented in the literature. A recent third position, outlined by Smith (1995), Samuelson and Smith (1998), and Plunkett and Elman (1997) offers yet another perspective on the word-learning problem.

The Domain-General View of Word Learning

Rejecting Quine's conundrum, proponents of the domain-general view of word learning suggest that word learning can be best accounted for through "dumb attentional mechanisms" such as perceptual saliency, association, and frequency. In comparing the differences in constraints theories and her own systems-theory view, Smith (1995, p. 4) wrote:

> The empirical focus [of constraints theories] becomes not the processes that enable children to interpret words in context, but whether children's biased learning has the properties needed to "solve the induction problem." The present thesis is that the induction problem is irrelevant to developmentalists. Learning is not necessarily hypothesis testing. Development is not induction.

It follows, therefore, that children do not need constraints or principles to forge word-to-world mappings. Rather, the process of mapping a word onto an object is straightforward. Children notice these objects, actions, and events that are the most salient in their environment. They associate the most frequently used label with the most salient candidate. In this way, ambiguity in the word-learning situation is removed. The most plausible word-to-world mapping is the one that surfaces as the only possibility. Thus, general cognitive mechanisms not only are sufficient to account for how young children first map words onto referents but can also combine in ways to account for the complexity of more-sophisticated word learning. To demonstrate how global cognitive mechanisms can more parsimoniously account for word-learning findings, Samuelson and Smith (1998) replicated a study conducted by Akhtar, Carpenter, and Tomasello (1996, Study 2). In the Akhtar, Carpenter, and Tomasello study (also described in chapter 5) 20-month-old children each played with three toys when the child's mother and two experimenters were in the room. A fourth toy was introduced after the mother and one of the experimenters left the room. When the adults returned, they looked into a box containing the novel objects (including the fourth object) and said (of no object in particular), "I see a gazzer!" In a later object-selection task in which the child saw all four objects, children consistently assumed that the toy that was introduced during the absence of the mother and one experimenter was the referent for the word "gazzer." Thus, children had apparently inferred that the object that the adults had *not* seen during play must be the one being called "gazzer." Akhtar, Carpenter, and Tomasello ascribed children's performance to a deep understanding of the referential intentions of other people.

Samuelson and Smith, who disagreed with this explanation, created the same outcome—a word-referent mapping—by making the target object the most "novel-in-context" item at the time that the name was offered. They did this by moving the target object to a location separate from the other objects and by putting it on a special glittery blue tablecloth. Their findings, they believed, showed that the ambiguous linguistic event of figuring out which object the speaker is naming "is resolved by mundane memorial and attentional processes" (1998, p. 100). Yet, although they believed their account to be more compelling for its parsimony, even Samuelson and Smith granted that social knowledge may have played a role in their experiment as well; they also granted that a social-communicative account is feasible *if* it incorporates what we know of how memory and attention work.

There is mounting evidence in favor of the social-pragmatic and the associationist account. Yet the Quinean problem refuses to go away. Any single object, action, or event presents an array of possible referents to be named. By way of example, even something as simple as a "sippy cup" has a lid, an elevated portion on the lid designed for optimal sucking (the mouthpiece), a base, and possibly even some pink flowers on its blue plastic. How is the child to know which of these multiple parts is graced with the name, "cup?" All of the parts move together when the cup is lifted, and some of the parts—such as the mouthpiece—may prove more salient than the whole object. Thus, neither perceptually based nor socially based theories assist the child in reaching the final destination that makes word-to-world mapping possible. Further, once a name is bestowed, it could be extended along the lines of perceptual similarity (a plastic tent), function (a regular tea cup), or taxonomic category membership (a squat red sippy cup with double handles). How is the child to know which aspect of the referent is being named and what governs extension?

Without recognizing the enormity of the problem, we are left with a three-legged chair analogous to the three families of theories just reviewed. Each leg makes a significant contribution in holding up the chair and in explaining the word-learning problem. Just as a three-legged chair is inherently unstable, scientific explanations of complex processes that force either/or decisions are not as powerful as those that embrace differing perspectives. Others, too, have recognized the force of explanations that integrate multiple causes for complex behavior. For example, Nelson (1996, p. 85) wrote, "There are no single effective pushes to the developing system, but rather a combination of influences that lead to observable change." Similarly, Karmiloff-Smith (1992, p. 193) urged us to adopt a more comprehensive view: "The flourishing new domain of cognitive science needs to go beyond the traditional nativist-empiricist dichotomy that permeates much of the field, in favor of an epistemology that embraces both innate predispositions and constructivism."

It is within this spirit of integration that the "emergentist coalition model of word learning" (Hollich, Hirsh-Pasek, & Golinkoff, 1998) was born. Representing the fourth leg of the chair, this model uses the support provided by the other legs, since it borrows from the strengths of the prior models. It also offers a developmental view of how children break the word-learning barrier and how they become expert word learners. The complexity of the word-learning process and the developmental changes that it undergoes demand a multifaceted theory.

AN EMERGENTIST COALITION MODEL
OF WORD LEARNING

The emergentist coalition model of word learning is a hybrid model that builds on and extends our developmental lexical principles framework (Golinkoff, Mervis, & Hirsh-Pasek, 1994). We (Hollich, Hirsh-Pasek, & Golinkoff, 1998; Golinkoff, Hirsh-Pasek, & Hollich, in press) posit a model of word learning that offers the child multiple cues to attach a novel label to a novel object. In the real world, as the research reviewed in this chapter has shown, children use social, perceptual, cognitive, *and* linguistic cues to learn new words. And in the real world, the same word-learning situation may offer combinations of these cues. Researchers have overlooked this possibility because the experiments that we conduct in the laboratory often manipulate only single cues. The emergentist coalition model embraces this complexity, incorporating the full range of cues to word learning, instead of forcing artificial choices among them. Thus, the first defining tenet of our model is that children mine a *coalition of cues* on their way to word learning. Figure 6.2 graphically depicts the multiple inputs that are available for word learning.

Although a range of cues is *available* from the start of word learning, not all the cues are *utilized* by children as they start their word-learning journey. *Not all cues for word learning are created equal.* The weighting of the cues changes over time. Younger children, just beginning to learn words, can detect and make use of only a subset of the cues in the coalition. Older, more experienced word learners can detect and make use of a wider subset of cues, relying on some cues more heavily than on others. For example, the model posits that social cues such as eye gaze, which are subtle and may demand at least a primitive theory of mind, are harder to use for word learning than is a cue such as perceptual salience. When given a choice between attaching a new name to a boring object that an adult is looking at and attaching a new name to a colorful, exciting

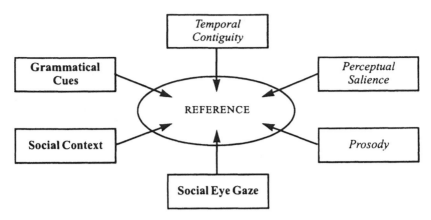

FIGURE 6.2. Change in relative weight of cues for word learning over developmental time. Italicized boxes represent phase 1; boldfaced boxes represent phase 2.

object, the child who is just beginning to learn words should rely on perceptual salience before relying on the subtle social cue of eye gaze. Thus, the second major tenet of the theory is that the cues for word learning change their weights over developmental time. Figure 6.2 graphically depicts how reliance on these cues shifts with development.

Because the child makes differential use of the available cues with development, this model holds that principles for word learning are emergent. They develop over the course of the 2nd year of life as children gain word-learning experience. Unlike other constraints posited in the literature, the emergentist coalition model states that *not all of the principles are available from the start of word learning.* Therefore, lexical principles are the products and not the engines of lexical development. For example, children do not start word learning with the novel-name nameless-category principle (N3C). Mervis and Bertrand (1994) have shown that the N3C principle is not in place until after the vocabulary spurt. The authors tested 19-month-old children, some of whom had and some of whom had not experienced a vocabulary spurt. They presented the children with four objects, three whose name they knew and a new object whose name the children did not know. Prior to the vocabulary spurt, when children were asked to retrieve an object required with a novel name, they did not assume that the name mapped to the unnamed object. However, if they had had a vocabulary spurt, they readily selected the unnamed object to be the referent of the new name. Also not present at the start of word learning, when children happily use their idiosyncratic names for objects is the principle of conventionality (Clark, 1983). The third tenet of this model, then, is that the principles for word learning are emergent and not given a priori.

The developmental cast of this model makes it imperative to study the origins of word learning as well as the transformation that takes place in the 2nd year of life, when the child becomes an expert word learner. To validate the model, it is essential to collect data that demonstrate that children detect and utilize multiple cues for word learning, that their reliance on these cues changes over the course of development, and that principles for word learning emerge from word-learning experience.

Our current work is designed to assess these claims within the context of the principle of reference, which states that words map onto the child's representation of objects, actions, and events. We began our research program guided by three hypotheses: (1) that even 12-month-olds are informed by multiple cues to word learning, such as perceptual salience and social information (e.g,. handling and eye gaze); (2) that perceptual salience would be more heavily weighted for the novice than for the expert word learner than would social cues; and (3) that the word-learning principles themselves develop along a continuum from immature to mature—that the principles themselves change in character over the course of development.

EVIDENCE FOR THE MODEL

To examine the development of the lexical principles, we needed a method that could be used equally effectively with children in the age range of interest: 12–24 months. We needed a method that would enable researchers to manipulate the multiple cues (e.g., perceptual and social) ordinarily available in the word-learning situation and to study their interactions over time. For these reasons, we developed the Interactive Intermodal Preferential Looking Paradigm, which uses three-dimensional objects instead of video presentations.

The Interactive Intermodal Preferential Looking Paradigm (Interactive IPLP)

Our new method for investigating early word learning is based on the Intermodal Preferential Looking Paradigm developed by Golinkoff and Hirsh-Pasek (Golinkoff, Hirsh-Pasek, Cauley, & Gordon, 1987; Hirsh-Pasek & Golinkoff, 1996) to study lexical and syntactic comprehension. Borrowing from Baldwin's (1991, 1993) successful "bucket task," described earlier in this chapter, our Intermodal Preferential Looking Paradigm (Golinkoff, Hirsh-Pasek, Cauley, & Gordon); and Fagan's (1971; Fagan, Singer, Montic, & Shepard, 1986) infant intelligence test, we arrived at the paradigm shown in Figure 6.3.

Each infant is seated on his or her blindfolded mother's lap, facing the experimenter and our testing apparatus. After some preexposure to the toys—

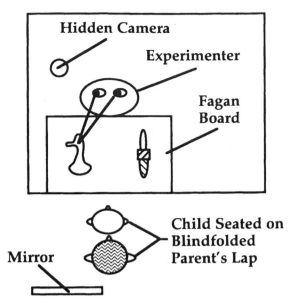

FIGURE 6.3. Interactive Intermodal Preferential Looking Paradigm.

familiar toys on some trials and unfamiliar toys on others—the toys are fixed with velcro onto one side of a two-sided black board (40 by 50 cm), approximately 11 cm apart. The board can be rotated almost 360°, so that the toys can go in and out of view for a specified period of time. The board is high enough so that the experimenter can hide behind it while children are inspecting the toys during test trials. Coding is done off-line from videotaped records.

Using this apparatus, it is possible, within a controlled setting, to examine word learning with both familiar and novel test objects and to provide some social interaction. Familiar object trials allow us to ask whether the child can "play our game." Children who cannot look at the correct *familiar* object when it is asked for by name are very unlikely to succeed with novel objects in a word-learning task. The use of unfamiliar objects given novel names and presented under various conditions permits us to probe *which* cues children use and what *combinations* of cues they use to guide word learning.

Both familiar and novel trials begin with a period of object *exploration* in which the child has an opportunity to play with the test objects. For novel objects, this period of exploration is followed by a trial that checks on object *salience*. For novel objects, this period of exploration is followed by a trial that checks on object *salience*. The *training* phase occurs as the experimenter attracts the infant's attention and attempts to teach the child a name. In the training phase, with the experimenter in full view, we can explore whether infants are even capable of attending to salience or social cues. Finally, there is a *test-*

ing phase to see whether the name offered has been mapped to the object. That is, even if children attend to the cues offered during the training phase, the main question is whether they *use* these cues in the service of word learning. Figure 6.4 reviews the sequence that occurs on the trials in which novel objects are used.

A number of variables, such as the side on which an object appears and which object is requested, are counterbalanced. The typical independent variables are gender, age, and condition. The logic of the design, as with our other Intermodel Preferential Looking Paradigm (Golinkoff, Hirsh-Pasek, Cauley, & Gordon, 1987; Hirsh-Pasek & Golinkoff, 1996), is that children will choose to look at objects that match the linguistic stimulus more than they will look at ob-

Exploration (26 s)   (Interesting Toy)

Exploration (26 s)   (Boring Toy)

Salience (6 s)
"Eve, look at the board!"
"What do you see?"

Salience (6 s)
Eve, look at the board!"
"What do you see?"

Training (≈16 s)
"Eve, look at the modi."
"It's a modi, a modi."
"Eve, see the modi!"

Testing (6 s)
"Eve, where's the modi?"
"Do you see the modi?"

Testing (6 s)
"Eve, where's the modi?"
"Do you see the modi?"

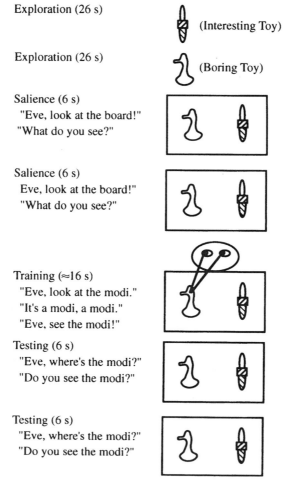

FIGURE 6.4. Sequence of Events in Presentation of Trials with New Objects.

jects that do not match the linguistic stimulus. Thus, the dependent variable is visual fixation time to the target versus the nontarget object.

Does the Method Work?

Children at three ages were tested in the Interactive IPLP: 12- to 13-month-olds just at the beginning of word learning; 19- to 20-month-olds, who may or may not have yet experienced a vocabulary spurt; and 24- to 25-month-olds, who typically have sizable production vocabularies. To determine whether the method was a viable one, children's responses to the test trials using two pairs of familiar objects (e.g., a ball versus a book) were examined across a number of experiments. Even 12-month-olds distributed their looking times to examine both stimuli. That is, they looked at and noticed both objects. Important for validation, however, was the fact that even the youngest children made a clear choice when they heard the name of a novel object. They looked for a significantly longer time at the familiar target item (i.e., the item requested) than they did at the nontarget item. Thus, this method is successful for 12-month-olds, and, as an added bonus, there is very little subject loss.

More than 23 experiments with hundreds of children have now been conducted. Here we present a selective review that speaks to our hypotheses.

Evaluating the Hypotheses

Hypothesis 1. *Can we find evidence that children utilize multiple cues in word learning?* As a start, we asked whether both perceptual salience and the subtle social cue of eye gaze play a role in word learning for children at different ages. A subsidiary question was whether 12-month-olds could even *follow* another's gaze to a focal point in the context. If they could follow the speaker's eye to the target object, could they show that they were affected by both perceptual salience and eye gaze in affixing a label? For the two older groups (19- to 20-month-olds and 24- to 25-month-olds), we expected to see that perceptual salience and social eye gaze continued to be factors in affixing a novel label to a referent.

To test this hypothesis, two conditions were created: In the *coincident* condition, the toy that coincided with children's preferences—the interesting toy— was labeled. If children use both social eye gaze and perceptual salience, they should learn best in this condition, where the cues are in alignment. In the *conflict* condition, the toy that did not coincide with the children's preferences— the boring toy—was labeled. Because the coalition of cues is disrupted, learning a novel word should be more difficult in this condition.

In the *exploration phase,* we presented the children with two novel objects, one at a time, for them to play with, and we offered no labels. We gave the children a boring toy and an interesting toy. To confirm our intuitions about which toy was boring and which toy was interesting, we placed the objects side by side on the board during a *saliency trial.* Results confirmed that, across all three age groups, children looked for a longer time at the interesting toy than at the boring toy when neither was labeled.

Following the salience trial, the *training trial* began. The experimenter first captured children's attention by locking eye gaze with them and calling them by name. Then, with both toys displayed but out of the child's reach, the experimenter gazed back and forth from the target toy to the child while labeling the toy five times. Using infant-directed speech, the experimenter said, for example, "Eve, this is a danu. See the danu?" In the coincident condition, the experimenter looked at and labeled the interesting toy; in the conflict condition, the experimenter looked at and labeled the boring toy. Coding for visual fixation time during the training trials provides valuable information about whether children can *attend* to the cues offered. Visual fixation times from the test trials that followed reveal whether the child can *use* the cues in the service of word learning.

In the *test trials,* the experimenter, now hiding behind the board, once again captured the child's attention and then asked for the object that was labeled during training. For example, the experimenter said, "Eve, where's the danu? Can you find the danu?" Children who had learned the name of the correct toy would be expected to look for a longer time at the target than at the nontarget.

Do children use multiple cues in word learning? The answer is yes, with some qualifications. The clearest case, shown in Figure 6.5, is made by the 24- and 25-month-olds. These post–vocabulary spurt children learned the names of the novel objects in both the conflict and the coincident conditions. However, in the coincident condition, where the perceptually interesting toy was labeled, children looked for a much longer time at the target object during test trials, than they did in the conflict condition, where the boring object was labeled. This suggests that children were lured by the perceptual salience of the interesting toy but were able to overcome this attraction when the boring toy was the focus of the experimenter's attention. These children attended to both perceptual and social information when linking a word to its referent.

The 19- and 20-month-olds also learned the labels of the objects in the conflict and the coincident conditions. Their pattern of results, however, looked different from the pattern the 24- and 25-month-olds produced. The 19- and 20-month-olds preferred the interesting object during the test trials in both conditions. Yet they looked at the interesting object for a much shorter time when the boring object was labeled in the conflict condition. These children could not overcome the lure of perceptual salience to the extent that the older group could. Nonetheless, the very fact that they learned the labels and looked at the boring object for a longer time in the conflict than in the coincident condition suggests that they were influenced by the cues of both perceptual salience and social eye gaze.

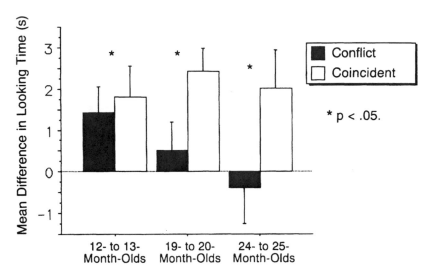

FIGURE 6.5. Mean Difference in Visual Fixation Time to the Interesting versus Boring Object in the Conflict and Coincident Conditions.

The 12- to 13-month-olds present a picture that is dominated by the effects of perceptual salience. During test trials, they looked at the interesting toy for a significantly longer time than at the boring toy, regardless of condition. This finding apparently confirmed our hypothesis that 12- to 13-month-olds would attach a label to the most interesting object—regardless of which object the experimenter labeled. However, in that children may have merely been looking at the interesting object, the experiment did not allow us to evaluate this alternative. Had these children learned any labels at all, or were they merely attending to the most salient object with no attempt to label it?

We reasoned that if children had learned a label in either condition, they should look for a longer time *toward* an object when it *is* labeled and *away* from that object when another novel label is introduced. Borrowing from Woodward, Markman, and Fitzsimmons (1994), the experimenter introduced a new name after the training and test trials. That is, the experimenter asked for the "danu" (the trained name) on the first set of test trials and then asked for the "glorp" (a novel name not previously heard) on a subsequent test trial. Would children look away from the object that had been labeled "danu" (as if recognizing that the name-referent relationship was being violated) when they heard the word "glorp"? Would children then return their gaze to the target object when the experimenter asked again for the "danu" on a final test trial? If children looked away from the target when a new name was introduced and looked *back* when they heard the original name, then they had probably affixed the name to the target object.

As Figure 6.6 shows, this is exactly what happened. Interestingly however, it happened only in the coincident condition. Even though the pattern of results is similar in the conflict condition, these results failed to reach significance. Why should children demonstrate that they had learned the novel labels only in the coincident condition, when the experimenter labeled the object that the babies were most interested in? For these babies, learning took place when the social and perceptual cues *coincided*. However, in the conflict condition, when multiple cues failed to coincide, infants showed less evidence of word learning. They wanted to look at the interesting object despite the fact that the experimenter persisted in labeling the boring object. The fact that the cues were not in alignment apparently did not permit word learning to occur in the conflict condition. This additional experiment, then, demonstrates that even 12-month-olds are able to use multiple cues for word learning, although it appears that for them, the cues must *overlap* for learning to occur.

The first question addressed in these two experiments was whether babies could show evidence of using multiple cues in word learning. Clearly, at all three ages, children were influenced by both perceptual salience and social eye gaze. Even the youngest learners indicated that they detected social eye gaze in attaching a label to a referent, but they were not able to overcome the effects of perceptual salience in the way that the 19- and 20-month-olds began to and the 24- and 25-month-olds clearly did.

Hypothesis 2. *Can we find evidence that the weightings of the cues shift over time, changing the complexion of word learning?* We hypothesized that 12-month-olds, with an immature principle of reference, would be more influenced

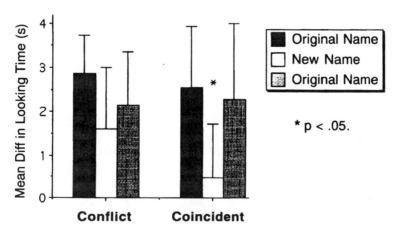

FIGURE 6.6. Mean Visual Fixation to the Target When Requested by Original Name, New Name, and Original Name Again.

by perceptual cues than by social cues when attaching a word to a referent. The novel word might be associated with the most interesting perceptual object in the immediate context. Older children, in contrast, might operate with a more mature principle of reference, using subtle social cues such as eye gaze more than perceptual salience. These children would "read" the speaker's intent when affixing a label to a referent—even when the object to be labeled was the more boring alternative. Older children might assume that the referent referred to what the speaker had in mind rather than to what they themselves had in mind.

The experiments already described give us preliminary answers to this question. For 12- to 13-month-olds, perceptual salience is dominant relative to social eye gaze. For 19- to 20-month-olds, perceptual salience still predominates, but social eye gaze has gained in importance. Finally, for the sophisticated 24- to 25-month-olds, social eye gaze can be used to override perceptual cues for word learning. Figure 6.7 depicts these trends. It appears that perceptual salience dominates at the outset and, over time, loses its relative potency to social cues, which increase in strength. It seems that children were starting to take the speaker's point of view. Although these data are convincing, it is possible that young infants' sensitivity to social cues was *masked* because of their undue reliance on perceptual salience. It is also possible that the particular social cue that we used—eye gaze—was too subtle to be relied upon. Eye gaze is signaled only by a turn of the head and eyes in the direction of an object. This is not an easy cue for children to detect (e.g., Butterworth & Grover, 1990). Social cues such as touching and handling may provide more information to children who are trying to map a word to an object. The only way to evaluate the claim that over time children become more sensitive to social cues in word learning, is to examine young children's ability to utilize a *range* of social cues in a task that seriously minimizes perceptual salience.

What would happen if perceptual salience were roughly equal between the two novel objects and more pronounced social cues were included? The next series of experiments was designed to test just that. In the first experiment, we tested whether 12- to 13-month-olds could respond to eye gaze when the objects were of equal salience. The rest of the experiment paralleled the previous eye-gaze experiment.

Results indicated that 12- to 13-month-olds were largely indifferent to social eye gaze. Even in the training trials, they did poorly at following the gaze of the experimenter to the labeled toy. This suggests that social eye gaze alone, without the additional cue of perceptual salience, was insufficient to promote word learning. The second experiment added a more potent social cue: touching. Here the experimenter touched *and* looked at the target during training. However, the experience in training did not translate into word learning in the test trials. Children looked at the target for roughly the same amount of time that they looked at the nontarget.

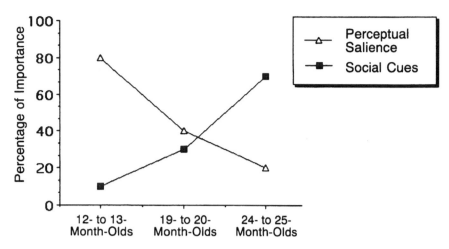

FIGURE 6.7. Decline of the Relative Importance of Perceptual Salience and Increase in the Importance of Social Cues during Development.

Frankly, we added an even more pronounced social cue: handling. During training, the experimenter looked at, touched, and slowly rotated the object while labeling it. Children followed the experimenter's lead to the target object even longer during training. Yet again, however, word learning did not occur. These experiments underscore the earlier conclusion that young children, at the start of word learning, do not know the significance of social cues for attaching a label to a referent. Although they show us that they can follow some of these cues during training (in particular, eye gaze in combination with handling and touching), they do not seem to use social information in the service to word learning; they act as though they do not know that it is relevant.

In sum, the claim that social cues increase in prominence over development holds for more than just eye gaze. Twelve- to 13-month-olds appear incapable of relying on a range of social cues for word learning—even when perceptual salience is no longer a factor.

Hypothesis 3. *The child moves from an immature to a mature principle of reference.* The very fact that older children use social cues to connect words with referents in a way that younger children do not suggests that the older children are approaching word learning as a fundamentally different task. What are the 12-month-olds doing with the word-learning input that they receive that allows them to learn any words at all? We suggested that young children are sensitive to a coalition of cues for word learning. Yet young learners may not know which of the many cues in the coalition can be relied on for word learning. For example, and as we discovered, younger children do not appear to realize that social cues are among the most reliable for word learning. As a consequence, the learner may act conservatively, requiring converging data to form word-referent connections. Children with an immature principle of reference may need to hear a novel word more times than do children with a mature principle of reference, and they may need to have multiple, overlapping cues for word-referent mapping.

To test this hypothesis, we asked what it would take to get 12-month-olds to learn a word. Could they do so if they were offered numerous, overlapping cues and if the new word was repeated more times than in the original studies? In what we affectionately called the "bludgeoning" experiment, we gave 12-month-olds every word-learning advantage. Using objects of equal salience, we loaded the training phase of the experiment with various cues. The experimenter looked at, touched, and handled the target object while repeating its name a full 10 times. The results were clear: On the whole, 12-month-olds learned the novel words. When the child is "bludgeoned" by the presentation of many converging cues in the coalition and is thereby given more time on the task, the supports are sufficiently strong to allow word learning to occur. Perhaps this is why word learning takes place so slowly in the real world outside of the laboratory. Children may require more support than they generally receive, both in frequency and in exposure time, to tie a word to its referent. Once they become able to weight the cues more veridically, they require less support for word learning to occur.

Is Early Word Learning Specific to Words or Will Any Auditory Stimulus Do?

If the earliest word learning is dependent upon hearing a word frequently in the presence of overlapping cues, then couldn't any auditory signal come to be associated with a referent by using "dumb attentional mechanisms," as Smith (1995) has posited? On that view, any sound that is frequently offered in combination with other cues in the coalition should act as a label for the immature word learner. The next set of experiments suggests, however, that all sounds are not equally effective potential associates to objects.

These studies followed the same course as the "bludgeoning" study: In the training phase, children heard either mouth sounds (such as "psst, psst" and "click, click" made at the side of the mouth) or object noises (such as "boing, boing"). We presented these sounds in the same way as the object labels in the "bludgeoning" study: We offered the noises 10 times, produced them concurrently with eye gaze and object motion, and embedded them in sentence frames (e.g., "Elmo, look at the [boing]"). Would children attach the mouth sounds and object noises to the target objects as readily as they did the real words? If so, it would seem that, for 12-month-olds, words have no special status for forming links with referents and that perhaps word learning starts out primarily as an associative process in which any auditory stimulus will do. If not, it would seem that words do have some special status for the young child, even for the 12-month-old.

The results suggested a more complex picture than we expected. Children seemed to differentiate between object noises and mouth sounds. They failed to learn the object noise–referent links, but they happily learned the mouth sound–referent links. The particular mouth sounds that we selected are actual sounds in human languages, although not in English. "Pss" is a phoneme in Greek, and some African languages use the click sound phonemically. This outcome leads to the additional question: Could *any* noise produced by the mouth—even a nonlanguage sound such as a bird chirp imitation—be attached to a referent? Perhaps, by 12 months of age, babies do privilege language and language-like sounds over other nonlinguistic sounds. This result contrasts with those of Woodward and Hoyne (1999), who found that 13-month-olds formed "hook-ups" between sounds and objects as readily as they did between words and objects. The discrepancy between our findings and those of Woodward and Hoyne (1999) are likely a function of the directions given to the babies in the two conditions. In our study, the mouth sounds and nonlinguistic sounds were embedded in linguistic frames identical to those used when labels are offered. For example, the experimenter said during training, "Elmo, look at the [boing]" or "Elmo, look at the psst." During test trials, the experimenter then requested the sounds in the same way. Woodward and Hoyne, in contrast, presented words and object noises in different frames. For words, they used typical naming frames—as in "Look, it's a toma"—whereas, for object noises, they did not use a labeling frame. Instead, they said, for example, "Look at this. [Squeak.] Yea, see it? [Squeak.]" It is difficult to conclude, therefore, that children hearing object noises recognized that the noises were being offered as *object names*. The same criticism carries forward to the test trials in the Woodward and Hoyne study. In the word condition, the experimenter asked the child, "Can you get the toma?" In the sound condition, however, the experimenter asked, "Can you get one of these?" and then triggered the noisemaker. Because the object (or mouth) noises were not presented in the same way as new labels, it is difficult to conclude that Woodward and Hoyne's 13-month-olds treated labels and noises equally—even though the same response (selecting the target object) resulted. This is tantamount to saying that children can pick the correct object at test for very different reasons. In one case (words), the children may have been selecting an object name; in the other case (noises), they may have been selecting an object by its *associate* rather than its name. Woodward and Hoyne's experiment does not allow them to discriminate between these possibilities. We do know (from the work of Waxman & Markow, 1995) that, in an object-categorization task, babies at this age respond differently when researchers offer them sentence frames that contain names (e.g., "Look, a car!") than they do when researchers offer them sentence frames that do not contain names (e.g., "Look at that!"). Only in the former condition do babies categorize the objects, indicating their sensitivity to frames containing labels. There is, therefore, good reason to believe that Woodward and Hoyne's 13-month-olds may not have been learning object *names* in the noises condition.

The present results suggest that the frequency with which an auditory stimulus is heard and the presence of overlapping cues are not the only ingredients for word learning. Rather, even by the tender age of 12 months, babies privilege language and language-like sounds. Balaban and Waxman (1996) reached the same conclusion with 9-month-olds. A word encouraged infants to form categories, whereas a tone matched in duration and pitch did not. Because we have not yet conducted a study with mouth sounds that are *not* found in human languages, we cannot conclusively claim that our data demonstrate language-specific effects. Nonetheless, it is clear that object noises do not work as labels. Not just any auditory signal will do.

Children with an Immature versus a Mature Principle of Reference.

Looking at these results as a whole, we can begin to paint a portrait of the child in possession of an immature principle of reference. These children differ from children with a mature principle of reference in several aspects. First, they use their own perspective on the word-learning situation almost to the exclusion of the speaker's perspective. That is, they link words to referents by attending primarily to what *they* find interesting in the environment (perceptual salience) rather than to what the speaker is indicating. Once in possession of a more mature principle of reference, children are able to shift their perspective to that of the speaker. When that occurs, we see a fundamentally different word learner, able to serve as an apprentice to the expert word learners around him or her. Second, immature word learners need far more support for word learning than do mature word learning. Unless they are exposed to numerous cues in alignment and frequent labeling and are allotted more time for the task, they will not learn new words. Finally, even immature word learners are willing to privilege language and language-like noises for attaching a label to a referent. The studies on mouth sounds and object noises will have to be conducted with 19-month-olds to see whether reference is more language specific than mouth specific in more experienced word learners.

Creating portraits of the immature and the mature word learner is only the beginning of the story. With a focus on *process* (parallel to that in Samuelson & Smith, 1998), it is important to ask what mechanisms cause the 12-month-old to abandon a focus on less-reliable cues (such as perceptual salience) in favor of a focus on more-reliable cues (such as social cues). On this account, how does the child move from learning one word a week to learning many words a day? And why does the child shift from needing multiple overlapping cues for word learning to needing only single subtle social cues such as eye gaze? Clearly there is much more work to be done, and we contend that it can best be accomplished within a framework that embraces the complexity of word learning: the emergentist coalition model.

THE ADVANTAGE OF THE EMERGENTIST COALITION FRAMEWORK

Why posit a hybrid model for word learning? Does a coalition model help us understand the complexity of word learning, or does it undermine any attempts at a parsimonious theory? For years scientists have endorsed one model of explanation over the others in an attempt to find the "smoking gun" in word-learning theory. Constraints/principles theories hold largely that the constraints for word learning are available at the outset. This approach addresses the issue of how children start the daunting task of word learning, but it offers little insight into how they mature into expert word learners. The theory is fundamentally nondevelopmental.

Social-pragmatic theories, on the other hand, eschew constraints, claiming that the rich social encounters in which the child engages guide word learning. As children become more socially sophisticated, they become better word learners who reach expert status under their apprenticeship to interactive adults. This theory helps us to understand how children, already beyond the fundamentals of word learning, become increasingly proficient, but it tells us little about infants' capacity for word learning at the start. These theories—which, like the constraints/principles theories are nondevelopmental—state that children are capable of utilizing sophisticated social cues from the outset. Our research clearly shows that this is not the case.

Finally, the newer connectionist and associative models of word learning contend that children start the task with "dumb attentional mechanisms" that are molded through experience into mature word-learning strategies. These theories provide a developmental account of both the starting points and the novice-to-expert shift but fail to solve the Quinean problem of helping children know what to look for in the vast array of possible word-to-world mappings. Surely the child does not randomly sample the numerous possible mappings before arriving at the right links between word and referent. This process would generate numerous errors that would become evident in early word production and comprehension. And this process, during which it might take years for a child to discover which of the many available cues were relevant for word learning, would surely stall word-learning progress.

This leaves us with theories that cover part, but not all, of the job of word learning. By putting these theories into a larger framework, however, we can account for both the character of early learning and the vocabulary spurt. Under the emergentist coalition model, children are surrounded from the outset by numerous cues for word learning. Using what Hirsh-Pasek and Golinkoff (1996) have called "guided distributional learning," children selectively attend to some of the information in the input over other information. For example, for children just beginning to play the word-learning game, bright colors, rather than texture, appear to be particularly salient in the environmental input; handling, rather than social eye gaze, is privileged in the social input. Further, at the outset, children seem to attend more to perceptual salience than to social cues even though both are available in the word-learning situation.

With the salient cues as their jumping-off point, infants—now known to be remarkably capable statisticians (Aslin, Saffran, & Newport, 1998; Saffran, Aslin, & Newport, 1996)—do a kind of distributional analysis of word-to-referent mappings. Imagine a child, for example, who hears the word "dog" uttered when the dog is running through the living room and again when the child's mother is talking about the dog on the phone as the child plays with a toy train. "Dog" could refer to either the dog or the toy train. Because the train is clearly the most salient object in the second instance, the child might well at first conclude that the train is the referent for the word "dog." But the selective part of guided distributional learning is supplemented with a distributional arm that helps to straighten out the misconception. Distributional analysis will help the child conclude that the dog, not the toy, is the referent. For example, after the child hears the word in the context of a dog sleeping, going for walk, and playing ball, the choices will be limited, and the child will be able to deduce the true referent. Notice that even distributional analysis on its own, however, will not be effective. Without being "guided" by selective attention to cues, the child may wrongly attribute the term to the dog parts or to the environment in which the dog was found. Whenever the dog appears, so, too, does the fur, the paw, and the floppy ears. Thus, it is a combination of selective cues and distributional cues across a number of available inputs that permits word learning. This selective input distinguishes the coalition model from the social and connectionist models that offer the child little mental word-learning preparation. Our model borrows the idea of selective input from constraints models and borrows the distributional analysis from the connectionists: This model is hybrid at its core.

Though the coalition model has a place for constraints or principles, unlike other constraint theories, it also supports development and change in those principles over time. The shifting of weights in the model, as children move from immature to mature learners, is demonstrated in the studies already discussed. Principles have some foundation at the outset but are not fully formed. They are emergent. The experiments previously described illustrate the emergent quality of word learning. Yet they fall short of explaining the mechanisms that account for the change from immature to mature word learners. It is, therefore, incumbent upon us to ask why the child would abandon a somewhat successful word-learning strategy in favor of a different strategy. To fulfill the promise of a true hybrid model, in short, we must do more than just characterize shifts in the weights of the cues used for word learning: We must explain them.

Our current research, which is attempting to address this very question, has produced data that suggest that young children must learn that social cues are more reliable than perceptual cues for linking word and referent. How might that occur? Let's return to the telephone example. The mother on the telephone is likely to say any number of words while the child is playing with the toy train. This stands in contrast to the dialogue that is likely to occur when the mother is looking directly at the toy as she labels the toy as "train." Notice that when the mother is on the phone, uttering various irrelevant names as the child plays with the target toy, the child may hold multiple wrong names for the object alongside the correct label. The only reliable or consistent label for the toy is provided when the mother looks at the toy while labeling it. That is, whenever she looks at the toy, she says, "train." The co-occurrence of these two cues provides a statistically consistent label. After numerous instances, the child should come to realize that the eye gaze that co-occurs with labeling is indeed a reliable cue that may be relevant for word learning. In the coalition model, we build a baby who attends to eye gaze from the outset of word learning but who does not use eye gaze in the service of word learning. The child has to learn through experience which cues facilitate the process of learning. Reliability of cues in the labeling context may therefore provide the catalyst that shifts the balance from weighting the cues of perceptual salience to weighting the more statistically reliable cue for labeling—social information. In this way, the child may come to rely on social cues and to use the speaker's intent to inform word-to-referent connections. Put simply, children will hear more word-referent pairings for the correct choice, and will be wrong less of the time, if they attend to social cues. Hence, children come to trust social cues. Attempts to model this process of cue reliability and validity may bear out the scenario painted here and begin to explain how principles of word learning emerge from the rather meager beginnings in the 12-month-old to the successful strategies of the 24-month-old (see Hollich, 2000).

The coalition model thus offers a way of characterizing the shift from novice to expert word learner and a potential mechanism for explaining that shift. It is a developmental model in which the child actively attends to the input and uses guided distributional learning to construct better and better strategies for word learning. Some people may deem this view unparsimonious, in that it offers, under one heading, multiple explanations for word learning. There is no competition among theories in this context, since no one theory can win out over the others. Instead, this hybrid model capitalizes on the many strengths of the different theories of word learning. Word-learning strategies emerge and change over the course of development as success strengthens some strategies over others. In reality, children are faced with multiple inputs that must be coordinated in language learning, and our theories must accommodate this richness. If we are to understand lexical development, we must abandon the search for a "smoking gun" explanation. We must appreciate instead that, as in other areas of development, the answers will come from complex theories of the ways in which children process varied inputs and of the interactions among these inputs over time.

ACKNOWLEDGMENTS

A grant from NSF (SBR9615391) and a grant from NICHHD (HD25455-07) to Kathy Hirsh-Pasek funded this research. The order of authorship of these authors is purely arbitrary. We thank Rebecca Brand, Camille Rocroi, He Len Chung, Michelle McKinney, and Beth Hennon for their insights and dedication to this project.

REFERENCES

Akhtar, N., Carpenter, M., & Tomasello, M. (1996). The role of discourse novelty in early word learning. *Child Development, 67,* 635–635.

Akhtar, N., & Tomasello, M. (1996). Twenty-four-month-old children learn words for absent objects and actions. *British Journal of Developmental Psychology, 14,* 79–93.

Aslin, R. N., Saffran, J. R., & Newport, E. L. (1998). Computation of conditional probability statistics by 8-month-old infants. *Psychological Science, 9,* 321–324.

Balaban, M. T., & Waxman, S. R. (1996). Do words facilitate categorization in 9-month-old infants? *Journal of Experimental Child Psychology, 64,* 3–26.

Baldwin, D. A. (1991). Infants' contribution to the achievement of joint reference. *Child Development, 62,* 875–890.

Baldwin, D. A. (1993). Infants' ability to consult the speaker for clues to word reference. *Journal of Child Language, 20,* 395–418.

Baldwin, D. A., Markman, E. M., Bill, B., Desjardins, R. N., Irwin, J. M., & Tidball, G. (1996). Infant's reliance on a social criterion for establishing word-object relations. *Child Development, 67,* 3135–3153.

Bloom, L. (1993). *The transition from infancy to language: Acquiring the power of expression.* Cambridge, England: Cambridge University press.

Butterworth, G., & Grover, L. (1990). Joint visual attention, manual pointing, and preverbal communication in human infancy. In M. Jeannerod (Ed.), *Attention and performance XIII* (pp. 605–624). Hillsdale, NJ: Erlbaum.

Clark, E. V. (1983). Meanings and concepts. In J. H. Flavell & E. M. Markman (Eds.), *Handbook of child psychology: Vol. 3. Cognitive development* (pp. 787–840). New York: John Wiley & Sons.

Dromi, E. (1987). *Early lexical development.* Cambridge, England: Cambridge University Press.

Evey, J. A., & Merriman, W. E. (1998). The prevalence and the weakness of an early name mapping reference. *Journal of Child Language, 25,* 121–147.

Fagan, J. (1971). Infant recognition memory for a series of visual stimuli. *Journal of Experimental Child Psychology, 11,* 244–250.

Fagan, J., Singer, L., Montic, J., & Shepard, P. (1986). Selective screening device for the early detection of normal or delayed cognitive development in infants at risk for later mental retardation. *Pediatrics, 78,* 1021–1206.

Gelman, R., & Greeno, J. G. (1989). On the nature of competence: Principles for understanding in a domain. In L. B. Resnick (Ed.), *Knowing and learning: Essays in honor of Robert Glaser* (pp. 125–186). Hillsdale, NJ: Erlbaum.

Golinkoff, R. M., Hirsh-Pasek, K., Bailey, L. M., & Wenger, N. R. (1992). Young children and adults use lexical principles to learn new nouns. *Developmental Psychology, 28,* 99–108.

Golinkoff, R. M., Hirsh-Pasek, K., Cauley, K. M., & Gordon, L. (1987). The eyes have it: Lexical and syntactic comprehension in a new paradigm. *Journal of Child Language, 14,* 23–45.

Golinkoff, R. M., Hirsh-Pasek, K., Hollich, G. (in press). Emerging cues for word learning. In B. MacWhinney (Ed.), *The emergence of language.* Hillsdale, NJ: Erlbaum.

Golinkoff, R. M., Mervis, C. B., & Hirsh-Pasek, K. (1994). Early object labels: The case for a developmental lexical principles framework. *Journal of Child Language, 21,* 125–155.

Golinkoff, R. M., Shuff-Bailey, M., Olguin, R., & Ruan, W. (1995). Young children extend novel words at the basic level: Evidence for the principle of categorical scope. *Developmental Psychology, 31,* 494–507.

Hirsh-Pasek, K., & Golinkoff, R. M. (1996). *The origins of grammar: Evidence from early language comprehension.* Cambridge, MA: MIT Press.

Hollich, G. (2000). *Making the implicit, explicit: A computational account of word learning.* Paper presented to ICIS conference, Brighton, England.

Hollich, G. (1999). *Mechanisms of word learning: A computational model.* Unpublished dissertation, Temple University.

Hollich, G., Hirsh-Pasek, K., & Golinkoff, R. (1998). Introducing the 3-D intermodal preferential looking paradigm: A new method to answer an age-old question. In C. Rovee-Collier (Ed.), *Advances in infancy research* (Vol. 12, pp. 355–373). Norwood, NJ: Ablex.

Karmiloff-Smith, A. (1992). *Beyond modularity.* Cambridge, MA: MIT Press.

Markman, E. M. (1989). *Categorization and naming in children: Problems of induction.* Cambridge, MA: MIT Press.

Markman, E. M., & Hutchinson, J. E. (1984). Children's sensitivity to constraints on word meaning: Taxonomic versus thematic relations. *Cognitive Psychology, 16,* 1–27.

Markman, E. M., & Wachtel, G. F. (1988). Children's use of mutual exclusivity to constrain the meaning of words. *Cognitive Psychology, 20,* 121–157.

Merriman, W. E., & Bowman, L. L. (1989). The mutual exclusivity bias in children's word learning. *Monographs of the Society for Research in Child Development, 54* (Serial No. 220).

Mervis, C. B., & Bertrand, J. (1994). Acquisition of the novel name-nameless category (N3C) principle. *Child Development, 65,* 1646–1663.

Mervis, C. B., Golinkoff, R. M., & Bertrand, J. (1994). Two-year-olds readily learn multiple labels for the same basic-level category. *Child Development, 65,* 1163–1177.

Nelson, K. (1988). Constraints on word learning? *Cognitive Development, 3,* 221–246.

Nelson, K. (1996). *Language in cognitive development.* New York: Cambridge University Press.

Newcombe, N. S., & Huttenlocher, J. (in press). *Making space: An interactionist account of development in the spatial domain.* Cambridge, MA: MIT Press.

Pinker, S. (1994). *The language instinct: How the mind creates language.* New York: William Morrow.

Plunkett, K. (1997). Theories of language acquisition. *Trends in Cognitive Science, 1* (4), 146–153.

Quine, W. V. O. (1960). *Word and object.* Cambridge, MA: MIT Press.

Saffran, J. R., Aslin, R. N., & Newport, E. L. (1996). Statistical learning by 8-month-old infants. *Science, 274* (5294) 1926–1928.

Samuelson, L. R., & Smith, L. B. (1998). Memory and attention make smart word learning: An alternative account of Akhtar, Carpenter, and Tomasello. *Child Development, 69,* 94–104.

Smith, L. B. (1995). Self-organizing processes in learning to learn words: Development is not induction. In C. A. Nelson (Ed.), *Basic and applied perspectives on learning, cognition, and development: The Minnesota Symposia on Child Psychology* (Vol. 28, pp. 1–32). Mahwah, NJ: Erlbaum.

Spelke, E. S. (1990). Principles of object perception. *Cognitive Science, 14,* 29–56.

Tomasello, M., & Barton, M. (1994). Learning words in non-ostensive contexts. *Developmental Psychology, 30,* 639–650.

Tomasello, M., Strosberg, R., & Akhtar, N. (1996). Eighteen-month-old children learn words in non-ostensive contexts. *Journal of Child Language, 23,* 157–176.

Waxman, S. R., & Kosowski, T. D. (1990). Nouns mark category relations: Toddlers' and preschoolers' word-learning biases. *Child Development, 61,* 1461–1473.

Waxman, S. R., & Markow, D. B. (1995). Words as invitations to form categories: Evidence from 12- to 13-month-old infants. *Cognitive Psychology, 29,* 257–302.

Woodward, A. L., & Hoyne, K. L. (1999). Infants' learning about words and sounds in relation to objects. *Child Development, 70,* 65–72.

Woodward, A. L., Markman, E. M., & Fitzsimmons, C. M. (1994). Rapid word learning in 13- and 18-month-olds. *Developmental Psychology, 30,* 553–566.

CHAPTER 7

Counterpoint Commentary

LOIS BLOOM: What Can We Take for Granted in Word Learning?

One thing that all of the contributors to this volume seem to agree on and that I think we should be grateful for is that *it is a child* who acquires a language and *not* a device, as the world according to MIT would have it. Each of us believes in the importance of the child and the child's development and learning for acquiring a vocabulary of words. That said, it is also clear that our views differ in a number of respects. Our theories differ in focus and perspective and, even more important, in the *mechanism* we propose for explaining word learning. Each of us emphasizes a different kind of mechanism—each of us focuses on a different *aspect* of the word-learning scenario—as the driving force for acquiring a vocabulary of words. And each of us seems to take something in the others' theories for granted.

Focus and Perspective

First I cannot help but note that I am the only one represented in this volume who listens to children learning to talk—who actively watches children's spontaneous acts of expression and interpretation as opposed to observing their responses to manipulations of word-learning events in an experiment. Children's spontaneous behaviors have by and large been ignored or, even worse, dismissed. But, I suggest, with all due respect, that we ignore children's spontaneous behaviors—what they *do* in the everyday events of their lives—at the peril of the theories that we construct to explain those behaviors. What children do in their activities of daily living has everything to do with learning words. Children do not just wait around for *other* people to construct the word-learning scenario for them. Not on your life. Instead, *they create the word-learning process themselves*. The words they learn are words *they* want to learn, the words *they* need to learn. They are the words that are relevant to what *they* have in mind. Experiments can illuminate features of word learning that may be difficult to isolate in spontaneous behaviors. Sometimes, however, experiments begin to assume a life of their own and become increasingly removed from the real-life processes entailed in word learning. A word-learning experiment is a

kind of performance, a demonstration of what children can do in different circumstances. And, more often than not, children are smart enough to learn to
play the game. We need to ask ourselves, however, whether learning to play the
game captures the important variables in real-life word-learning scenarios. All
of this is to say that we need as much information as we can possibly get about
how children go about the business of word learning, and *we cannot take children's everyday behaviors for granted.*

In addition to the differences in the kinds of data that we, as researchers, use
to build our theories, we also differ in the starting points for our inquiries into
how children learn words. In my mind, the clearest difference is whether we begin with the child or with the other people in the child's social context. On one
hand, children cannot be separated from their experiences with other persons—
all social contact is somehow represented in the child's mind, and some might
even say that all social contact takes place in the child's mind. On the same
hand, and most assuredly, children acquire the words that they learn from the
world around them—from what other people say to them and to each other.
Words come from other persons, plain and simple, in anybody's theory. But that
said, and now getting to the other hand, whose act is the learning of words any-
way? And that is where we differ.

Socially based theories give major responsibility for word learning to the
adult, whose job, presumably, is to get words into the child's head. More recent
social theories take into account the child's ability to "read" another person's
pragmatic signals as clues to the person's intentions, even suggesting that it is
not until a child is able to do so—to see another's point of view—that the child
is ready for serious word learning. The two seem to be correlated: Children begin to learn a vocabulary of words in earnest at about the time that they give evidence that they appreciate what other people have in mind. But that is the only
real connection, a simple correlation: Both things seem to happen at about the
same time. The causal connection proposed is not the one that I would favor.
More likely, children are able to detect the word-learning cues offered to them
in an experiment because they have begun to learn words and what words do.

The result of more than a generation of research in infant cognition and emotion is the impressive evidence that very young infants give, already in the 1st
few months of life, that they can take another person's feelings and even something of another's thoughts into account in their own behaviors (see L. Bloom,
1993, for review). Reading other people's intentions is not a late development—coming midway through the 2nd year—that triggers word learning.
Instead, it is a gradual development that begins in early infancy and evolves
along with many other language-related behaviors that emerge in infancy for
language learning. The social experiences that contribute to language learning
begin virtually at birth and, to be sure, *we cannot take a child's social experience for granted.*

Mechanisms for Word Learning

The social context; neural networks; association processes; and lexically specific constraints, principles, and biases are *mechanisms outside of the child's intentionality,* outside of the child's control—*external* to the child. One might argue that these mechanisms are, instead, internal because they are presumably "in the child's mind." However, because they are external to the child's agency, they are external to the control that the child exerts over the word-learning process. Associations and neural connections have to figure into anybody's theory. But as mechanisms, they are removed from conscious action, and, although *we cannot take neural connections and associations for granted,* such mechanisms are not enough.

And so we come to word-learning constraints, principles, biases, default assumptions, and the like, which received a great deal of attention in the word-learning literature of the 1990s. An unfortunate myopia plagued studies of word-learning constraints at the beginning of the decade, due primarily, I argue, to the dependence on Quine's fictitious word for a fictitious rabbit, spoken in a fictitious language, by an "hitherto untouched peoples" (1960, p. 28). The result was almost a decade of research driven more by the "logic" of Quine's dilemma than by the psychology of the young language-learning child. More recently, the welcome marriage of constraints theories to pragmatics by the architects of the word-learning constraints position, Ellen Markman (with Amanda Woodward), and Roberta Golinkoff and Kathy Hirsh-Pasek (this volume), has happily contextualized principles of word learning in the larger contexts in which real words are actually learned. We *cannot take for granted the pragmatic cues to a word's meaning*—children's word learning depends on them.

The question that has been posed in the past about word-learning principles remains, however: To what extent are principles, biases, default assumptions, and the like explanatory rather than merely *descriptive* of the results of the process? I have proposed that "linguistic assumptions acquired early in language learning can be expected to 'bootstrap' subsequent language learning . . . [but] they are assumptions the child comes to as a consequence of learning language" (L. Bloom, 1993, p. 245; see also, e.g., L. Bloom, 1981). The original idea that constraints on word learning were innately determined has, by now, been largely abandoned. But one assumption that took the place of that notion is that the constraints (or principles) are *developmental*—that they develop in conjunction with or (as I would argue) because of word learning. As such, they succeed in describing at least some of what words do: For example, words stand for shared items of experience; words pick out items relative to each other, to contrast one item with another; and words bring together items that go together with the same name. Learning these things is what it means to learn words.

Similarly, Clark's (1990) principles of contrast and conventionality are two defining features of language, and to learn a language is to learn these two principles. For example, contrast has to do with learning words, because that is *what words do:* they mark contrasting states of affairs. Thus, it is not at all clear that the word-learning principles (constraints or biases) can exist prior to or independently of language learning. *As a description of word learning, however, constraints and principles cannot be taken for granted.*

The Child as Mechanism

The theory I have proposed takes the child's contents of mind very seriously: Representations in consciousness are a child's intentional states, and intentionality is the mechanism for language acquisition, in general, and word learning, in particular. Children's cognitive development has many facets, not the least of which are the symbolic capacity, conceptual structure, and concepts that emerge in the first 2 years of life to provide the substrate for language learning. These aspects of infant cognition have been stressed in research since the 1970s, and they are the results—the products, if you will—of the processes of a child's thinking. This was Piaget's original insight, by the way—a fact about his theory that has been forgotten or *is* perhaps taken for granted—that all understanding is the result of the forms of active thought. I have focused on the relationship between what the child has in mind—what the child's active thought processes *are about*—and what is going on in the context of the everyday events in which the child is acting and interacting. And I have proposed three principles—relevance, discrepancy, and elaboration—as generalizations that describe this dynamic relationship between intentional states and context for word learning. The child's intentionality will have to embrace attributions of the intentional states of other persons, to be sure. But it is the *child's* intentionality that is primary, fundamental, and most basic for word learning. *Intentionality and the child's cognition cannot be taken for granted.*

Returning to the question that begins this commentary—what can we take for granted in word learning?—the answer is *none of the things* that have been emphasized in this book can be taken for granted. Each of us has argued persuasively in behalf of a piece of the puzzle, a piece of the process of how children learn words. Each of us is right in what we have chosen to focus on, and whether one is more right than the others remains to be seen. But it seems to me that we have arrived at a good place as a consequence of this last quarter-century of inquiry into how children learn words—we have at least laid out the playing field. We will have to wait and see how others who come after us will take the inquiry into the 21st century, and *let's hope that none of what we have emphasized here will be taken for granted.*

LINDA B. SMITH: Avoiding Associations When It's Behaviorism You Really Hate

"Association of ideas" is an unfashionable term—much used in the 19th century, it has almost disappeared in this one—but the time may have come to put it back to work again. The reason for its disappearance was the doubt, earlier, whether ideas and thought exist at all. We have seen that Thorndike raised this question about cats; John B. Watson took it further, and suggested that human thinking is only a series of tiny muscular contractions, each contraction providing a stimulus to the next one, so that in thinking one is really talking to oneself under one's breath. In that case ideas would not exist. . . . We now know however that ideas do exist . . . and we also know that connections can be set up between them. (D. O. Hebb, *Textbook of Psychology*)

The chapters in this volume present wonderful insights into early word learning. Many of the authors remark on babies' attention to and learning about relations—relations between forms and referents, between speakers' actions and speakers' intentions, between direction of gaze and objects, between syntactic cues and meanings. They use such words as "links," "maps," "correspondence," "predicts," and "expectations" in their discussions of what babies know about learning words. They avoid references to "associates" and "association." Among cognitive developmentalists "association" is still a very unfashionable term—a term to be raised only if the purpose is to dismiss it.

My fellow contributors to this volume offer three reasons for running from associative accounts: Associative learning implies that (1) contiguity is everything, (2) we can learn anything, and (3) we have, more or less, the mental lives of rats. They are wrong. Associative learning implies none of this. My fellow authors confuse associative learning with the worst of American behaviorism. As Hebb (1949) notes in his history, associative learning was on the other side of the behaviorist firestorm. It went underground in the behaviorist heyday and was at the vanguard of the cognitive revolution (e.g., Hebb; Minsky & Papert, 1969). Radical behaviorists hated the idea of associations. Why? Because associative learning is about ideas, about internal mental events, about the processes that *make* cognition.

Here, then, is the take-home message: Today's associative learning is not your father's behaviorism. Associative mechanisms do not imply what developmentalists take them to imply. Indeed, way too much is known about associative processes—from neuroscience, from behavioral experiments, from mathematical and computational modeling—for reflexive rejections to have a place in developmental discussions of mechanism any longer (see also Kelly & Martin, 1994). Although there is not enough space in this brief commentary to provide even a partial tutorial, I present three brief lessons about associations, each motivated by my colleagues' confusions. I encourage readers to pursue a more thorough study of the field.

Three Lessons

Predictability and Causality. Classical conditioning is a basic form of associative learning. It consists of learning the relation between pairs of sensory events, one of which, the unconditioned stimulus (UCS), has a preexisting connection to a measurable response. Classical conditioning is not the only form of associative learning, and it is *not* a candidate model for word learning. Nonetheless, it is useful to consider just what knowledge organisms acquire in this most rudimentary form of learning. What is learned is the predictive relation between the conditioned stimulus, or CS (the neutral stimulus), and the UCS (the consequential sensory event), *whatever that predictive relation is.* If the CS reliably precedes the UCS by a short time, organisms learn that the CS predicts that the UCS will occur after a short delay; if the CS reliably precedes the UCS by a long time, organisms learn that the CS predicts that the UCS will occur after a long delay. If the UCS precedes the CS (backward conditioning), organisms learn not to expect the UCS to occur immediately after the CS occurs. In brief, the evidence of the past three-quarters of a century shows that just about any set pattern of paired experiences leads to learning and what, precisely, is learned is the predictive relation between the cues. Indeed, classical conditioning is so much about making predictions, about expectations, that the Rescorla and Wagner model (1972) of classical conditioning forms the basis for several successful formal models of human causal reasoning (see Cheng & Holyoak, 1995). Here is the lesson: *Associative learning, even in its most rudimentary form, is neither about contiguity nor about counting the pairings of events in experience; it is about prediction and forming expectations.*

Attention and Constraints. Because attention is very much at the heart of all forms of learning, it is a centerpiece of several of the chapters in this volume. Simply, we learn about what we attend to, and we learn *what to attend to.* Over the past quarter century, considerable theoretical and empirical work in cognitive psychology has yielded a nearly unified theory of the associative basis of attentional learning. The foundational ideas are those of Rescorla and Wagner (1972); Mackintosh (1975); Shepard, Hovland, and Jenkins (1961); and Medin and Schaffer (1978). The mathematical unification of these ideas into a single theory is gaining momentum through the work of Nosofsky (1986) and Kruschke (1992, 1999). The central idea is simple but powerful: As organisms learn associations among cues and outcomes, they also learn which cues to attend to. The power of these ideas as realized in current formal theories is evident in the success of these theories in explaining (in fine experimental detail) phenomena from many divergent fields and paradigms. The associative mechanisms behind attentional learning instantiated in, for example, Kruschke's models of adult category learning (e.g., 1992, 1999) constitute the accepted explanation of attentional learning in psychology—at least they do outside of developmental psychology. There is simply no equally specified or empirically supported contender of how organisms—including people—shift attention to task-relevant properties. Thus, for *any* of the attentional phenomena that are part of early word learning, attentional learning via associative mechanisms is, prima facie, a candidate explanation, one to be dismissed only when an *equally specified* alternative is offered that can explain and unify as many phenomena.

Science seeks unified explanations. It is important, then, that attentional learning via associative mechanisms may explain word-learning phenomena beyond the shape bias. Consider the recent finding that words become special in their ability to refer (Namy & Waxman, 1998; Woodward & Hoyne, 1999). Recall that Namy and Waxman presented 18- and 26-month-olds with a triad of objects: an exemplar and two choice objects. In one condition, the experimenter named the exemplar object with a novel name and, using that name, asked the child to select among the two choice objects. In the second condition, the experimenter referred to the exemplar with a hand gesture rather than with a spoken name and, using the gesture, asked the child to select among the two choice objects. The younger children, 18-month-olds, chose taxonomically in both conditions. Apparently, for younger children, any associate of an object can work to push attention to similar kinds. The older children, in contrast, chose taxonomically only in the name condition; they responded randomly when signaled to make a choice by a gesture.

Some contributors to this volume have suggested that this fact shows that, at least for older children, word learning cannot be *merely* associative learning. If it were, they reason, the older children would associate the gesture with the object. This reasoning is flawed, however, because associative learning does not imply that any cue can be linked with any other cue. Indeed, a powerful (and well-studied) phenomenon in associative learning—blocking—provides a mechanistic explanation of Namy and Waxman's (1998; and Woodward & Hoyne's, 1999) results. Blocking is the name given to the following powerful fact about associative learning: If one already has learned a cue that reliably predicts an outcome, it is harder to learn a *new* cue that predicts the same outcome (see Mackintosh, 1975; Kruschke, 1999). In terms of Namy and Waxman's result, an already learned link between naming and the object of the speaker's attention *blocks* the learning of a link between a gesture and the object of the speaker's attention. Think of what the mere fact of blocking means: Associative learning based on the regularities in one's previous experiences *alters* what regularities will be learned in the future.

Associative learning is not the creation of isolated connections between stimulus events. The formation of initially simple associations *changes* what is attended to and, in so doing, changes what will be learned in the future. This is where the significance of a learned shape bias lies. And here is the lesson: *Learning is a historical process that leads to increasingly constrained destinies. Unbiased associative mechanisms become biased learning mechanisms.*

Universality and Specificity.   A number of phenomena, such as blocking, have been observed in a variety of learning domains and in a number of species (see Kruschke, 1999). This commonality suggests similar learning principles and a similarity of mechanisms both across domains within a single species and across different species. This does *not* constitute a weakness—a fatal flaw—in associative learning as a candidate mechanism for children's word learning. The argument that associative learning cannot be the basis of children's word learning because rats do not learn words and the related argument that associative learning, *if* involved, is unimportant because it cannot explain the differences between people and rats are both profoundly wrongheaded. Using associative mechanisms to explain word learning in children no more implies that rats should be able to learn words than the universality of the DNA code implies that we should have rat bodies. And the fact that the DNA code for protein synthesis is universal despite the fact that rats and people have very different bodies does not make the DNA code ipso facto uninteresting and unimportant in explaining either the differentiation of organs within a single body or bodily differences across species. In both cases—the same DNA code or the same associative mechanisms—the uniqueness of the outcome depends exquisitely on the particulars in the *history* of the processes and the cascading consequences within that history. In other words, what matters is development. I offer two striking examples of associative learning in developmental process.

The first example concerns suckling behavior in newborn rats. Shortly after birth and despite the severe immaturity of the sensory and motor system, the newborn rat moves itself to its mother's ventrum and suckles. This behavior—crucial to survival—is created by a complex chain of events that includes classical conditioning. First, research has shown that the scent of amniotic fluid on the mother's ventrum (deposited when the mother licks the pups and then herself after birth) is a crucial cue. Newborn rats fail to attach to nipples if the ventrum and nipples are washed (Teicher & Blass, 1976, 1977). Second, this scent cue is learned. Pedersen and Blass (1982) introduced an arbitrary smell (lemon) into the amniotic sac two days before birth. In this condition, rat pups did not suckle in the context of amniotic fluid but did so in the presence of a lemon scent. Third, recent research shows that the scent cue gains its power to initiate suckling through classical conditioning (Ronca, Abel, & Alberts, 1996; Abel, Ronca, & Alberts, 1998). The CS, the smell, is linked to the UCS, compression, through the birthing process. Abel, Ronca, and Alberts term this form of perinatal conditioning "intrinsic," because the associations learned are derived from the functional properties of birth. It is by virtue of the natural sequence of concordant events constituting the birth process that the conditioning occurs and that the congenital capability of suckling so crucial to survival appears.

The second example of how universal mechanisms lead to specific (and constrained) outcomes concerns imprinting and, in particular, a model of imprinting offered by O'Reilly and Johnson (1994). O'Reilly and Johnson used a recurrent network composed of the most general and universal processes: Hebbian learning, excitatory connections, and lateral inhibition. None of these is a prescription for imprinting or for its sensitive period, and each is evident everywhere in the study of brains of all species—the "common stuff" of brains. The experiences that O'Reilly and Johnson gave the network are also "common stuff"—looking at individual objects presented one at a time for varying durations, experiences that might correspond to 10 minutes or 1 hour of viewing the same object. That is all there is to the model. But the outcome of these experiences is preferential recognition of the first object seen and the emergence of a self-terminating sensitive period. Quite simply, if early experience consists of an object that persists for sufficient duration, the strength of that bias cannot ever be overcome; through lateral inhibition and recurrent connections, it maintains itself. If, in contrast, early experience consists of sufficiently many different nonpersisting objects, no preference emerges and the possibility of developing such a preference is lost. The point of this example—as in the example of suckling in baby rats and as in the associative-learning account of the shape bias—is that something special can develop out of the particular history of activity of general learning processes that subserve other specializations.

Here, then, is the third lesson: *Associative learning operates in particular contexts, as parts of particular causal chains and particular natural histories, and yields specific outcomes.*

A Note about Levels of Explanation

These three lessons are profoundly important for evaluating the different accounts in this volume. They mean that it is possible to build an associative-learning version of each of the alternative explanations—the social-pragmatic, the constraints, the many-principles, the active-child accounts. These associative-learning accounts would be implementation versions of their parent explanations, versions that mechanistically specify the undefined terms of "links" and "maps" and "predicts" and "expects" that fill the parent accounts. Specifying such implementation versions of the other accounts in this volume is a useful goal, since each account captures real and important truths about children; about language; and about how children become, in such a very short time, truly prodigious learners of words. But, at present, each is currently underspecified, couched in undefined folk-psychological terms. Because of this, none is a direct competitor of the associative-learning account; however, each could, instead, be realized in terms of associative mechanisms. Put another way, the associative-learning account resides at a different level of explanation than do the other accounts in this volume. It seeks to go behind folk-psychological terms to specify the processes and mechanisms out of which "beliefs" are made.

AMANDA L. WOODWARD:
There Is No Silver Bullet for Word Learning:
Why Monolithic Accounts Miss the Mark

Because of its sheer complexity, language acquisition is a stunning achievement. Far from being a unitary phenomenon, language is the coming together of such varied streams as phonological structure, syntax, social and communicative knowledge, and conceptual structure. Nowhere is this more evident than in development, where the separate streams can be seen to emerge and converge. Because of the nature of words and the nature of the problem posed by learning them, word learning embodies the complexity of language.

Words are inherently multifaceted. They are social signals; therefore, understanding the behavior of other people is an important component of understanding language for adults. The fact that words are also units in a formal system sets them critically apart from other kinds of social behaviors or signals. Words are symbols that stand for concepts. In this respect, they have a life of their own; for example, adults can understand them perfectly well when they occur outside of social interactions. The same may well be true for 1- and 2-year-olds, who—many studies have found—can learn and respond to words played over audio speakers (e.g., Hirsh-Pasek & Golinkoff, 1996; Naigles, 1990; Schafer & Plunkett, 1998; Werker, Cohen, Lloyd, Casasolo, & Stager, 1998). The link between words and concepts means that conceptual structure is a critical component of word learning. Each of these elements is equally critical to an understanding of words. The absence of any one of them is grounds for questioning whether a form really is a word. Debates about the status of potential word forms that lack one of these aspects illustrate this fact. The topics of these debates have included, for example, a lack of understanding of the referential nature or communicative function of words, as has been argued to occur in autism or in animal "word learning"; a lack of the correct underlying conceptual structure, as may occur with complexive terms or performatives; and the lack of an arbitrary, formal relationship between word and referent, as in early iconic forms or prelinguistic gestures.

A child learning words draws on their multifaceted nature. Words seldom come accompanied by an explicit account of their meanings. On the contrary, learners must puzzle out the meaning of a new word based on the available evidence. Words usually come embedded in rich linguistic social and physical contexts, providing some of the evidence that learners may recruit. It is clear that "expert" word learners, preschool-aged children, draw on these sources of information in word learning. Fifteen years of research has shown, moreover, that preschool-aged children have a set of default assumptions that inform their hypotheses about word meaning. These default assumptions, as well as the child's knowledge about syntax and communication, serve to constrain the problem space in word learning. Understanding the development of word learning, then, requires understanding how each of these sources of constraint arises. How does linguistic and social knowledge emerge and become recruited for word learning? Where do default assumptions come from? What is the nature of prelinguistic conceptual structure?

Several current accounts are at variance with this view of word learning. They propose, one way or another, that word learning is a monolithic phenomenon, which can be explained primarily in terms of only one kind of factor. One approach is to argue that only one of the many factors involved in word learning really matters. Another is to argue that all of the seemingly disparate factors that contribute to word learning are really instances of the same underlying factor or process. Both of these approaches threaten a comprehensive understanding of how children learn words.

A Single Root for Word Learning

The first approach is evident in chapter 5, where Akhtar and Tomasello make a strong argument that social-communicative understanding is the one critical factor behind word learning. While the authors grant, very reasonably, that other factors eventually contribute to word learning, they argue that these are "ancillary to the fundamental social-communicative process." They make this argument both definitionally, in terms of what words really are at the heart of it, and developmentally, in terms of the way in which words are first acquired. Yet it is not clear that this single-factor model works in either case. Words are, as I have noted, inherently multifaceted. If a baby had a "word" that she understood or used as a communicative signal but did not understand it as conceptually grounded or as a part of a formal symbol system, we would not be comfortable calling it a "word." Early nonlinguistic gestures are a case in point (see Petitto, 1988).

From a developmental standpoint, it is clear that multiple factors contribute to word learning from the very beginning. Consider an example: At the zoo, a father points toward an animal and says, "A bear!" His intention in uttering "bear" is to draw the baby's attention to that particular animal. A baby who is a skilled reader of intentions might thus hypothesize that "bear" named the specific intention of the moment (drawing attention to an item). If this were the case, then baby words would be very different from adult words, because the baby would not yet understand that particular words are independent of the particular communicative intentions they are used to convey. But, as it turns out, babies almost never make this error. Instead, they interpret "bear" as a category term, thus pulling away from the specific communicative interaction in which the word was introduced. They extend "bear" to other animals, not to other interactions, of the same kind. To do so, babies must draw on their category knowledge. This is true from the very beginning. Complexive terms and performatives may sometimes occur, but, as Huttenlocher and Smiley (1987) demonstrated, these are not typical of babies' first words. The vast majority of the time, young 1-year-olds use words as category terms. Clearly, more than an understanding of communicative intent must contribute to word learning from the beginning.

Even at the dawn of word learning, at 12–16 months of age, babies bring to the problem not only social knowledge but also an appreciation of the link between conceptual categories and names, as well as (the evidence suggests) assumptions about likely referents and the mutual exclusivity of forms. In fact, as it happens, there is more evidence for the use of the noun-category bias and default assumptions in word learning by babies under 18 months of age than there is for the use of social cues. By the time babies turn 2 years old, the age at which Akhtar and Tomasello's data (chapter 5) most clearly demonstrate the role of social knowledge in word learning—there is also clear evidence that babies, like older learners, have default assumptions about the likely meanings of new words and that they understand a number of the important formal features of words, including the fact that they constitute a distinct system in which different forms contrast in meaning and in which different form classes have different likely meanings. Each of these factors has been found to contribute to word learning in 2-year-olds. Therefore, at no point in early development are infants solely dependent on social-communicative knowledge in word learning. Multiple factors contribute from the start, which suggests that multiple factors are necessary to break into word learning. If babies had only the ability to read intentions, they might never successfully figure out what words do.

Questioning why word learning begins when it does, at the end of the 1st year of life, Akhtar and Tomasello conclude that the answer lies in developing social knowledge. This is certainly part of the answer, but within this same timeframe cognition is blooming across domains. There are developments in conceptual categories, problem-solving abilities, causal reasoning, and sensitivity to regularities in the speech patterns of their community. It could therefore be countered that this new richness in social, cognitive, and linguistic resources causes word learning to begin when it does.

Seemingly Distinct Factors Reduce to a Single Root

A second approach to the idea of word learning as a monolithic phenomenon is to attempt a unified account of the various factors that are at work. This is the approach of Hirsh-Pasek, Golinkoff, and Hollich in chapter 6. The authors begin by noting the diversity of information that children bring to bear in word learning. The goal of these authors is to create a single theory that can account for this diversity. As their account plays out, however, important aspects of this diversity are lost. The authors focus on how infants learn to select among the many environmental stimuli—potential "cues"—that might be relevant for word meaning. To start, the only factor that distinguishes cues is salience; some aspects of the environment (bright colors, perhaps) catch babies' attention more than others. Infants select the right cues by distributional learning over multiple repetitions of a word. Babies come to focus on the cues that occur most reliably with the referent. This leads infants to come to attend more to some cues (e.g., gaze) than to others (e.g., the salience of the potential referent). That is, specific constraints on word learning (e.g., the use of social cues) are proposed as the product of general process learning that occurs in the context of learning about words.

This is essentially the account that Smith formulates in chapter 3 to explain the shape bias and the emergence of other expectations about word meaning. The prior contingencies of word learning shape children's reactions to words, thus yielding systematic expectations about form-referent relationships—for example, the expectations that count nouns are extended to items with the same shape and that mass nouns are extended to items made of the same substance. In Smith's account, this claim is quite concrete: Children's word-learning abilities at any point in time are literally the sum total of their prior word-learning experiences.

It is certainly true that associative learning is a powerful engine of development, and it could well account for many of the expectations that children bring to bear in word learning. My concern is with the claim that the relevant knowledge for word learning derives *only* from the prior contingencies of word learning. This claim disregards the role of knowledge and other sources of constraint that arise outside of the word-learning arena. There is little debate about the fact that the concepts and assumptions that babies apply in word learning develop. The question of interest and controversy is how they develop. Do they develop based on word-learning experience alone? Or are they the product of development across contexts? If the latter is the case, then some sources of constraint could be in place at the start of word learning and could, therefore, help to get word learning off the ground. Here are three examples.

First, before infants learn words, certain aspects of the environment may stand out to them as readily extractable, informative, and useful units of analysis. Objects may constitute such a unit, as is evidenced by the literature on infants' object perception. Therefore, babies may favor objects in word learning, which involves the task of linking units with units. Imai and Gentner (1997) illustrated this in a study in which Japanese-speaking and English-speaking babies found complex objects compelling units in a word-learning task.

Second, prelinguistic infants understand aspects of human behavior and communication. This is Akhtar and Tomasello's point in chapter 5: Prelinguistic knowledge about attentional states and intentions in other people provides an important source of initial constraint in word learning. Prelinguistic infants follow eye gaze and points and use pointing to direct others' attention. This helps to explain why gaze and other attentional behaviors are "salient" to young word learners. They are salient because babies understand something about the relationship of these behaviors to attentional states in other people. Thus, gaze may not begin as equivalent to any other potential cue in word learning (such as the salience of objects), but it may carry with it special significance. This possibility gains support from the findings that I outline in chapter 4. Near the onset of word learning, at 13 months of age, infants use gaze and pointing to inform word learning. This very early attention to relevant features indicates prior learning, but it is learning that occurs before infants have a history of word learning under their belts.

Third, infants can form categories at various levels of abstraction (Mandler & McDonough, 1993; Quinn, 1987). By 1 year of age, babies use categories in such nonlinguistic contexts as making inductive inferences about shared properties. Waxman and Markow's (1995) work has shown that infants as young as 12 months of age understand the link between words and categories. This is well before infants have the extent of word-learning experience that Smith describes in chapter 3 as being critical to setting up word-category relationships. Moreover, babies continue to learn about categories outside of word-learning contexts, and they bring this knowledge to bear in word learning. A recent finding by Goodman, McDonough, and Brown (1998) illustrated this point: In these studies, 2-year-olds inferred the meaning of a new word based on the semantic context and their knowledge about kinds. For example, having heard "Mommy feeds the ferret," babies inferred that a ferret is a kind of animal—that is, something that eats.

Of course, it could be argued that the knowledge that provides a starting basis for word learning is the result of the same associative-learning processes that Smith describes in chapter 3 as operating for word learning. This may be the case, but then what we need is an account of how knowledge gained in different domains and learning contexts interacts. Here we could enter a debate about the right level of analysis. Will such an account be possible at the level of simple associations; will we have to jump up to the level of existing knowledge structures; or, as Bloom argues in chapter 2, is even this level inadequate to explain the integration of conceptual structure and the intentions of the child in word learning? At this point, our best accounts are at the middle level—that is, the level of knowledge and concepts.

Conclusion

Each author in this book is onto a critical piece of the story. I agree completely with Bloom's argument in chapter 2 that children are active agents in their own word learning. What needs to be determined is the tools they have at their disposal to achieve this learning. Akhtar and Tomasello are certainly right in positing in chapter 5 that one very important tool is social-communicative knowledge. Smith is certainly correct in positing in chapter 3 that another critical tool is the ability to derive expectations based on prior learning episodes. Hirsh-Pasek, Golinkoff, and Hollich rightly point out in chapter 6 the need for accounts of how word-learning abilities develop.

The problem arises from the natural tendency to search for a simple cause and to stretch it to account for as much of the data as possible. This approach will not succeed for word learning. Learning a word involves tying together different kinds of knowledge—social knowledge, knowledge about language, and knowledge about the world. Monolithic accounts are pleasing and elegant. However, this elegance comes at a high cost when it deals with an inherently multifaceted phenomenon such as word learning. If we accept these accounts, we run the risk of missing the richness that gives rise to the really impressive human cognitive achievements. In short, I wholeheartedly agree with Hirsh-Pasek, Golinkoff, and Hollich's conclusion in chapter 6 that a "smoking gun" will never be found for word learning.

MICHAEL TOMASELLO & NAMEERA AKHTAR:
Five Questions for Any Theory of Word Learning

For our commentary on the chapters in this volume, we would like to ask five very basic questions about the process of word learning, in each case contrasting our own views (also known as social-pragmatic theory) with those of the other theorists.

(1) Why Does Language Emerge When It Does?

Perhaps surprisingly, none of the theorists in this volume—nor any others we know of—has a concrete proposal for why language acquisition begins when it does. Could it be due to associative learning? The problem here is that human infants are very good at associative learning from very early in development—

as demonstrated by the research of Haith, Rovee-Collier, and many others—
and so, by this theory, language development should begin at an earlier age than
it does. Could it be due to some word learning constraints or principles that
emerge at the appropriate age? The problem here is that there is no independent
way to observe or measure constraints; they are inferred from the child's linguistic behavior, after the fact. And so there is no way to observe a constraint
in a language-independent way and then use that to predict the onset of language (this is why Smith, in chapter 3 of this volume, refers to constraints and
principles as "skyhooks"). And so the two major mechanisms discussed in this
volume—association learning and constraints/principles—have no answer to
the question of why language emerges precisely when it does near the end of
the first year of life.

We have an answer to this question. Language acquisition begins when it
does because it depends on a more fundamental skill, namely, the ability to
share attention with other human beings—which emerges near the end of the
first year of life. Thus, many different studies have found that children begin to
develop joint attentional skills at around 9 to 12 months of age (see Tomasello,
1995a, for a review). Most children also show their first signs of comprehending language at this same age, with the first linguistic productions coming soon
after (Fenson et al., 1994). Most importantly, in a recent longitudinal study
Carpenter, Nagell, and Tomasello (1998) found that children's skills of joint
attentional engagement with their mothers correlated highly with their skills
of language comprehension and production. Regression analyses found that
roughly half of the variability in the sizes of infants' word comprehension and
production vocabularies was predicted by one factor alone: the amount of time
infants spent in joint attentional interaction with their mothers during a 10-
minute observation session.

The reason that linguistic skills are so highly correlated with joint attentional
skills is that language is nothing more than another type—albeit a very special
type—of joint attentional skill; people use language to influence and manipulate one another's attention. Linguistic symbols are special in a number of ways,
most of these emanating from their social-conventional-historical nature, which
differentiates them from the gaze following, pointing, and other nonlinguistic
joint attentional skills. The social-conventional nature of linguistic symbols
means that children can only learn them in interaction with other persons, and
the fact that their function is to manipulate the attention of others means that
their communicative significance can only be learned by entering into an intersubjective (joint attentional) state with a mature language user—which thus
makes joint attentional skills a genuine prerequisite for the acquisition and use
of linguistic symbols. Joint attentional skills themselves emerge when they do
at around 9 to 12 months of age for several complicated reasons, mostly involving infants' dawning understanding of other persons as intentional agents

(see Tomasello, 2000, for the specific hypothesis). The essential point in the current context is simply that language is of a piece with other joint attentional skills, and indeed these other skills serve as a kind of "crane" for language acquisition—not as a skyhook out of nowhere, but as a crane grounded in basic human social and cognitive skills. The failure to appreciate language as a social-pragmatic-intersubjective skill has prevented the other theorists in this volume from giving a principled reason why language emerges when it does, whereas our appreciation of this fact provides us with a very natural developmental explanation.

(2) Can Association Do the Job?

Smith (chapter 3, this volume) argues that children's attention deployment is "dumb" and that word learning is initially a process in which children's attention is captured by something, which they then associate with some acoustic pattern they hear coming out of the mouth of an adult. This theory may explain why Pavlov's dog associated a bell with the arrival of food or why pet dogs around the world learn to anticipate dinner when they hear a particular sound sequence (e.g., a human voice saying "dinner"), but associations between sounds and perceptual experiences are not language. If they were, then many nonhuman animals, who are very skilled at processes of associative learning, would learn language.

We have concluded a series of experiments in which children show just how active and strategic is their attention deployment in word-learning situations (some of these were reviewed in chapter 5, this volume; for a full review see Tomasello, in press). Children (a) hear novel words and then skip over the next referents they see if the adult gives indications in her nonverbal actions that these are not her intended referents; (b) preferentially learn words for intentional over accidental actions no matter the order in which they see them; (c) learn a word for the element in the situation that is novel for the adult (not for themselves) who is saying the word excitedly, based on the premise that people get excited about new, not old things; and (d) learn new words for actions they know (from past experience) the adult is preparing to perform even if she never actually performs them. In all of these studies the classic bases of associative learning—spatial-temporal contiguity between stimuli—would not only have not helped the children, but would have actually led them to make incorrect associations between words and referents. The fact that in another recent study children were provided with very poor cues to adult referential intentions and so guessed that her intended referent was the most salient object in a situation simply shows that children sometimes use perceptual salience as a cue to adult referential intentions—presumably when they have no better cues available (Samuelson & Smith, 1998). Indeed, when perceptual salience and adult gaze direction were pitted against one another in a recent word-learning study, children of 24 months used gaze direction as their preferred referential cue (Moore, Angelopoulos, & Bennett, 1999).

In the context of Smith's proposals in chapter 3 (this volume), let us be clear about one thing. We are not proposing any "skyhooks" here. Children are learning words with well-known developmental mechanisms involving speech processing, cultural (imitative) learning, concept formation, and intention reading—to name only the most obvious. The point is simple: There can be "cranes" other than associative learning.

(3) Are There Word Learning Constraints?

In a word, no. There is no question that the process of language acquisition must be constrained, as must all developmental processes. But there are many aspects of children's cognitive and social development that may serve to constrain the word-learning process without positing that the child possess distinct entities in her brain called "word-learning constraints." Tomasello (1992b) put the question in this form: If a child were to have a constraint-removal operation (performed by a highly skilled and specialized neurosurgeon) would she then, every time she heard a new word, entertain as hypotheses all of those enumerated by Quine and other philosophers? Of course she would not, and the reason is that the process of word learning is constrained by the child's general understanding of what is going on in the social situation in which she hears a new word. We may thus imagine many scenarios more realistic than Quine's in which the native and the learner are actually engaging in some meaningful social interaction when the novel word is uttered; in such a case the learner will make a reasonable guess at the native's referential intentions given her intentional actions in context. For instance, if the child hears the adult say "gavagai" as a rabbit runs past, it makes a difference whether (a) they are in the process of hunting for dinner and the rabbit fits the bill; (b) they had been admiring the pet rabbit in its cage and they just now see it escaping; (c) they are meditating together and the rabbit's movements are disturbing them; or (d) they are playing a game in which in order to win one must find things of as many different colors as possible. Quine knew all of this, of course, as is clearly evident in his (1960) book, one quotation from which forms the epigraph to our chapter in this volume.

Hirsh-Pasek, Golinkoff, and Hollich (chapter 6, this volume) want it both ways. The original justification for constraints was Quine's problem of referential indeterminacy, which, for some theorists, required that there be a priori constraints to get the child into the system (Markman, 1989). In some places, the authors of chapter 6 seem to be arguing for a different kind of constraint— word learning "principles" that are "emergent [and] develop over the course of the second year of life as children gain word learning experience"—a position with which no one could have any quarrels (even Brown, 1973, outlined some things along these lines). However, and in seeming contradiction, in other places they say that their tier-one principles (reference, object scope, extendibility) are a priori and, indeed, "word learning could never begin without them." These are two very different positions, perhaps corresponding to Woodward's (chapter 4, this volume) "default assumptions" and "knowledge-based constraints." In our opinion, it is this kind of unannounced ambiguity that keeps constraints alive as a theoretical explanation. In their original formulation as *a priori* constraints that enabled language acquisition—as proposed so clearly and boldly by Markman (1989)—they clearly do not accord with the data. In their form as principles of word learning that the child induces a posteriori on the basis of primary word-learning experiences, no one doubts their existence in general (although we may still doubt any specific principles proposed [see question (5) below]).

And so our own view is that given a 1-year-old child who knows many kinds of things about objects, events, and properties in the world and who also knows at least some things about why people do what they do in specific situations (their intentions, including communicative intentions), the process of learning linguistic symbols is constrained enough without positing any additional specialized linguistic machinery.

(4) What is the Role of Social Context?

Social-pragmatic theorists are regularly characterized as "outside in" theorists (e.g., Hirsh-Pasek & Golinkoff, 1996) or, worse, as theorists who believe that "a language tutor/caregiver in the child's social context is the mechanism for word learning" (see Bloom, chapter 2, this volume). We are not sure how this misconception has arisen, since we have been very clear from the beginning that acquiring a piece of language requires *both* that the environment present a learning opportunity and that the child have the ability to take advantage of that opportunity (Tomasello, 1992b). Indeed, in the series of word-learning studies alluded to above, we were almost the opposite of tutors: We presented children with very difficult learning opportunities that required them to follow the vagaries of adult attention, and, indeed, the adult was not being sensitive to their communicative needs at all. Although adults may sometimes "scaffold" young children in language development—and this is more common in some cultures than in others—children clearly do not need such scaffolding to learn a language.

Children do, of course, need some kind of predictable social context in order to learn a language, and they do, of course, need to hear other people using language. If we imagine a child who grew up in a social world in which there were

absolutely no repetitions or consistencies of any of her social activities or interactions—so that no predictions of the behavior of adults were possible—it is
hard to imagine that language acquisition could take place. Nor would language
acquisition take place if there was no language spoken in the child's presence at
all. But given a normal, human, social and linguistic world, in which children
and their caregivers engage in similar activities day after day, with language integrated into those activities in a normal way, there do not need to be any special efforts on the part of the caregiver to "tutor" language-learning children.
Indeed, there are some cultures in which adults talk to their children very little,
and so they must learn much of their language from overhearing the speech of
adults to one another or from speech addressed to them by other children, who
are generally not such great tutors for very young children (Brown, in press).

(5) How Do Children Learn Words Other Than Object Labels?

Children talk about events and states of affairs in the world. Even when they
use the name of an object as a one-word utterance, "Ball," they are almost always asking someone either to *get* them the ball or else to *attend* to the ball.
Simply naming objects for no other purpose except to name them is a language
game that some children play, but these are typically only some children in
some Western middle-class homes and this game concerns only basic-level objects; no children anywhere simply name actions ("Look: Giving!") or relationships ("Look: Of!"). In terms of vocabulary items per se, Bloom (chapter
2, this volume) summarizes evidence that children learn as many non-object
words as object words in early development—and that is for English. There are
other languages (Mandarin, Korean, Tsotzil) in which object labels comprise
an even lower percentage of children's early vocabularies.

It is thus mystifying that theories of word learning continue to focus on the
acquisition of objects labels as if it were somehow the paradigm case. And it is
positively counterproductive to go on making principles of object-label learning if they are going to actually hinder the child in learning other kinds of words,
which many of them do. Just from the Hirsh-Pasek, Golinkoff, and Hollich list
(chapter 6, this volume), here are some word types that would be hindered by
the corresponding word learning principle (brief definitions from Golinkoff,
Mervis, and Hirsh-Pasek, 1994):

- *Reference* ("Words map to objects, actions, attributes"): Performatives
  such as *Hi, Bye, Please,* and *Thank You* are quite common in early language, and they are not referential.
- *Object scope* ("Words map to whole objects"): Verbs, adjectives, prepositions, and many nonprototypical nouns like *breakfast, party,* and *park* are

all quite common in early vocabularies, and they do not map to whole objects.

- *Extendability* ("Words extend to other referents"): Proper nouns such as *Daddy, Jeffrey,* and *Mickey Mouse* are quite common word types in early vocabularies, and they do not extend to other referents at all.
- *Categorical scope* ("Words extend to basic level categories"): Proper nouns such as *Daddy* do not extend, and commonly occurring pronouns such as *it, that,* and *she* extend to a wide range of objects well beyond basic level categories.

And so not only would these particular word-learning principles not help the child with words other than object labels (common nouns), they would in fact be a positive hindrance to the learning of all these other word types. This is most obviously true for the principle of Object Scope, which must be overridden for all non-object words. But even in the case of referring to objects, following the principles for proper nouns and pronouns (especially Extendibility and Category Scope) would be an unmitigated disaster.

Smith's association theory is also aimed specifically at object labels (chapter 3, this volume). It is unclear if this theory has anything interesting to say about other kinds of words, but on the face of it the theory could not even describe the difference between nonreferential performative expressions (*Hi, Bye,* and *Thank You*) and referential expressions, and it is hard to know what gets associated with what when the child is attempting to learn words like *of, from,* and *with,* whose meanings change radically in different syntactic contexts. And how does the association theory explain word-learning studies in which the child learns—for the exact same referential event—either an object word or an action word depending only on the way the adult sets up the social situation (Tomasello & Akhtar, 1995)? Like all association theories, Smith's theory has basically nothing to say about how children cognitively construe a referential situation before associating it with some linguistic expression.

Precisely how children learn all of the different kinds of words they need to learn in order to master a natural language is not at all an easy question, even for our own social-pragmatic theory. But some grapplings with the problems presented by verbs are presented in Tomasello, 1992a, 1995b; with the problems presented by prepositions in Tomasello, 1987, 1992a (and focused specifically on the issue of how some prepositions must be extracted from the syntactic contexts in which they are habitually embedded in Tomasello & Brooks, 1999); for adjectives in Akhtar and Montague, in press; and for nonreferential performative expressions in Tomasello, 2000. The main reason we believe that our approach has more promise than others in helping to account for the acquisition of the whole range of different word types—besides the fact that it does not have object-based word-learning principles that have to be overcome or a theory of associative learning that has no cognitive substance to specify the concepts being associated—is because it attempts to integrate the acquisition of language with other research on children's cognitive and social development in general. For instance, problems of verb learning can be informed by research on event cognition, and problems of performative learning can be informed by work on children's understanding of intentions and communicative intentions. The associative theory seems either unwilling or unable to take advantage of such research, and the principles-coalition model typically looks at language acquisition as a very specialized developmental process.

Conclusion

And so, our overall critique of the other theories is that (1) associations can never add up to anything other than, well, associations—they can certainly not add up to the reading of intentions and the manipulation of attention as characteristic of linguistic communication; and (2) linguistic constraints, or even principles of the type normally proposed, do not help in acquiring the majority of the word types of a language, and indeed in many cases they present serious obstacles to the process. Social-pragmatic theory has not solved all the problems of word learning—not by a long shot—but it at least gives us a fighting chance to tackle the very difficult empirical problems of language acquisition in all of their cognitive and communicative complexities. And of course we should stress that social-pragmatic factors are not the only factors that figure in word learning; clearly, processes of speech perception/production and various processes of general cognition are key, and there are very likely some principles of word learning that emerge during development as well. But it is crucial to begin in the right place, and social-pragmatic theory does that by explicitly recognizing the social nature of linguistic communication, thereby placing the social-pragmatic dimensions of the language acquisition process front and center, where they belong.

KATHY HIRSH-PASEK & ROBERTA MICHNICK GOLINKOFF:
The Whole *Is* Greater Than the Sum of the Parts,
or Why the Emergentist Coalition Model Works

Any adequate theory of word learning must address two key questions. First, how do infants break the language barrier by learning their first words? Second, what accounts for the change in the character of word learning that occurs in children at around 19–21 months of age? Theories must address these questions not only for object nouns but for the entire spectrum of word types, including verbs, adverbs, and adjectives. Because we did not believe that any of the "either/or" theories—be they constraints based, associationist, or social-pragmatic—could, in and of themselves, provide compelling answers to these questions, we developed the emergentist coalition model for word learning. This hybrid approach offers a theory that borrows the best from the alternatives. Yet the emergentist coalition model is not designed to be all things to all people. Rather, it offers an empirically testable alternative that allows us to address the two key questions of word learning and to chart the course of word learning as it changes over development. This essay highlights the problems inherent in the "either/or" theories and demonstrates the merits of a nonreductionist view of the word-learning problem.

Associationism Is Only Part of the Story: A Commentary on Smith

There is no question that children form associations between words and objects, actions, and events. The most salient object in the environment is likely to rivet the child's attention and hence be labeled by a sensitive parent or caregiver. There is also no question that infants are expert pattern analyzers who can generalize across a number of exemplars to extract the common element—be it shape or number. If there is one lesson that infant researchers learned in the last decade of the 20th century it is that babies as young as 8–10 months of age are already computing statistical relationships among the characteristics of the sounds they hear (Saffran, Aslin & Newport, 1996) and the sights they see (Younger & Cohen, 1983). "Dumb attentional mechanisms," as Smith (1995) has called them, can take the child at least part of the way, and complexity can arise out of simple relationships.

For Smith (chapter 3 in this volume), the answer to the question of how children learn their first words is relatively straightforward—they associate the word they hear with the referent they find most compelling and interesting. To the question of what drives the change in the character of word learning, Smith suggests that children learn to generalize once they have acquired a stock of words. That is, once they accumulate enough words, they learn that words tend to label categories of objects that share a similar shape. Having abstracted this principle, word learning becomes much more efficient, shedding its slow, one-word-at-a-time character. In chapter 3, Smith not only forwards this theory but also offers impressive evidence that children who have more words are faster at making this generalization. So what is wrong with this picture?

The problem with Smith's model is not with her argument that associationism plays a role but with her argument that it plays an exclusive role in explaining word learning. Data from our laboratories strongly suggests that association to the most salient objects cannot alone account for the earliest word learning. Rather, attention to a myriad of cues is implicated in word learning.

Just as construction jobs cannot be completed without both cranes and sky-hooks, explanations for word learning require biased, or "guided," attention to a coalition of cues.

The evidence for our claim comes from an experiment outlined briefly in chapter 6 and reported at length in Hollich, Hirsh-Pasek, and Golinkoff (in press). We presented infants with both an interesting and a boring object. We labeled either the interesting or the boring object five times while looking at the object and the child's eyes alternately. For example, we said to baby Irving, "Irving, it's a modi!" In the first two test trials, we placed the two objects side by side on our rotating board. Using the Interactive Intermodal Preferential Looking Paradigm, the experimenter (hiding) requested the labeled object by asking, "Irving, where's the modi?" We hypothesized that children who had originally heard the interesting object labeled in the *coincident* condition would look for a longer time at the interesting object than at the boring object. Children who had heard the boring object labeled in the *conflict* condition would look for a longer time at the boring object than at the interesting object—if they had learned its name. The third and fourth test trials pointed out the weakness in the associationist theory. In the third trial, we asked infants to look at the "glorp." Because children had not been trained with the name "glorp," we expected that they would look away from the named "modi" and toward the unnamed object. Then, in the final test trial, or "recovery" trial, the experimenter again requested the original "modi." Children who had truly learned the label, we predicted, would look again at the original object.

When we conducted this experiment, we anticipated that the youngest children would use pure associationism to solve the task. That is, we hypothesized that 12-month-old first-word learners would focus on the most salient object in *both* the coincident condition (in which the labeled object coincided with the children's preferences) and the conflict condition (in which the labeled object did not coincide with the children's preferences). Regardless of which object the experimenter labeled, a child who was motivated (as a "dumb attentional mechanism" theory predicts) to attach a label to the most attractive object present would, we expected, think that the label was for the interesting object. Thus, we predicted that children would affix the name "modi" to the *interesting* object in both conditions. We anticipated that they would then demonstrate reduced looking time at the interesting object on the "glorp" trial and then recovery to the interesting object in the fourth test trial. To our surprise, that is not what happened!

In the coincident condition, when we labeled the interesting object, children did seem to learn the name for that object. They did exactly what we expected: They demonstrated reduced looking time at that object in the third test trial and recovery in the fourth trial. In the conflict condition, however, the children did not learn the label for the interesting object, as both we and the "dumb attentional" explanation had predicted. They did not look for significantly less time at the interesting object in the third trial when they were asked for the "glorp." In fact, whether the infants heard "glorp" or "modi," they seemed fixated on the interesting object. It appeared as if children in the conflict condition had learned no name at all.

How can we begin to make sense of this finding? First, the data offer conclusive evidence—contrary to our hypothesis—that children are *not* associating labels only with the most interesting object, the one that grabs their attention. Second, it appears that, though children in this task could not use the social information offered by eye gaze in service to word learning, they nonetheless attended to eye gaze. How do we know this? Even though the children spent the majority of their time in the conflict condition looking at the interesting object at the same time that the label was offered, their continued attention to the interesting object even during the "glorp" trial indicates that they did not form a mismapping. Only in the coincident condition, when all the moons were in alignment, so to speak, did children map the novel word to an object. Children, it seems, respond to the coalition of cues available to them. Word-to-world mapping, however, is fragile for children who are just breaking the word-learning barrier. If anything disrupts the alignment of cues, they do not learn a label at all. Association to the most interesting object surely controlled their attention and played a role in the labeling. It did not, in and of itself, however, *determine* the acquisition of a label.

This finding has been secured by another of our laboratory tests, in which children played with the interesting and boring objects and then went through a labeling phase in which the experimenter hid from view. We expected that children who were merely associating words to interesting objects would learn the word in this circumstance as easily as in the situation in which there was a visible experimenter. Interestingly, they did not. In this case, infants learned nothing at all.

Finally, under an associationist account with only cranes to work with, all associations should be created equal. That is, without a bias to look for shape or color, for example, infants learning their first words should show no inherent bias to attach words to objects of similar shape over objects of similar color. Smith and other associationists have explicitly made this claim (1995; see also chapter 3, this volume), arguing that the shape bias comes about because of the association between count nouns and bounded objects. This implies that if count nouns labeled objects of similar color, a color bias should develop. Recent research in our laboratory is investigating this issue. In one experiment, Hollich (1999) presented 12-month-olds with three objects that shared either similar shape (but not color) or color (but not shape). He labeled each exemplar three times and then tested to see whether children would extend the new label to an object of similar shape or color. The results suggested that, even at this very young age, a shape bias is present; however, no color bias was detected. One could argue, as Smith (personal communication, 1999) has, that, by 1 year of age, children may have already heard more words associated with shape than with color. However, the result seems to fly in the face of the claim that children will abstract a shape bias only after they have accumulated over about 50 object names. Further, to the extent that one can always rescue the associationist theory by positing past experience (cranes all the way down), the theory becomes unfalsifiable.

In sum, then, associations surely play a role in early word learning. It is unimaginable that children could learn words if they could not form some associations between words and salient objects, actions, and events. Further, these associations probably play a larger role in early acquisition than they do in later acquisition, when the child has more tools in his or her repertoire. However, as our results have shown, even at the youngest age, association does not rule the day. Children do not just associate words with salient objects. An appeal to "dumb attentional mechanisms" does not tell the entire story. Children are surrounded by a complex web of word learning cues—some perceptual, some social, and some linguistic. It is in the interaction of these cues that children—with their own cognitive predispositions—learn their first words.

Social-Pragmatic Information Plays but a Role:
A Commentary on Akhtar and Tomasello

There is no question that children attend to social cues in the environment from the time that they are born (see Adamson, 1995, for a review). Considerable data exist on infants' attention to gazing and pointing, for example, in the second 6 months of life (Carpenter, Nagell, & Tomasello, 1998; Corkum & Moore, 1995). Indeed, recent reports suggest that, in certain settings, infants can follow eye gaze at 6 months of age (Morales, Mundy, & Rojas, 1998). Thus, the issue is not whether infants are social beings born into a social world but whether they can *recruit* social cues for the purpose of word learning. In chapter 5, Akhtar and Tomasello suggest that infants can do so from the start, that word learning is fundamentally a social activity. Only a social theory, they claim, can explain how words are learned in the context of language use. Although we do not want to downplay the importance of the social environment, it is our belief that appeals to social understanding can explain neither the way children learn their first words nor the change in the character of word learning over time. In fact, our data suggest that, at first, if information is in conflict with other cues in the word-learning situation, children cannot use that social information to learn words. As with associationistic accounts, attention to social information is only part of the story.

Evidence for the claim that social cues are not dominant in first word learning comes from Experiment 4 in Hollich, Hirsh-Pasek, & Golinkoff, in press). Again, children first played with one of two objects, although here the objects were of equal perceptual salience. During the training phase, only one of the toys was labeled, as in the experiment previously described. Even in the absence of perceptual salience, children were unable to use the minimal social cues of eye gaze and body orientation to learn the label for the object that the experimenter labeled. Children did not follow the experimenter's gaze during training. When we changed the training phase to include pointing to and handling the object (see Experiments 5 and 6), children spent significantly more time looking at the labeled toy. Thus, children could clearly follow these more blatant social cues during the labeling phase. Nonetheless, there was no evidence that they had learned the label—that they had used the social cues to inform their word learning. The ability to *utilize* social information in word learning seems to be a skill separate from being able to *follow* social cues. Only at 19 and 24 months of age were children able to use the social cues in service to word learning. These findings are consistent with the "glorp" data previously presented. At 12 months of age, children *notice* social information but fail to *use* it exclusively to map words to objects.

The results of these studies are not incompatible with the data presented by Akhtar and Tomasello in chapter 5, which offer evidence that children notice social information in the latter half of the 1st year of life. Infants 9–12 months old can engage in interactions with other people. They can follow another's gaze. In one notable experiment reported by Baldwin and Tomasello (1998), babies also checked a speaker's line of regard to see which of two objects was being labeled (see also chapter 4 in this volume). Notably, the outstanding evidence they cite in favor of infants' ability to note referential intent, however, comes from studies of children who are *18 months or older.* As Akhtar and Tomasello argue, the ability to recognize referential intent may well be the cornerstone for rapid word learning. Attention to social information in the first 18 months serves as the backdrop for this discovery.

Akhtar and Tomasello suggest that word learning is social all the way down. However, social information does not seem to control word learning until the child enters the period of the naming explosion. If all of word learning can be explained through appeal to social understanding, then this theory is at a loss to explain how children learn their first words and why the character of word learning changes over time. To explain early word learning, Akhtar and Tomasello (chapter 5 in this volume) suggest that any words uttered prior to the time that they are socially infused are *really* not words at all. They write:

> If our purpose is trying to explain how children come to use conventional symbols
> to communicate with others . . . then a sound-referent pair that is neither used nor

comprehended as a communicative symbol (that is, in interaction with others) cannot be granted the status of a word.

By defining the earliest words as nonwords, the problem is solved tautologically.

Our position holds that the earliest words are indeed words. Rather than excluding them from the theory of learning, we view word learning on a continuum and ask what mechanisms can best explain word learning at each point in development.

Does the Child's Perspective Rule?
A Commentary on Bloom

L. Bloom's theory (see chapter 2 in this volume) offers one way to think about the role of social information and attentional cues (association) in a broader context. Bloom holds that the child's cognitive status, social information, and attentional engagement all work together to produce word learning. In many ways our view is sympathetic with Bloom's. She has long recognized the value in having an active child who balances and coordinates multiple inputs in the solution to such complex problems as word learning. Indeed, after we read her chapter, it became clear that the child's intent must figure more prominently in our own view of word learning (although we had already incorporated her views into our theory of early language comprehension—see Hirsh-Pasek & Golinkoff, 1996). We find Bloom's approach to word learning compelling; however, we believe that it does not go far enough. The principles of relevance, discrepancy, and elaboration that mediate between effort and engagement in Bloom's model are not yet well defined. They seem more descriptive than explanatory and run the risk of constituting a circular defense.

Take the principle of relevance as an example. Sperber and Wilson (1986, p. 46) define relevance as "the single property that makes information worth processing and determines the particular assumptions an individual is most likely to construct and process." L. Bloom refines the definition by noting that relevance is *not* the same as salience. Rather, relevance in word learning is determined by three factors: the child's focus of attention, the child's engagement in whatever is the focus of attention, and the conceptual structure or the knowledge base that the child brings to the task. Bloom argues that we do not need internal word-learning principles, because the child will attach a word to the object, action, or event that is most relevant in the labeling context.

The problem is that it is very difficult to know independently what counts as relevant for the child. Indeed, as Golinkoff (1986) has shown, mothers notoriously make incorrect assumptions about what their children want in a situation that has few degrees of freedom—meal time. Research by Tomasello and

Baldwin, among others (see Baldwin & Tomasello, 1998, for a review), suggests that, by about 18 months of age, the child—rather than simply affixing the label to the toy that *he or she* is playing with—will take the perspective of the speaker into account. Knowing that the child has allocated attention to the toy and that he or she is engaged with it, is not enough to ensure label learning. Instead, we need some independent assessment of the child's cognitive intent—a construct that, although critical, is very difficult to measure. We are therefore left in the awkward position of assuming that whatever gets a label must have been that which is the most relevant for the child. That which is most relevant gets the label and that which gets the label is the most relevant. This excellent descriptive principle becomes grounded in a circular defense.

Even if we could conclusively and independently determine which toy was relevant, we would need to explain why children generally find "whole" toys, rather than interesting toy parts, relevant. That is, we might still require such principles as whole object (Markman, 1989) or object scope (Golinkoff, Mervis, & Hirsh-Pasek, 1994) to explain why children reliably make certain labeling decisions over others. Relevance might not be enough of an explanation to account for word learning.

In sum, L. Bloom's perspective captures the multifaceted nature of word learning and does much to put the child back in the word-learning equation. An understanding of the mechanisms of and the changes that occur in the course of word learning, however, will require a better understanding of the principles forwarded by Bloom and the ways in which they guide change over time.

Pulling the Pieces Together:
A Commentary on Woodward

Like L. Bloom, Woodward proposes that word learning is a complex process. It is the product of multiple sources of evidence, including linguistic information (e.g., morphology), social-pragmatic information (e.g., pointing and gazing), and even default assumptions such as the whole-object assumption and the taxonomic constraint (Markman, 1989)—both of which are apparent at the beginning of word learning. Woodward (chapter 4 in this volume) writes, "No single factor can account for the word-learning success of young children."

Having offered a superb review of the literature supporting her view, Woodward holds that infants are actively responding to different sources of input from the time they utter their first word. The changing character of word learning reflects a quantitative rather than a qualitative shift in word-learning strategy. As children bring more and different kinds of knowledge to the task, they become increasingly proficient in finding the mappings between words and referents.

Woodward's summary sets the stage perfectly for the emergentist coalition model. The challenge for both views is to demonstrate how multiple sources of information interact over time, how word-learning principles emerge in development, and how the seemingly quantitative growth of knowledge can lead to qualitative shifts in the way children approach the word-learning task. Philosophically, Woodward's view is aligned with our own. By going beyond the step of the hypothetical statement that cues must interact, to the step of a test of how these multiple cues interact to produce word learning in the 2nd year of life, however, the emergentist coalition model takes the theory to its next level.

The Emergentist Coalition Model:
A Falsifiable Word-Learning Theory

The emergentist coalition model stands at the confluence of the current theories of word learning. By assuming that perceptual salience, or attention-grabbing properties of the child's environment, will weigh heavily on children's first mapping between words and their referents, we adopt the best of the associationist view as we shed the myopic perspective that all is constructed from cranes alone. Perceptual salience stands with social and linguistic cues in the child's arsenal of word-learning tools. Children who are just breaking the language barrier seem to give undue—although not exclusive—significance to salience information even though other information is available.

Similarly, though social cues are available from birth, children do not harness this information in the service of word learning until the latter half of the 2nd year of life. Repeated exposure to reliable social information in the word-learning context encourages children to place more emphasis on this information, thereby enabling them to become apprentices to more experienced language users. Once children are able to detect and use social intent, the very character of word learning changes. At 18–21 months of age, babies are still lured by perceptual cues, as our research shows (Hollich, Hirsh-Pasek, & Golinkoff, in press). Yet they can overcome the attraction to an interesting object, for example, and succeed in properly attaching a label to a boring object. Just 3–6 months later, these children can use social cues to determine a word's referent even when the perceptual cues are in *conflict* with the social information available (see Moore, Angelopoulos, & Corkum, 1999).

It appears that young word learners are conservative—they look for overlap between multiple interactive cues in context. Children equipped with some immature word-learning principles cull from the information around them to determine which objects, actions, or events will be associated with which words. At first constrained by the need for overlapping cues, children soon learn which cues are more reliable for word learning, probably through statistical calculations—"guided distributional learning" (Hirsh-Pasek & Golinkoff, 1966)—of the varied cues contained in the input. Eventually the child comes to rely more heavily on social and linguistic cues than on perceptual salience to solve the mapping problem. With this new strategical savvy, the very nature of word learning changes from its slow and laborious beginnings to a process that advances at a rapid clip.

In our laboratory we are, at present, conducting word-learning simulations (Hollich, 1999), so that we can better understand the ways in which multiple inputs overlap and differentially contribute to the course of word learning. Such models allow us to chart with precision the biases that children may bring to the task as well as the strategies that they will use to learn words at any given point in time. We do not intend for the model to be all things to all people. Instead, by taking the best from the available theories, we offer a hybrid that emphasizes the mechanisms of word learning and takes process seriously. This model allows us to chart both the process that children use as they break the language barrier and the way in which it changes as they become expert learners in their 2nd year of life.

REFERENCES

Abel, R. A., Ronca, A. E., & Alberts, J. R. (1998). Prenatal sensory stimulation determines suckling onset. *Developmental Psychobiology, 32,* 91–99.

Adamson, L. (1995). *Communication development during infancy.* Madison, WI: Brown & Benchmark.

Akhtar, N., & Montague, L. J. (in press). Lexical acquisition: The role of cross-situational learning. *First Language.*

Baldwin, D. A., & Tomasello, M. (1998). Word learning: A window on early pragmatic understanding. In E. V. Clark (Ed.), *Proceedings of the 29th Annual Child Language Research Forum* (pp. 3–23). Stanford, CA: Center for the Study of Language and Information.

Bloom, L. (1981). The importance of language for language development: Linguistic determinism in the 1980s. In H. Winitz (Ed.), *Native language and foreign language acquisition* (pp. 160–171). New York: New York Academy of Sciences.

Bloom, L. (1993). *The transition from infancy to language: Acquiring the power of expression.* New York: Cambridge University Press.

Brown, P. (in press). The conversational context for language acquisition: A Tzeltal (Mayan) case study. In M. Bowerman & S. Levinson (Eds.), *Language acquisition and conceptual development.* Cambridge, England: Cambridge University Press.

Brown, R. (1973). *A first language: The early stages.* Cambridge, MA: Harvard University Press.

Carpenter, M., Nagell, K., & Tomasello, M. (1998). Social cognition, joint attention, and communicative competence from 9 to 15 months of age. *Monographs of the Society for Research in Child Development,* (Serial No. 255).

Cheng, P. W., & Holyoak, K. (1995). Complex adaptive systems as intuitive statisticians:

Causality, contingency, and prediction. In H. Roitblat, J. Meyer, et al. (Eds.), *Comparative approaches to cognitive science: Complex adaptive systems* (pp. 271– 302). Cambridge, MA: MIT Press.

Clark, E. V. (1990). On the pragmatics of contrast. *Journal of Child Language, 17,* 417– 431.

Corkum, V., & Moore, C. (1995). Development of joint visual attention in infants. In C. Moore & P. J. Dunham (Eds.), *Joint attention: Its origins and role in development* (pp. 61–83). Hillsdale, NJ: Erlbaum.

Fenson, L., Dale, P. S., Reznick, J. S., Bates, E., Thal, D. J., and Pethick, S. J. (1994). Variability in early communicative development. *Monographs of the Society for Research in Child Development, 59* (5, Serial No. 242).

Golinkoff, R. M. (1986). "I beg your pardon?": The preverbal negotiation of failed messages. *Journal of Child Language, 13,* 455–476.

Golinkoff, R. M., Mervis, C. B., & Hirsh-Pasek, K. (1994). Early object labels: The case for a developmental lexical principles framework. *Journal of Child Language, 21,* 125–155.

Goodman, J. C., McDonough, L., & Brown, N. B. (1998). The role of semantic context in the acquisition of novel nouns. *Child Development, 69,* 1330–1334.

Hebb, D. O. (1949). *The organization of behavior.* New York: John Wiley & Sons.

Hirsh-Pasek, K., & Golinkoff, R. M. (1996). *The origins of grammar: Evidence from early language comprehension.* Cambridge, MA: MIT Press.

Hollich, G., Hirsh-Pasek, K., & Golinkoff, R. M. (in press). Breaking the language barrier: An emergentist coalition model for the origins of word learning. *Monographs of the Society for Research in Child Development.*

Huttenlocher, J., & Smiley, P. (1987). Early word meanings: The case of object names. *Cognitive Psychology, 19,* 63–89.

Imai, M., & Gentner, D. (1997). A crosslinguistic study of early word meaning: Universal ontology and linguistic influence. *Cognition, 62,* 169–200.

Kelly, M. H., & Martin, S. (1994). Domain-general abilities applied to domain-specific tasks: Sensitivities to probabilities in perception, cognition and language. In L. R. Gleitman & B. L. Landau (Eds.), *Lexical acquisition* (pp. 105–141). Cambridge, MA: MIT Press.

Kruschke, J. K. (1992). ALCOVE: An exemplar-based connectionist model of category learning. *Psychological Review, 99,* 22–44.

Kruschke, J. K. (1999). *Toward a unified model of attention in associative learning.* Manuscript submitted for publication.

Mackintosh, N. J. (1975). A theory of attention: Variations in the associability of stimuli with reinforcement. *Psychological Review, 82,* 276–298.

Mandler, J. M., & McDonough, L. (1993). Concept formation in infancy. *Cognitive Development, 8,* 291–318.

Markman, E. (1989). *Categorization and naming in children.* Cambridge, MA: MIT Press.

Medin, D., & Schaffer, M. (1978). Context theory of classification. *Psychological Review, 85,* 207–238.

Minsky, M., & Papert, S. (1969). *Perceptrons.* Cambridge, MA: MIT Press.

Moore, C., Angelopoulos, M., & Bennett, P. (1999). Word learning in the context of referential and salience cues. *Developmental Psychology, 35,* 60–68.

Morales, M., Mundy, P., & Rojas, J. (1998). Following the direction of gaze and language development in 6-month-olds. *Infant Behavior and Development, 21,* 373–377.

Naigles, L. (1990). Children use syntax to learn verb meanings. *Journal of Child Language, 17,* 357–374.

Namy, L. L., & Waxman, S. R. (1998). Words and gestures: Infants' interpretations of different forms of symbolic reference. *Child Development, 69,* 295–308.

Nosofsky, R. M. (1986). Attention, similarity and the identification-categorization relationship. *Journal of Experimental Psychology: General, 115,* 39–57.

O'Reilly, R. C., & Johnson, M. H. (1994). Object recognition and sensitive periods: A computational analysis of visual imprinting. *Neural Computation, 6,* 357–389.

Pedersen, P. E., & Blass, E. M. (1982). Prenatal and postnatal determinants of the first suckling episode in albino rats. *Developmental Psychobiology, 15,* 349–355.

Petitto, L. A. (1988). "Language" in the prelinguistic child. In F. S. Kessel (Ed.), *The development of language and language researchers* (pp. 187–221). Hillsdale, NJ: Erlbaum.

Quine, W. V. O. (1960). *Word and object.* Cambridge, MA: MIT Press.

Quinn, P. (1987). The categorical representation of visual pattern information by young infants. *Cognition, 27,* 145–179.

Rescorla, R. A., & Wagner, A. R. (1972). A theory of Pavlovian conditioning: Variations in the effectiveness of reinforcement and nonreinforcement. In A. H. Black & W. F. Prokasy (Eds.), *Classical conditioning II.* New York: Appleton-Century-Crofts.

Ronca, A. E., Abel, R. A., & Alberts, J. R. (1996). Perinatal stimulation and adaptation of the neonate. *Acta Paediatrica* Suppl., *416,* 8–15.

Saffran, J. R., Aslin, R. N., & Newport, E. L. (1996). Statistical learning by 8-month-old infants. *Science, 274* (5294), 1926–1928.

Samuelson, L. R., & Smith, L. B. (1998). Memory and attention make smart word learning: An alternative account of Akhtar, Carpenter, and Tomasello. *Child Development, 69,* 94–104.

Schafer, G., & Plunkett, K. (1998). Rapid word learning by 15-month-olds under tightly controlled conditions. *Child Development, 69,* 309–320.

Shepard, R. N., Hovland, C. L., & Jenkins, H. M. (1961). Learning and memorization of classifications. *Psychological Monographs, 75* (13), 517.

Smith, L. B. (1995). Self-organizing processes in learning to learn words: Development is not induction. In C. A. Nelson (Ed.), *Basic and applied perspectives on learning, cognition, and development.* Hillsdale, NJ: Erlbaum.

Sperber, D., & Wilson, D. (1986). *Relevance: Communication and cognition.* Cambridge, MA: Harvard University Press.

Teicher, M. H., & Blass, E. M. (1976). Suckling in newborn rats: Eliminated by nipple labage, reinstated by pup saliva. *Science, 193,* 422–425.

Teicher, M. H., & Blass, E. M. (1977). First suckling response of the newborn albino rat: The roles of olfaction and amniotic fluid. *Science, 198,* 635–636.

Tomasello, M. (1987). Learning to use prepositions: A case study. *Journal of Child Language, 14,* 79–98.

Tomasello, M. (1992a). First verbs: A case study of early grammatical development. Cambridge, England: Cambridge University Press.

Tomasello, M. (1992b). The social bases of language acquisition. *Social Development, 1* (1), 67–87.

Tomasello, M. (1995a). Joint attention as social cognition. In C. Moore & P. J. Dunham (Eds.), *Joint attention: Its origins and role in development* (pp. 103–130). Hillsdale, NJ: Erlbaum.

Tomasello, M. (1995b). Pragmatic contexts for early verb learning. In M. Tomasello & W. E. Merriman (Eds.), *Beyond names for things: Young children's acquisition of verbs* (pp. 115–146). Hillsdale, NJ: Erlbaum.

Tomasello, M. (in press a). *The cultural origins of human cognition.* Cambridge, MA: Harvard University Press.

Tomasello, M. (in press b). Perceiving intentions and learning words in the second year of life. In M. Bowerman & S. Levinson (Eds.), *Language acquisition and conceptual development.* Cambridge, England: Cambridge University Press.

Tomasello, M., & Akhtar, N. (1995). Two-year-olds use pragmatic cues to differentiate reference to objects and actions. *Cognitive Development, 10,* 201–224.

Tomasello, M., & Brooks, P. (1999). Early syntactic development: A construction grammar approach. In M. Barrett (Ed.), *The development of language.* Hove, England: Psychology Press.

Waxman, S. R., & Markow, D. B. (1995). Words as invitations to form categories: Evidence from 12- to 13-month-old infants. *Cognitive Psychology, 29,* 257–302.

Werker, J., Cohen, L. B., Lloyd, V. L., Casasolo, M., & Stager, C. L. (1998). Acquisition of word-object associations by 14-month-olds. *Developmental Psychology, 34,* 1289–1309.

Woodward, A. L., & Hoyne, K. L. (1999). Infants' learning about words and sounds in relation to objects. *Child Development, 70,* 65–72.

Younger, B. A., & Cohen, L. B. (1983). Infant perception of correlations among attributes. *Child Development, 54,* 858–867.

Index

Abel, R. A., 172–173
Acredolo, L., 101, 105, 131n.5
Adams, F., 15n.2
Adjective learning, 130
Adults. *See* Caregivers
Affect. *See* Emotional expression
Agency of children, 21, 36–41, 165–166, 168
Ahn, W., 81
Akhtar, N., 15, 29, 37, 95, 96, 115–130, 130n.2, 142–144, 175, 176, 178–186, 190–192
Alberts, J. R., 172–173
Allport, A., 54
Altem, W. M., 54
Angelopoulos, M., 95, 96–97, 128, 182, 194
Anglin, J. M., 94, 102
Animacy, 66–68
Animal artifact categories, 66–68
Animal research, 3, 7–11
Antonyms, 5
Aslin, R. N., 4, 116, 160, 187
Associative learning, 23–24, 54–55, 169–170
Associative model of word learning
animal artifact categories, 66–68
assessment of, 118–120, 159, 169–170, 177–179, 181–182, 185–190
and attention, 170–172
and blocking, 171, 172
concluding comments on, 76–77
and description of associative learning, 54–55
developmental trend in novel-noun generalization, 60–69
and first hundred nouns, 56–58
introduction to, 14, 51–52
longitudinal study on, 69–71
and MacArthur Communicative Development Inventory, 58–59

and novel-noun generalization based on nouns already known, 69–76
and objects with eyes and feet, 66–68
and predictability, 170
and shape bias, 14, 52–54, 59–77, 171, 177, 189–190
and solid versus nonsolid things, 65–66
and specificity, 172–173
statistical regularities among early learned nouns, 55–60
taxonomic versus shape bias, 68–69
training study on, 71–76
Astington, J. W., 95
Attention, 28, 29, 96–98, 125, 170–172, 178, 180–181
Auditory stimulus versus words, 156–158
Augustine, St., 24
Austin (chimpanzee), 3, 9, 11
Au, T. K., 65, 88

Bailey, L. M., 92, 138
Balaban, M. T., 90–91, 100, 158
Baldwin, D. A., 12, 24, 90, 91, 95, 96, 97, 99, 100, 120, 125, 128, 142, 147, 191, 193
Banigan, R. L., 92, 94
Barnes, H., 32
Barr, D. J., 95
Barrett, M., 118, 119, 120
Barton, M., 12, 95, 120, 142
Bates, E., 6, 11, 12, 32, 33, 35, 37, 117, 118
Bauer, P., 68
Baumberger, T., 33
Beckwith, R., 30, 31, 35, 41, 42
Behaviorism, 169
Benedict, H., 82
Bennett, P., 95, 96–97, 128, 182
Bertrand, J., 55, 84, 85, 92, 94, 105, 141, 146

Printed in the United States
205983BV00003B/55-60/A

9 780195 130324